Transforming
ANXIETY,
Transcending
SHAME

REX BRIGGS, M.S.W.

Health Communications, Inc.
Deerfield Beach, Florida

www.hci-online.com

Briggs, Rex
   Transforming anxiety, transcending shame / Rex Briggs.
     p.   cm.
   Includes bibliographical references and index.
   ISBN 1-55874-722-2 (trade pbk.)
    1. Anxiety.   2. Shame.   I. Title.
   RC531.B753   1999
   616.85'223–dc21   99-41648
                                                         CIP

Publisher: Health Communications, Inc.
            3201 S.W. 15th Street
            Deerfield Beach, FL 33442-8190

Cover design by Lisa Camp
Inside book design by Dawn Grove

What People Are Saying About
Transforming Anxiety, Transcending Shame. . .

"Thought-provoking, yet practical, *Transforming Anxiety, Transcending Shame* gives anxiety sufferers understanding into what previously seemed mysterious and frightening. It provides help in living life the way we were intended to live it."

John C. Friel
author, *Adult Children: The Secrets of Dysfunctional Families* and *The 7 Worst Things Parents Do*

"Rex Briggs has written a very important book. He makes a clear case that anxiety is not to be demonized but to be learned from and used to enhance our humanity. *Transforming Anxiety, Transcending Shame* will be rewarding reading for anyone who believes that self-understanding can lead to self-determination. If you suffer from anxiety, then this book is for you. In a direct, perceptive way, Mr. Briggs prescribes a more powerful approach to healing than any medication or specialist's approach. Here is a practical manual on how to reclaim your birthright as an assertive, loving, sexually healthy and resilient member of our society."

R. Reid Wilson, Ph.D.
author, *Don't Panic: Taking Control of Anxiety Attacks*

"A most gentle beginning place for people who suffer from excessive anxiety. The approach is non-medical without denying the contribution of biology; spiritual without being preachy or parochial; and kindly without avoiding a call to honest self-confrontation. The simplicity of style should not be confused with superficiality: The ideas are grounded and important."

Sally Winston, Psy.D.
founder and codirector, The Anxiety & Stress Disorders Institute of Maryland

"Rex Briggs's book is a wonderful gift to people who suffer from anxiety disorders. He focuses on shame with a message of spiritual growth through learning techniques to transform anxiety. I recommend it to everyone who wants to escape from their prison of fear."

Robert L. Dupont, M.D.
author, *The Anxiety Cure: An Eight-Step Program for Getting Well*
founding president, The Anxiety Disorders Association of America
president, The Institute for Behavior and Health, Inc.

"If you're getting tired of managing your anxiety, let Rex Briggs help you transform it! This comprehensive, well-written and practical book shows you how to turn anxiety's energy into fuel for personal growth."

Robert Gerzon
author, *Finding Serenity in the Age of Anxiety*

"*Transforming Anxiety, Transcending Shame* is an excellent book that many will find helpful on their journey to recovery from anxiety. I especially like the way he transforms cold, clinical jargon and diagnostic categories into human terms as well as the many practical exercises that are included."

Reneau Z. Peurifoy, M.A., M.F.T.
author, *Anxiety, Phobias & Panic, Overcoming Anxiety* and
Anger: Taming the Beast

"By combining his own experience with anxiety with his professional expertise, Rex Briggs has written an encouraging and practical book that gives anxiety sufferers the building blocks to create a more fulfilling life."

Mani Feniger
author, *Journey from Anxiety to Freedom*

Thank you to my wife, Myrna,
and my sons, Austin and Tannen,
who have patiently tolerated the highs and lows
of writing and seeking publication.
I'd also like to dedicate this book to my mother.
Even though she's been gone nearly twenty years,
I still miss her.

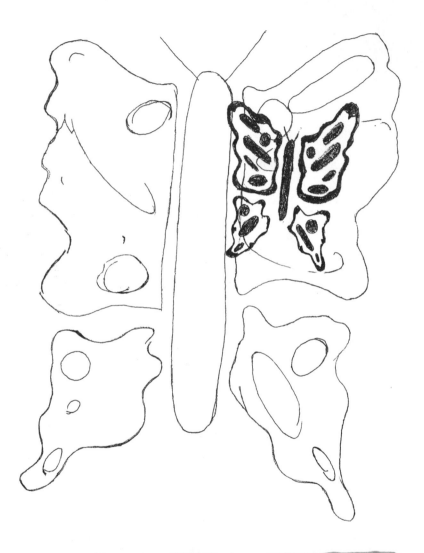

Upon learning that his father's book *Transforming Anxiety, Transcending Shame* would be published, Austin Briggs, then fourteen, drew this conceptualization of what the front cover should look like. The transformation of a caterpillar into a butterfly is symbolic of the transformation people experience when they learn to deal with their anxiety in a healthy, liberating way. After freeing themselves from an insular existence in a cocoon of anxiety, they can test their wings and take flight, able to fully experience and enhance the beauty of the world around them.

Contents

List of Figures ix
List of Tables xi
Acknowledgments xiii
Foreword by John Bradshaw. xv

Introduction. 1

1. Moving from Fear to Freedom:
   A Shift of Thinking and Attitude. 9
2. What Is Anxiety, Anyway?
   What Are Anxiety Disorders?. 25
3. Understanding, Coping with and Healing
   from Shame 49
4. Learning to Walk Before We Run 79
5. Knowing Your Rights and Setting
   Your Boundaries 111
6. Healthy Anger: A Prerequisite in
   Intimate Relationships. 135

7. Coming Out of Hiding: Allowing Yourself
   to Love and Be Loved 159
8. Repairing Your Shame-Plagued Sexuality 179
9. Learning to Grieve Our Daily Losses 205
10. Learning to Communicate with Yourself
    and Others 223
11. The Big Picture: Spiritual and
    Existential Issues in Recovery 249
12. Sailing Out of the Harbor: Embarking on
    Your Own Journey 275
13. The Sky's the Limit 293

Appendix A: My Sixteen-Week
   Anxiety Treatment Program 319
Appendix B: Other Resources 325
Appendix C: Anxiety Disorders—
   Behaviors and Symptoms 327
Bibliography 329
Index 333

Figures

2.1   Anxiety: From Freedom to Fear 34

2.2   As Anxiety Grows, One's World Narrows 35

5.1   Others' Needs Are More Important 129

5.2   One's Own Needs Are More Important 130

5.3   Everybody's Needs Are Important 131

Tables

4.1 Scale of Physical Anxiety Symptoms 102

5.1 Passive Behavior, Assertive Behavior, Aggressive
Behavior. 117

6.1 Levels of Anger 142

6.2 Options for Dealing with Emotions 145

Acknowledgments

Without my editor, Kathleen Fox, this book would have been neither readable nor saleable. She is truly a talented professional.

I also want to acknowledge the generosity of the late Arthur Hardy, M.D., who donated countless hours to me over the phone when I first began this work, just because he wanted to help people suffering with anxiety.

Thanks also to the staff and members of the Anxiety Disorders Association of America (formerly the Phobia Society) for their painstaking efforts in leading the way to better understanding and treatment of excessive anxiety.

Thanks to Bill Harlan for his encouragement and support as this work evolved.

Finally, I'd like to say thank you to the many people I've had a chance to meet in my practice over the last twenty-one years. They have placed their trust in me and have taught me countless lessons as we've learned and grown together.

Foreword

When I was doing my own recovery work, it became clear to me that shame is one of the major destructive forces in our lives. I understood clearly for the first time that I needed to address this issue and I seriously began to study the role of inappropriate shame in my own life and was amazed to find the harm it had done. It was immensely helpful to know that respected authors and therapists had discussed shame in the context of recovery from codependency and addictions and their work helped me to find my way. In my own work, *Healing the Shame That Binds You*, I describe shame as the core problem that lurks behind addictions, codependency and other obsessive conditions. Now, in *Transforming Anxiety, Transcending Shame*, Rex Briggs illustrates the connection between shame and anxiety-related conditions by his willingness to share personal experiences and his own commitment to practicing what he preaches.

The July 1999 issue of *The Journal of Clinical Psychology* cited recent studies indicating that 19 million Americans suffer from anxiety-related disorders each year, are three to five times more likely to go to the doctor, and are six times more likely to be hospitalized than non-anxiety sufferers. Over 40 percent of these patients are also suffering from depression or alcohol and drug abuse.

Anxiety disorders lead the list of mental health problems of people seeking help. Furthermore, statistics show that these anxiety disorders are even more prevalent than depression, alcohol or drug abuse.

While other writers in this rapidly growing area of specialization have suggested confronting shame issues as one of the many steps necessary for anxiety recovery, Rex Briggs is the first to demonstrate just how central a factor shame is in this debilitating condition. His ability to help readers understand anxiety as a messenger, rather than an illness, is of great value. This information helps the serious anxiety sufferer to curtail the tendency to interpret frightful physical symptoms catastrophically, thus saving frequent trips to the doctor and unnecessary medical expense.

Rex Briggs's practical suggestions in first managing and ultimately eliminating unnecessary anxiety are invaluable. His ideas move far beyond the usual symptom-management approach to anxiety treatment and provide a foundation for a sweeping life transformation.

Transforming Anxiety, Transcending Shame makes a significant and valuable contribution and is a strong source of help for anyone suffering from excessive anxiety. Unfortunately, in today's hectic society, this condition seems to affect most of us.

John Bradshaw
author, *Healing the Shame That Binds You*

Introduction

Life ought to be a rich and exciting experience, full of joy and limitless possibilities. However, for those of us who suffer from excessive anxiety, it is instead a fearful and limited experience. Our lives are governed by our fears. We cut ourselves off from the choices that would enrich us, because we have been hurt before and we are afraid we will be hurt again. Instead of a wide-open landscape to be explored and enjoyed, life for us is a tunnel that becomes increasingly narrow as we proceed through it. And as we make our way fearfully through that tunnel, most of us are convinced that the tiny light at the end of it can be nothing else but an oncoming train.

This book is about expanding that tunnel, opening it up again to the wide range of exciting choices that are our birthright. But before we can get out into a bigger and more beautiful world, it helps to explore and accept the reality of the dark and narrow one we have been living in.

Let me begin by telling you what it felt like for me when I was groping blindly in that fearful, anxiety-ridden existence:

Morning after morning I'd awaken with knots in my stomach. So how's life going to poop on my parade today?

Even before I opened my eyes, my morning began with a critical review of concerns and possible problems. Why did I say that? Now what do they think of me? I wonder what my clients need today? Do I have what it takes to help them? What does the future hold?

But I never had a chance to stay in bed and wallow in my worry. My bowels made sure of that. I would trot to the throne, distress churning my stomach into a frenzy. If the worry and obsession began earlier than the alarm clock, which they often did, going back to sleep after a trip to the bathroom was unheard of. I'd try to settle into bed for another hour or half hour, but I never could relax. My mind was fully engaged by now, the adrenaline beginning its surge through my system and the muscles bracing for all sorts of imagined danger.

At the office, I greeted my colleagues with a forced smile. What do they really think of me? *A bit of last-minute preparation before my first client arrived—always prepare for all possibilities.* What will I do if they're angry at me? What if I get sick? What if I begin to feel sad or sexual, for God's sake?

The morning passed. Lunch with other staff members found me entertaining; I always talk when I'm nervous. What if they know what I'm really feeling?

Ditto for my afternoon. The hours would be punctuated by my colleagues from next door asking me to stop the nervous foot-bouncing that would reverberate through the walls. My stomach constantly churned as it critically evaluated my hourly performances. Maybe I'm allergic to dairy products. Maybe if I just quit coffee.

Evenings with my wife were times to recoup. I'm so tired. What a headache. I wonder if this gut-ache is an indication of something more serious. "What do you think, Myrna?" I think she's really getting sick of this.

Weekends were something I always looked forward to but rarely enjoyed. I couldn't handle all that unstructured time. I've got to stay busy.

And so went my life. It hadn't always been this way. I'd had a star-studded academic career. Honors classes, scholarships, president of this, captain of that. I knew how to play the academic game. The rules were clear; the pats on the head came easily. The structure of my life was set up by class schedules, study time and extracurricular activities. I had ignored occasional bouts of stomach trouble in graduate school. My body's messages weren't coming through at that time because the symptoms weren't intense enough to get my attention.

Like many people who suffer with excessive anxiety, I was the firstborn in my family. (Research tells us that excessive-anxiety sufferers are typically firstborn, lastborn or the "responsible child" in the family.) I was praised a lot, and I learned to perform—until performing itself became a pressure. It became difficult to manage living up to my reputation. Anything less than perfect and "looking good" simply wasn't good enough.

I didn't realize until I entered therapy just how much I depended on external accolades to buoy my self-esteem. It didn't just feel nice to be the leader or the team captain or the president; it felt necessary. While I was boisterous throughout my life, I kept myself fairly well-concealed. Nobody really knew me. I was living a shame-based, image-oriented lifestyle, attempting to compensate for the emptiness I felt inside.

Then real life began. Maintaining a marriage and beginning a career as a counselor in a mental health center weren't nearly as structured and clear-cut as school had been. The pats on the head didn't come as frequently. The people who paid for my services expected results. Outside of work, I had to reach out to meet new people and develop common interests.

Three years into life after graduate school, my sense of security began to unravel. I couldn't maintain my own image anymore—an image I wasn't consciously maintaining to begin with. The pressure I put on myself to be there for everyone else, to be supportive, to be good and to be entertaining was too much. The gulf between what I felt like inside and what I projected outside was widening, and I felt more and more uncomfortable.

I went to my physician for answers. I was poked and probed. Tests were run—upper GIs, lower GIs, blood scans, etc. "Young man, you have a nervous stomach," the doctor told me. "Irritable bowel," it was called. He had all sorts of medications to suggest. They helped somewhat in relieving my symptoms, but they didn't do anything for my anxiety.

A close friend and colleague eventually suggested I seek out a therapist. *Me?* The idea was unsettling. But because my pain was great enough by then, I went.

For the previous few years, I'd begun to take a special

interest in working with people who suffered with panic attacks. *(Those poor people. I'm glad I never feel that way!)* It finally dawned on me, while I sat in my therapist's office, that I, too, suffered with a form of anxiety. I was affected by constant anxiety, more formally referred to as generalized anxiety disorder.

For two years in therapy, I explored all the subtle happenings in my life that had led to my perceived need to maintain an image. Specifically, I learned to recognize my shame (a term fully explained in the remainder of this book).

I began to see my symptoms as messengers instead of curses. With the help of my therapist, I learned to listen to the deep inner messages my body was trying to convey. I gradually became aware of feelings that I had previously learned were unacceptable or unwanted—feelings that had been ridiculed, criticized or just plain buried.

I learned what was reasonable to expect from myself and others. Having learned to expect too much, I had developed a pattern of being either overly responsible or too scared to try. Both of these patterns, of course, produced anxiety.

I learned that anger was essential in healthy relationships and that I could share my frustrations in constructive ways. I found out that such sharing dovetailed with establishing and maintaining loving relationships with my friends and family.

I began to build my confidence by facing things in my life that I had previously avoided—decisions, people, responsibility, conflict and grief.

As the weeks passed, slowly but surely, my joy in life

began to grow. I started to develop a sense of healthy power and self-confidence. My expectations about life changed from nervous questioning of my capability to exciting anticipation of my future. My worries and self-doubts began to fade. I eventually realized that I wasn't looking over my shoulder anymore, wondering when *it* (my anxiety) was going to get me.

After my first stint in therapy ended, I kept remarking to my wife, "I can't believe my life can be this good." No more stomachaches, no more gas, no more worry, no more cramming to prepare for every possibility, and much less second-guessing of myself. I luxuriated in life as it unfolded, enjoying one day at a time, one moment at a time.

Not surprisingly, I became more effective with my clients. Slowly, I began to share my own experience with them when it seemed to relate. As I did, we began to develop a common language. Together we began to understand the commonalities of our condition, from the inside out, and to use what I had learned in my recovery to facilitate theirs. I also sorted through the growing data in the treatment community, incorporating strategies that worked and discarding those that didn't.

As my practice grew over the years, I worked with hundreds of people suffering from different forms of anxiety. I began to recognize common denominators. No matter whether people had been labeled with a diagnosis of obsessive-compulsive disorder, agoraphobia, generalized anxiety disorder, simple phobias, social phobias or post-traumatic stress, the similarities became obvious.

Regardless of their specific diagnosis, excessive-anxiety

sufferers generally felt powerless, lacked self-confidence, weren't realistic about what they could expect of themselves or others, avoided confrontations, and second-guessed their own emotions and feelings. Their sense of identity was often based on external accomplishments and could be easily rocked by criticism. They were sensitive but censored their responses because they feared other people's reactions. When they felt safe, they really enjoyed people and were quite humorous, but frequently they would feel trapped and obligated. They had learned to try to deal with most of life's challenges by themselves. They tended to be awfully harsh on themselves, but they could be forgiving of others who tended to take advantage of their unequal generosity. I realized all these characteristics grew out of shame.

Shame is a significant factor in the development of excessive anxiety. In my opinion, it is the most important dynamic people must face in eliminating excessive anxiety from their lives. It also can impede recovery. It is essential to deal with shame if a person is to move beyond symptom management to really becoming healthy.

This book is not intended to fully describe the dynamics of shame. Many authors have already done a fine job of that. (See the bibliography for some excellent references.) Rather, I am seeking to use what has been written about shame, and blending it with what I have learned through my own recovery and years of work with clients. Many others have written about shame as it relates to alcoholism and codependency. This will be the first book to explore shame as the driving force in the development of excessive anxiety. My goal is to offer a plan of recovery from excessive anxiety that is easy to understand and practical in its application.

This recovery plan has been developed over the years through my work with clients. As I began to teach my clients the same things I was learning, we began to realize that the goal of recovery was not just to survive, but to flourish. We began to understand that recovery meant not just managing our symptoms, but transcending them. We needed to understand that we were good people who were just temporarily stuck and needed to find some new methods of appreciating life. We could use the raw personality traits we possessed—our creativity, our sensitivity and our intelligence—to enhance our lives instead of creatively destroying ourselves. We could use our sensitivity as an asset instead of criticizing ourselves for it.

In the following pages, I will share with you the methods I have arrived at with the help of my clients. I also have included exercises you may want to do in order to further your own recovery. Please note, however, that this book is not intended by itself to "cure" your excessive anxiety. If anxiety is causing significant problems in your life, I strongly recommend that you seek help through therapy, Twelve-Step groups and other resources.

It is possible to turn your perceived liabilities into strengths and to move beyond your fears. I hope this book is a useful tool for you as you move toward recovery and empowerment. It's a challenging journey, but the transformation from a life of fear to a life of fulfillment is well worth each step along the way.

MOVING FROM FEAR TO FREEDOM: A SHIFT OF THINKING AND ATTITUDE

*The successful person has the habit of doing
the things failures don't like to do. They don't like
doing them either necessarily. But their
disliking is subordinated to the strength
of their purpose.*

—E. M. Gray, *The Common Denominators of Success*

Carla originally came to my anxiety program for help
with paralyzing panic attacks that left her feeling frustrated
and inadequate, believing she could not even travel across
town. She was committed to change and made rapid
progress, beginning to try new things and enlarging her
world. At one of our last sessions, she told the following
story:

*Last week I went downhill skiing for the first time. It was ter-
rifying. My husband was busy teaching the kids how to ski, so I
was left more or less on my own. I started down the first part of the
beginner's slope, and I got so scared I literally couldn't move. I went
off to the side and just sat there for probably two hours, feeling
angry and scared and terribly ashamed of myself. The only reason
I didn't quit was that in order to quit I had to get down the hill.*

*After a long time, I finally put my skis back on and started to
work my way slowly down. I kept falling, and eventually, when
I was stuck halfway under a pine tree, my husband came by. He
helped me get up, showed me how to control my skis a little and*

helped me get down the rest of the way. Then he went with me a couple more times, and it still wasn't fun; but I managed to make it down the slope.

A couple weeks later we went back again, and this time I took a lesson. I told the instructor how scared I was, and he was great—he acknowledged my fear, but he was so sure I could do it anyway that somehow I did. By the end of the lesson, I was swooping down the beginner's slopes (which had somehow become much less steep than they had been the first time), doing turns and having fun. It was great. We've gone skiing several times now, and next winter I'm going to buy my own skis.

I asked Carla if she could explain why, when the first experience was so frightening, she decided to go back the second time. She finally said, "I guess going back in spite of the fear was better than thinking of myself as the kind of person I would be if I didn't go back."

Learning to go on in spite of our fear is the bottom line of recovery from excessive anxiety. Recovery isn't not being afraid; it's being afraid but taking action anyway.

Susan Jeffers, Ph.D., discusses this in her provocative book *Feel the Fear and Do It Anyway*. She says, "If you knew you could handle anything that would come your way, what would you possibly have to fear? The answer: nothing."

Underneath every one of our fears is simply the fear that we can't handle whatever life may bring us. This fear, based on our belief that we are inadequate and powerless, comes from shame experienced early in life. We become more capable of overcoming our fears as we recover from the effects of shame.

To recover from excessive anxiety
means dealing with our shame.

Carla had some help in getting over her fear of skiing. But neither her husband nor the ski instructor could have forced her to keep on trying. They could offer information, encouragement and support, but she had to do the work. The turning point for her wasn't the lessons. It was the moment when, in spite of her fear and her shame, she got up and started down the hill. The help she got was extremely important, but her willingness to push through her fear and use the help was what made the difference.

Dr. Jeffers says we can change our relationship to our fears by accepting the following five truths:

1. The fear will never go away as long as we continue to grow.
2. The only way to get rid of the fear of doing something is to go out and do it.
3. The only way to feel better about ourselves is to go out and do it.
4. Not only are we going to experience fear whenever we are on unfamiliar territory, but so is everyone else.
5. Pushing through fear is less frightening than living with the underlying fear that comes from a feeling of helplessness.[1]

Isaac Marks, M.D., in *Living with Fear*, suggests five similar

---

[1]Susan Jeffers, Ph.D., *Feel the Fear and Do It Anyway* (New York: Fawcett Books, 1992), 30.

truths that help to demystify and conquer anxiety:

1. Anxiety is unpleasant but rarely dangerous.
2. You should avoid escape.
3. You should face the fear.
4. The longer you face your anxiety, the better.
5. The more rapidly you confront the worst, the more quickly your fear will fade.[2]

In order to recover from the excessive anxiety that hampers us, we need three things: the desire to change, the tools to make the changes and the discipline to use those tools. You already have the desire to change, or you wouldn't be reading this book. Therapy, books like this one and support groups can give you some tools to change your behavior. The discipline comes when the long-term goal of becoming a healthy, self-confident person becomes more important than your short-term comfort or your fears.

The shift in thinking that focuses our attention on the long-term goal doesn't just magically happen. We can't be sure exactly what made Carla, sitting in terror on a ski slope, finally get up and start down the hill. Part of it was the foundation of growing confidence she had been building through many smaller steps as she practiced facing situations that were fearful for her. She also explained it as something she had to do in order to respect herself. Her integrity was involved. Her desire to be competent and confident outweighed the pain and discomfort of making the effort to overcome her fear.

As you are reading this book, you may very well be in the same state Carla was in when she sat, afraid and ashamed, on the ski slope. You may be tired of living in fear, tired of

[2]Isaac Marks, M.D., *Living with Fear* (New York: McGraw Hill, 1978).

feeling "less than," tired of not feeling comfortable in the world. You have narrowed your world more and more, making choices intended to keep you safe, but you don't feel safe—you just feel stuck. You have come to believe you just can't handle it.

In the same way that Carla reached a point of being able to get up and move on, you will begin to change when the time is right for you. The balance will shift, and your integrity will become more important than your discomfort. You will find your own motivation to change.

> *Some people say that you have to like yourself before you can like others. I think that idea has merit, but if you don't know yourself, if you don't control yourself, if you don't have mastery over yourself, it's very hard to like yourself. . . . Real self-respect comes from dominion over self, from true independence.*
>
> —Stephen Covey, *The 7 Habits of Highly Effective People*

Finding Your Motivation to Change

Many of us are motivated to change only when the pain of staying the same becomes greater than the fear of doing something different. As long as we can keep our lives narrow and manageable, as long as we are comfortable, we aren't likely to grow.

Those who suffer with excessive anxiety put way too high a priority on being comfortable. They attain comfort by avoiding whatever is difficult or frightening; but as they avoid, their lives slowly become more and more limited. As they avoid, their integrity suffers and their shame increases.

I remember a client who suffered with all types of fears. Rich was afraid of traveling, public presentation and a host of other things. He had worked for a long time for a man who did not force him to do anything in his job that he was not comfortable with but who in exchange expected him to work unreasonable hours and participate in unethical business practices. Unhappy but in a familiar and undemanding situation, Rich made little progress in therapy.

One day he called me to say that he had finally quit his job and wanted my help as he looked for another one. Losing his financial security gave him a strong motivation to consider changes. For a short period, he made tremendous progress. Then he found a job and told his new boss about all of his fears and concerns. His new boss assured him he wouldn't be expected to travel or make presentations. He felt safe again. And soon his growth came to a standstill.

Motivation for many of us comes at a time of crisis or change in our lives. Maybe the death of a parent makes us aware of our own mortality. We sense that we have become the "older generation," and that it's time to grow up. Milestone birthdays, when we turn thirty, forty or fifty, can urge us to make the most of our lives. Children being born or leaving home, divorces, serious illnesses, or other significant events often make us stop and evaluate our lives.

But it isn't necessary to wait for a crisis in order to motivate yourself to change. One important motivator is to consciously establish your "mission" in life.

What do you see as your purpose in life? What kind of person do you want to be? These are important questions, yet I find many of my clients have never thought about them in a meaningful way. If we have no sense of a larger purpose, no goal to work toward, then we find it harder to motivate ourselves to make the effort to push through our fears and discomfort.

If you haven't thought about your life's goals and purposes, try this simple exercise.

Imagine yourself as a spectator at your own funeral. What would you want people to be saying and thinking about you as they grieve and remember your life? If your life ended right now, what would people say about you? How would you be remembered? Would you have accomplished what you wanted to do? Would you have been the kind of person you wanted to be?

This exercise can help you establish your own definition of "success." It's helpful to write it down. Create your own "mission statement" about the kind of person you want to be. Then you can evaluate whether the way you are living now is helping you work toward success as you define it.

If it isn't, what would you need to do differently in order to be remembered the way you would like to be? And when would you need to begin doing it? Someday? Next year? Or today?

I think it was the awareness of her "mission" that made the difference for Carla. It gave her the motivation to come back and master the challenge of learning to ski instead of creeping down the slope and running away. It helped her to face her shame-based belief that she was inadequate. In facing her demons, she felt empowered. In the same way, an awareness of your larger goal and purpose can help motivate you to maintain the discipline necessary for recovery.

Ships in a harbor are safe,
but that's not what ships are built for.

–John Shedd

From False Safety to Genuine Safety

Keeping a low profile may have provided temporary safety for a child in a stressful situation, but continuing to do so is limiting for adults. Ironically, while staying trapped in the false security of a constricted life may *feel* safe, getting out there in the world is the only way to genuinely *be* safe. Just ask Carla which felt safer: sitting paralyzed with fear on the ski slope or swooping down it with confidence?

Authentic safety is a genuine sense of empowerment that comes from solid self-confidence and feeling comfortable with ourselves and others. It includes such things as knowing what is reasonable to expect from ourselves and others, knowing our rights, setting healthy boundaries, facing conflict with reasonable assurance, involving ourselves in healthy intimate relationships, meeting life's sadness and loss head-on, and being willing to accept responsibility for the decisions and choices inherent in managing our own lives. The only way we develop that confidence is by interacting with other people. We can't learn it by withdrawing, hiding or sitting on the sidelines. Those ways of coping may have helped us to survive as children, but they stifle us as adults.

Excessive-anxiety sufferers confuse *being* safe with *feeling* safe. Since our feelings were shamed in growing up, we don't feel comfortable with many of our emotions or the situations that evoke them. So we live our lives on the principle that "If I'm really careful, nothing bad will happen to me." Unfortunately, that translates into "If I'm really careful, nothing bad—*or good*—will happen to me."

Shutting Out
Parts of Life Doesn't Work

We may think it would be nice if we could just shut out the so-called bad things, such as sadness, anger, tragedy, hurt and disappointment. Many of us learned to do this as children, and we still live life that way. But what happens is that we shut out all the good things as well. Our bodies don't know how to screen out painful feelings without screening out the enjoyable feelings as well. We end up unintentionally throwing out the baby with the bathwater. As one of my clients put it, "I think I've shut out all the difficult things in life so well to protect myself that I really can't feel life's joy, love and enthusiasm, either."

We must learn to face both extremes in life, or else we risk losing both. Life is a series of contrasts, and it's our ability to allow ourselves the experience of hate and grief that enables us to fully savor the ecstasy of love and joy.

Rationally, that makes sense. If we don't have the experience of conflict, we can't very well appreciate the sense of accomplishment and satisfaction that comes from participation in a win-win resolution. If we've never experienced both the pain and relief that come from utter grief, we can't value the contrast with some of life's exquisite joys.

Many of us have tried to walk a narrow path through our lives, hoping not to suffer any really "low" lows, but paying the price of not enjoying any really "high" highs. After a while we begin to feel like observers of our lives instead of participants, gradually coming to believe more and more "I can't."

For many years I had fallen into a pattern of thinking, *If something is uncomfortable, then don't do it.* As a result, my life had slowly become smaller and smaller. I felt relatively comfortable as long as I avoided this, that and the other. When I began therapy, I became temporarily more uncomfortable as I began to face these situations, emotions and people that I had previously been dodging. In time, as I faced these different circumstances, my confidence grew. My comfort level also increased somewhat, but I still encountered discomfort as I continued to grow.

Recovery is about long-term effectiveness, not short-term comfort.

Remember, recovery is not about being comfortable. Recovery is hard work. It is sometimes frightening. It is about learning to do something different. Living a robust, vigorous and fertile life means being confident, not necessarily comfortable.

I have learned to look at discomfort differently. I used to believe, "If I'm uncomfortable about something, that's a good reason not to do it." But as I explored the implications of this approach, I realized my integrity and self-confidence eroded every time I opted for short-term comfort. Now I have a new attitude: "If the situation causes me this much anxiety, it's a clear indication of just how important it is for me to face."

Sometimes, of course, I still respond to discomfort with a first impulse to run or to avoid. However, I need to keep in mind my bigger goal in life, which is to feel adequate, self-confident and effective. Having such a goal helps me overcome the fear and become willing to make myself uncomfortable. I know it will be rewarding in the long run.

> *Courage is the price that life exacts for granting*
> *peace.*
> *The soul that knows it not, knows no release*
> *From little things;*
> *Knows not the livid loneliness of fear,*
> *Nor mountain heights where bitter joy can hear*
> *The sound of wings.*
>
> —Amelia Earhart Putnam, "Courage"

There Are No Right or Wrong Decisions

It may seem to us as if successful people possess some magic formula for making the "right" decisions. We think of this as a black-and-white area. We are often afraid that we might make a "wrong" decision. Life became much easier for me when I realized there was no such thing as a "wrong" decision; there are simply decisions to make.

Our challenge, once we have made a decision, is to make it a right one. And often the way we do that is by making a whole series of other decisions.

Stewart Emery, in his book *Actualizations*, describes an apt analogy for this decision-making process. On a flight to Hawaii, the pilot explained to him the inertial guidance system. The purpose of that system was to get the plane within one thousand yards of the runway in Hawaii within five minutes of the estimated arrival time. Each time the plane strayed off course, the system corrected it. The pilot explained that they would arrive in Hawaii on time in spite of "having been in error 90 percent of the time." Emery then goes on to say, "so the path from here to where we want to be starts with error, which we correct, which becomes the next error, which we correct, and that becomes the next error, which we correct. So the only time we are truly on course is that moment in the zigzag when we actually cross the true path."[3]

The challenge in life is not gathering enough information so that we never make wrong decisions. Instead, it's learning from every situation we go through, so that we may become more skilled in our ability to get ourselves back on course.

We also may think that successful people are lacking in fear. It's easy to assume we are the only ones suffering from fear and anxiety. Sometimes this is because we mistakenly compare our insides to someone else's outsides. Getting up in front of a group to speak, for example, might be frightening for you. Your stomach quivers, your palms sweat, and

[3]Stewart Emery, *Actualizations* (Garden City, N.Y.: Dolphin Books, Doubleday & Co., 1977, 1978), 19.

you have trouble breathing. You may watch others and be amazed at how calm and confident they seem. But, instead of comparing how you feel with how they look, try asking them how they feel when they're speaking. You might be surprised at how often they say something like, "Oh, I was so scared. My palms were sweating, and I couldn't breathe, and I felt like I was going to throw up."

As Dr. Susan Jeffers points out:

> *If everyone feels fear when approaching something totally new in life, yet so many are out there "doing it" despite the fear, then we must conclude that fear is not the problem.*
>
> *The real issue has nothing to do with fear itself, but rather how we hold the fear. For some, the fear is totally irrelevant. For others, it creates a state of paralysis. The former hold their fear from a position of power (choice, energy and action), and the latter hold it from a position of pain (helplessness, depression and paralysis).*[4]

One Step at a Time

I don't mean to say that going out and taking on your greatest fears with reckless abandon is the way to go. While in some cases that may be just fine, most of the time we have to learn to take things one step at a time. One purpose of this book is to give you some tools that will help you start taking those small steps.

Many of us haven't learned how to leave ourselves a way to win. We tend to approach life in a black-and-white fashion, having very high standards for ourselves. We may try to

---

[4] Jeffers, 33.

take on big goals in one big step. If we make it, we think, *Ah, I was just lucky,* or we criticize the way we did it. If we don't meet the goal, we think, *See, I'm a failure.*

Instead of taking on overwhelming goals, we must learn to break down our goals into manageable steps. With each step, our confidence grows. We may say to ourselves, *I didn't think I could take the previous step, but I did.* That encourages the next step, the next and the next—until finally we may obtain our ultimate goal. But even if we don't reach that particular goal (maybe the goal changes, or it doesn't seem nearly as attractive once we get closer), we still have the confidence we gained from each little step we took along the way.

Later chapters in this book will describe how to break down anxieties into small steps and how to practice "desensitizing"—confronting your small fears in small ways so you can gradually learn to deal with the bigger fears that hold you back from fully enjoying life.

Does It Matter?

You might ask, "But what's wrong with my fears? Maybe my life is just fine the way it is. If change is such a struggle, why bother? Does it really matter?"

No one can answer that question except you. But my suggestion is yes, it does indeed matter. George Bernard Shaw, in *Man and Superman,* put it this way:

> *This is the true joy in life, the being used for a purpose recognized by yourself as a mighty one, the being a force of nature instead of a feverish selfish little clod of ailments and grievances*

complaining that the world will not devote itself to making me happy.

I am of the opinion that my life belongs to the whole community and, as long as I live, it is my privilege to do for it whatever I can. I want to be thoroughly used up when I die, for the harder I work the more I live.

I rejoice in life for its own sake. Life is no brief candle to me. It is a sort of splendid torch which I've got to hold up for the moment and I want to make it burn as brightly as possible before handing it on to future generations.[5]

Suggested Exercises

1. Consider what you would like your friends, family and colleagues to say about you after your death. This will help you develop your definition of success. Then spend some time writing your own mission statement.
2. How does your mission statement fit in with the way you are living your life right now? (Consider E. M. Gray's quote at the beginning of this chapter.)
3. Can you identify the ways that you avoid or sidestep situations rather than face them? What happens to your sense of integrity when that happens?
4. Consider beginning a journal, paying particular attention to your avoidance behavior. What are your thoughts and physical symptoms before, during and after such behavior?

[5]George Bernard Shaw, *Man and Superman* (New York: Viking Penguin, 1903, 1987).

WHAT IS ANXIETY, ANYWAY?
WHAT ARE ANXIETY
DISORDERS?

Fear is an instructor of great sagacity.

—Ralph Waldo Emerson

All of us are anxious from time to time. We worry about our kids or our jobs or what someone else might think about us. We get nervous about trying something new. We are sometimes afraid. Once in a while we can't sleep because something is bothering us. All of that is perfectly normal.

For some of us, though, anxiety is part of our everyday lives to such an extent that it gets in our way. It keeps us from doing as well as we could or from being the kind of persons we would like to be. If you are one of these people, you might suffer from excessive anxiety, like many of the clients I see in my practice:

Ed is thirty-nine, a bank vice president who perspires all the way through his suit jacket when he gives reports to his colleagues. He fears he may lose his job. He also fears being promoted, because then he would be required to do even more public speaking, and he's afraid he couldn't handle it.

Frank is a forty-six-year-old accountant who feels "on edge" all the time. Although at times he is less tense, he has trouble relaxing and never quite feels at ease.

Bev, twenty-two, is a hardware store cashier. She has dreams of becoming a teacher, but she dropped out of college after several panic attacks during classes.

Christie is a thirty-four-year-old housewife who increasingly stays at home because she feels nervous when she goes out in public.

Bernice, sixty-seven, is a retired nurse whose husband died two years ago. She feels overwhelmed by all the decisions she has to make alone now and wakes up a lot at night "hearing noises."

Ted is fifty and lives alone. He has to go through a ritual of checking all the electrical outlets in his house and making sure he has locked the door, sometimes as many as a dozen times, before he can leave the house.

Kelly is twenty-eight and has two young children. She has increasingly felt nervous being alone with her kids because she wonders if she might lose control and hurt them.

Sam is a thirty-seven-year-old business owner. Recently he stopped flying to business meetings because he is afraid he will become claustrophobic and embarrass himself during the flight. Driving to meetings takes much more time, and he has lost business because of it. He can't understand where this discomfort has come from, since he has flown frequently before with no fears at all. Lately just the thought of flying upsets his stomach.

For every one of these people, the bottom line is simply the fear that they can't handle whatever life may bring them.

Some people who suffer from excessive anxiety might be diagnosed as having specific illnesses. The *DSM-IV*, a diagnostic manual for health professionals, lists the following as anxiety disorders:

- Simple phobias
- Social phobias
- Generalized anxiety disorder
- Panic disorder
- Agoraphobia
- Obsessive-compulsive disorder
- Post-traumatic stress disorder

All of these categories are described with lists of behaviors and symptoms (see Appendix C). There is certainly some value to this. It establishes diagnostic criteria that are helpful for professionals. It can help determine whether a person is suffering with a simple obsessive anxiety or whether that person may be psychotic.

But these categories are not sufficient to describe a sufferer's dilemma. Often a person seeking help may have symptoms that fit into several categories, not to mention a few that may not fit any category. It is difficult, if not absurd, to spend much time trying to fit a person into a specific diagnostic "box." This is the drawback to trying to define anxiety the way the *DSM-IV* does, as a disease or a deviation from the "normal."

Instead, I find it more helpful to think of anxiety as a reaction to stress that can be placed along a continuum from "normal" to "excessive." The book *Anxiety Disorders and Phobias: A Cognitive Perspective*, by Aaron T. Beck, Gary Emery and Ruth L. Greenberg, offers the following definition:

> *Anxiety is generally considered a normal reaction if it is roused by a realistic danger and if it dissipates when the danger is no longer present. If the degree of anxiety is greatly disproportionate to the risk and severity of possible danger, and if it continues even though no objective danger exists, then the reaction is considered abnormal.*[1]

Anxiety is a normal human reaction that is meant to help keep us safe. Beck, Emery and Greenberg say that normal, healthy anxiety has four functions:

1. Acting as a check against carelessness
2. Mobilizing our bodies in response to danger
3. Acting as a spur to maturation
4. Acting as a signal flag for underlying conflicts

[1]Aaron T. Beck, Gary Emery, and Ruth L. Greenberg, *Anxiety Disorders and Phobias: A Cognitive Perspective* (New York: Basic Books, 1985), 10.

A Check Against Carelessness

Anxiety is intended and designed to protect us against behavior that may be careless or beyond our own capabilities. An example of this is the "visual cliff reflex." It has been discovered that many infant mammals, including humans, "freeze" when they come to the edge of a drop-off. This inhibition keeps us from advancing into possible danger. It has been theorized that this response can be exhibited in adulthood by a sense of dizziness and immobility in response to heights or ledges.

This useful function of anxiety is related to children's fears of venturing into unfamiliar or dangerous places before they have the needed skills or abilities to deal with those situations. This might include being afraid of water before one learns to swim or being afraid of heights before learning to climb. "Social" fears, such as being frightened of meeting strangers or being separated from a parent or caretaker, can also be explained in this way.

These fears keep us from getting into situations that are beyond our abilities. They usually are eased as we learn more about the new situation and become more confident.

Mobilizing Our Bodies
in Response to Danger

The experience of pain impels a person to take action in order to reduce or end the pain. The function of anxiety is similar to the function of pain. It helps us deal with a real or perceived threat. Reflex actions, such as eye blinking, gagging, coughing, vomiting, diarrhea, dodging, ducking, flinching, retracting or stiffening, may all be understood in this context. The problem arises when we react not to an actual danger, but to our misperception or exaggeration of that danger, either external or internal.

Anxiety activates the nervous system to prepare our body to fight or flee, whether the perceived danger is real or imagined. When people feel endangered, they become hypervigilant—looking for early warning signals that may indicate danger. Along with that hypervigilance, people often have repeated thoughts or images of possible threats. During this time there is increased muscular activity (for example, stretching, flexing or pacing) as we prepare ourselves for defense. Our heart rate increases and our breathing changes, to literally get us ready for greater strength or greater speed.

Inhibition is a mechanism our body uses to curtail risky behavior and buy time to determine appropriate strategies. Often during this time people may experience a sense of mental blurring and difficulty in recalling abstract information as their minds center more on survival. Our movements may stiffen, and we may feel choked up, have difficulty pronouncing words or staying steady.

Demobilization shuts down our bodies and reflects a sense of helplessness in the face of overwhelming threat. Often a person who feels demobilized also begins to feel weak and faint.

A Spur to Maturation

For most people, anxiety acts like a nudge or a spur to push them to learn healthier and more functional behaviors and habits. For example, if you are a student and go in unprepared to take a test, your anxiety is trying to knock you in the head: "Remember this feeling—and study next time!"

If you go to a party and you feel uncomfortable, your anxiety pushes you to learn new social skills. If you don't know how to dance, you might decide to take lessons. Likewise, when you first drive a car, you're uncomfortable, awkward and jumpy. With practice, your confidence increases, until you have developed a new habit and it becomes natural.

A Signal Flag for Underlying Conflicts

As children grow and explore, trying to learn how to operate in and master their surroundings, anxiety is a normal and common response to both real and imagined threats in their world. Children need a great deal of security early in life. Anything physical, emotional or financial that threatens that security can be traumatic. If those feelings of insecurity are not settled and healed, they can become stirred up again later in life when a person goes through a stressful circumstance, such as a divorce or job change. This can culminate in excessive anxiety.

Let's take Hazel as an example. She was the oldest of five children who grew up on a small farm. Their father worked long hours and would periodically go on drinking binges and disappear for a few days. Mom was the steadying force in the family. She, too, was very busy, if not with house and farm work, then in picking up the loose ends when Dad was drinking. His drinking and absences were never discussed.

Because Hazel was the oldest child, she would take care of her brothers and sisters while Mom was busy, particularly when Dad was gone.

Hazel is now thirty-two, working as a nursing home administrator. She and Josh have been married for eleven years and have two children. Josh's work as a carpenter is sporadic, and sometimes Hazel suspects he doesn't really make much of an effort to find jobs. He has frequently lost jobs due to his inability to get along with bosses and coworkers.

When Josh is out of work, Hazel has stomachaches, is frequently nauseated and suffers from sleeplessness. Josh tells her she worries too much. She wonders if she's just expecting too much. Her doctor recommended that she come to my office after finding no physical cause for her stomachaches. Hazel reports that she has not shared her concerns with anyone. In fact, she doesn't have many friends. Most of her life revolves around work and her children.

Hazel's physical symptoms are a classic example of her body's attempts to get her attention and encourage her to notice issues in her life that need to be faced. In this case, roles and responsibilities that she had as a child in her family were repeating themselves in her adult life, and her body was keeping score.

Anxiety Is the Body's Attempt to Keep Itself Safe

When we focus on the healthy functions of anxiety, we begin to realize that it is there to keep us safe. People who suffer from excessive anxiety are creative—they either read danger into a situation where there is none, or they create anxiety through internal conclusions based on faulty thinking and catastrophization. Once we understand this, we can then see anxiety attacks and persistent worrying as an ineffective method of keeping us safe from supposed danger.

In *Managing Your Anxiety*, Christopher McCullough and Robert Mann describe anxiety as "warning signals that indicate a need to reduce both external and internal sources of stress." In his yet unpublished manuscript *The Wisdom of Anxiety*, McCullough depicts anxiety as "an informer whose messages such as panic attacks, phobias, and the like hold important secrets to wellness." He says further in the same manuscript that past treatments for anxiety have often focused on eliminating physical symptoms and have assumed the goal was to "attack and conquer" anxiety.

Beck, Emery and Greenberg suggest that "anxiety is not the pathological process in so-called anxiety disorders any more than pain or fever constitute a pathological process in infection or injury."

Thomas Moore in *Care of the Soul* surmises that "our work in psychology would change remarkably if we thought about it as ongoing care rather than a quest for a cure." Moore, in his therapeutic work with people, helps them to perceive depression and anxiety as messengers requesting necessary changes.

If, instead of regarding it as an illness, we see anxiety as a normal human response to perceived danger or to vulnerability (real or imagined), we can then move away from trying to find a diagnostic container for symptoms. Then we can place whatever symptoms arise on the continuum from normal to excessive. With this model (figure 2.1), we are reminded that those with normal anxieties enjoy seemingly unlimited choices. They take for granted a general sense of safety and freedom, and project a vivacious spontaneity and potency as they approach life's challenges and excitement.

As people struggle with their self-esteem and shame, their choices seem more and more limited. They question their own safety. They may feel trapped. They approach life with an attitude of passivity, bitterness and helplessness. That attitude can range from mild to severe, depending on the depth of their shame-based beliefs.

The more that people believe they are without choices and resources, the more their lives narrow and the more pronounced their excessive anxiety becomes. Their symptoms feel more and more paralyzing until they figuratively transform, as the chart below shows, from standing straight and tall to curled up in a ball.

Figure 2.2, on pages 35 through 37, gives other specific examples of the ways someone's life can become progressively affected by anxious beliefs. As you look at these examples, remember that they are not rigid divisions or labels. Use them as a guideline to compare to problem areas in your own life. They may help you decide which of your anxiety symptoms are mild and which may be more severe.

Anxiety: From Freedom to Fear

Choices

Freedom

Sense of Safety

Potency

Spontaneity

NORMAL   EXCESSIVE ANXIETY

FIGURE 2.1

As Anxiety Grows, One's World Narrows

NORMAL ANXIETY

Parenting	Family	Being Alone	Work
Some worrying about kids participating in sports, driving, etc., but letting them participate.	Discomfort over disagreeing with parents or spouse, but speaking up anyway.	Missing spouse when he or she is out of town.	Passing nervousness when asked to see supervisor.
Frequent worrying and cautioning kids to be careful.	Feeling fearful about conflict but dealing with issues anyway.	Not sleeping well, double-checking door locks, feeling unsafe when spouse is gone.	Assuming when boss calls you in that you've done something wrong.
Not letting kids take part in riskier activities such as karate or football.	Worrying and planning for days before confronting a family member.	Making plans for nightly events with friends while spouse is gone.	Chronic worrying about doing a good job, but still working effectively.
Not letting kids take swimming lessons, go away on visits or to camps.	Manipulating, passive/aggressive behavior, etc., to avoid overt conflict.	Manipulating events to try to get spouse to stay home.	Chronic worrying about doing a good job, which affects job performance.
	Chronic peace-making or manipulating to avoid conflict among others.	Going to a hotel or relative's house when spouse is gone.	Calling in sick when scheduled to do presentations, etc.
Discouraging kids from learning to drive, having friends, getting jobs.	As an adult, subservience to or dependence on elderly parents.	Feigning illness to try to keep spouse from leaving.	Turning down opportunities or promotions because of fears.
Not letting kids out of your sight.	Denying your own needs and rights because of fear of conflict.		Losing job because of anxiety-related poor performance.

EXCESSIVE ANXIETY

FIGURE 2.2

NORMAL ANXIETY

Victim of Violence	Housekeeping	Enjoying Free Time	General Approach to Life
Feeling grief, loss, hurt and anger over incident of sexual violation.	High standards of cleanliness.	Difficult time relaxing. Family, career or other stressors encourage worry and feelings of powerlessness or being trapped.	Living without unnecessary fear and limitations.
Withdrawing socially due to growing feeling of vulnerability.			
Developing various bodily symptoms as one attempts to repress and deny trauma.	Perfectionistic, unreasonable standards; constantly organizing and cleaning; may have strenuous rituals.	Emotionally unavailable due to constant busyness; may be short-tempered.	"If I go there I might have a panic attack" thinking leads to avoidance.
Traumatic memories stirring panic attacks.		Panic attacks occur more frequently; more avoidance.	
Fear of bodily symptoms (including panic attacks) leads to fear of going out in public.	Fears of germs and contamination keep one home and isolated.	Various physical manifestations of inner turmoil, i.e., headaches, dizziness, stomach problems.	Fear of panic attacks becomes a constant preoccupation.

EXCESSIVE ANXIETY

NORMAL ANXIETY

Social Situations	School	Flying
Feeling nervous about attending a party with strangers, but attending anyway.	Some concern about starting college.	Passing thought about risk when planning to fly.
Calling a friend to go to the party with you.	Seeking extensive reassurance from friends, others about going to college.	Temporary mild anxiety during takeoff or landing.
Obsessive worrying about what to wear, what to say, how to behave.	Obsessive planning, visits or calls to college.	Planning distractions such as reading to let you tolerate flying.
Going to party but clinging to friend or spouse all evening.	Choosing college close to home or where friend is attending.	Chronic white-knuckle discomfort during takeoffs, landings, any turbulence
Planning to go but getting stress-related headache or upset stomach at the last minute.	Paralyzing anxiety over taking tests or taking certain classes.	Needing alcohol or prescription drugs to tolerate flying.
Not even considering going to the party.	Avoiding classes or choosing major based on fears.	Only flying in emergency situations.
Avoid making friends so you won't get invited to social events.	Dropping out of school or not even considering going.	Never flying, even in emergencies.

EXCESSIVE ANXIETY

In addition to being in a lower place on the scale, normal anxiety tends to decrease as the person gets used to the new situations or behaviors. The first few days on a new job, for example, would normally produce feelings of anxiety, which would subside as the person learned the new responsibilities and became comfortable. People who have excessive anxiety don't follow this same pattern. Instead of becoming less anxious as they repeat a new experience, they become more anxious. Their interpretations tend to build layers of anxiety instead of removing layers.

What Causes Excessive Anxiety

Even when we broaden our definition of anxiety and place it on a continuum, we are still left with sorting through the various theories and explanations for the causes of excessive anxiety. Theorists have given many explanations, ranging from attributing anxiety to endocrine disorders, such as estrogen fluctuations, to considering excessive anxiety an organic disease.[2]

I don't see these theories as mutually exclusive. There is intriguing research, for example, showing that identical twins who are separated at birth have a higher incidence of developing similar symptoms, despite never knowing each other and being raised in totally different environments. This certainly suggests there may be genetic predispositions involved. Yet many persons have a history of disease such as cancer in their families but never develop it themselves. Is this because they eat differently, exercise more frequently or are exposed to fewer toxic elements than their relatives? We can't be sure.

[2]David Sheehan, *The Anxiety Disease* (New York: Charles Scribner's Sons, 1983).

Changes in Our Society Have Led to the Increased Prevalence of Anxiety

Unquestionably, we live in an increasingly stressful world. When we were a primarily rural society, people knew what to expect from day to day. Families and communities took care of their own and absorbed people's idiosyncrasies. Extended families and neighbors were involved in each other's lives and worked cooperatively.

But the days of community barn raisings are all but past. Fewer and fewer people end up living where they were born and raised. Families are split up when children go off to school or move across the country to start lives for themselves. They move to cities where they may not know anyone. Schools and universities encourage competition. People may feel the need to step on someone else to get or keep jobs.

Technology requires knowledge that is continually updated. To survive in the marketplace, one must stay ahead of the competition. Sharing information is discouraged. It is everyone for themselves.

There is a lot of external pressure in this type of society and little emotional support. Perhaps that is why anxiety disorders are the fastest growing psychiatric condition for which people seek help today. More people seek help for excessive anxiety than for either depression or alcoholism.

One theory is that at least some of us who suffer with anxiety may be more neurologically sensitive than other people. I don't have a hard time believing that. No one can argue with the very real pain and discomfort created by anxiety symptoms, whether it be chest pain, palpitations of the heart, headaches, difficulty breathing, blurred vision, difficulty swallowing, knots in the stomach or a myriad of other symptoms people may experience when they are anxious. That discomfort is genuine and not "just in their head." In that way, anxiety is organic.

However, to refer to anxiety as a disease implies that it is something that just happens to us, or that we are just unlucky enough to "catch." That is where I draw the line.

I am impressed by researchers who have included thousands of people in their studies and have found trends. But I differ with any of those researchers who imply they have "known" those thousands of people and who confidently report that some of them experience anxiety attacks "out of the blue." In my twenty years of practice, I have worked with over a thousand people suffering with one form or another of excessive anxiety. I have had the honor of getting to know most of them quite personally, and I can honestly say I have never met a person who did not have a good reason for having panic attacks. The reason was not necessarily rational or "real," but there was always a reason.

Anxiety Is Not an Illness, but a Human Fact

My concept of treatment for excessive anxiety has been shaped by my own suffering with excessive anxiety for years and by the sense of serenity and freedom I have felt since my own treatment.

I believe excessive anxiety is created by the way we think, the attitudes we hold and the beliefs to which we react. This places a lot of responsibility in the lap of the sufferer, but it also provides us with a lot of power. If this is a disease we are simply unfortunate enough to "catch," then we must rely on something or someone outside of ourselves to "cure" us. On the other hand, if this is a condition created by our thinking, which rests on our attitudes and beliefs, then we have the power to change that thinking, adjust those attitudes and explore those beliefs. We can make ourselves better!

I have seen many of my clients, through sheer effort and will, get themselves to a point where they no longer suffer with excessive anxiety and don't fear its return. Some of them use short-term medication, while others choose to recover without medication. They have begun to perceive their symptoms not as signals of danger, but as their body's method of calling attention to something inside them that needs to be changed.

Excessive Anxiety
Is Related to Our Thinking

Excessive anxiety doesn't "just happen." It is related to a stimulus, which can be either an external event or an internal thought. The problem is not that we have a reaction to the stimulus, but that our reaction (or overreaction) is based on a certain way of thinking about the stimulus.

Life and learning unfold for everyone in part as a result of stimulus and response. If someone were to brush against you in a crowded hallway, for example, you would likely have very little response:

x ——————————————————————————————► x
Small Stimulus   Small Response

If, on the other hand, someone were to walk by and slap you in the face, you would likely have a much stronger reaction:

X————————————————————————————►X
Large Stimulus   Large Response

For those who suffer from excessive anxiety, a small stimulus (a feeling of temporary weakness, a pain in the gut, a loved one coming home late) may lead to an inappropriately large response *(Uh-oh, this is the big one! Maybe I have a tumor. They've wrecked the car and gotten hurt; I just know it.")*:

x ——————————————————————————————►X
Small Stimulus   Large Response

As time goes on, we get so focused on our large response that we lose sight of the subtle things that may have set off that response. In fact, we may become convinced that our response (a panic attack, a headache, chest pain, etc.) may have come out of nowhere.

As we begin to understand that excessive anxiety is related to our thinking, it is helpful first of all to redefine some familiar terms: *fear, anxiety, panic* and *phobia.* The following definitions are adapted from Beck, Emery and Greenberg's *Anxiety Disorders and Phobias.*

Redefining Fear

It is useful to think of fear as based on knowledge and information rather than simply as emotion. For example, if we look at a situation in our lives and say to ourselves, *I don't have what it takes to deal with this,* then we experience fear. This is a normal response. Shame-based anxiety sufferers, however, have had their confidence badly undermined. They are using flawed information, so they conclude *I don't have what it takes* much more often than other people. Fear, defined in this way, is the cognitive component in the development of excessive anxiety.

Redefining Anxiety

Once we evaluate a situation and decide we are incapable of dealing with it appropriately, we respond emotionally. Our fear, combined with our emotion, expresses itself in the form of anxiety. Anxiety, then, is the emotional component in the experience of excessive anxiety.

Redefining Panic

When we have evaluated a situation, decided we can't handle it and begun to feel the emotion of anxiety, our body prepares itself to either fight or flee. *Panic* refers to the physiological process that our body goes through as it prepares to protect itself against danger (real or imagined). Panic, then, is the physiological component in the experience of excessive anxiety.

Redefining Phobia

A phobia is no more than a belief system that says "I can't." To feel anxiety as we approach new experiences is normal. If people are nervous but face a situation *(I'm scared, but I'll try),* their confidence is likely to rise. Then their anxiety will be reduced the next time. But once they begin to believe that they "can't" or that they "don't have what it takes to deal with a situation," then their anxiety increases with each experience. Eventually, a pattern of avoiding such experiences—a phobia—is formed. This is the belief component in the experience of excessive anxiety.

The Thinking Process of Excessive-Anxiety Sufferers

According to Beck, Emery and Greenberg, those who suffer from excessive anxiety generally go through a process of thinking that follows these steps:

1. **Minimization.** This is the thinking process by which we downplay our capabilities or personal resources. We convince ourselves we aren't really very capable or very smart, that we don't have the knowledge, the experience, or the ability to handle a situation.

2. **Selective Abstraction.** This is a process by which we overemphasize our perceived weaknesses. It would be normal to feel uncomfortable in certain situations because of our own perceived social inadequacies (such as not knowing the right fork to use or being unsure of the right way to behave). But we are overemphasizing if we avoid certain situations because of one symptom that would probably be minor to anyone else. For example, one man I worked with stayed away from social gatherings because he was afraid he might blush.

3. **Magnification.** This is "making mountains out of molehills." While selective abstraction is concentrating on our perceived weaknesses, magnification

overemphasizes the importance of those weaknesses or symptoms. The man who was afraid of blushing, for example, would anticipate that he might blush. He would exaggerate the importance of that particular response. *People will really think I'm stupid if I blush.*

4. **Catastrophization.** This takes magnification even one step further. It is exaggerating the importance of an action or a symptom, imagining the most horrible consequences that could possibly take place. For example, one woman I worked with did everything she could to avoid confrontation. She said she and her husband never fought. She was involved in a therapy group I was leading when she reported she and her husband had had their first argument. She was quite distraught. As she described the incident, she began by describing the details of the argument and ended with her fears that she would be thrown out of the house and left penniless on the streets. One of the other group members pointed out that she had simply had her first argument—which for her was actually an important step along the way to recovery. But she had taken the consequences of that argument to the worst possible alternative.

The following diagram, developed by Albert Ellis, Ph.D., can help anxiety sufferers understand the thinking process that leads to anxious behavior.[3]

EVENT ➞ THOUGHT ➞ FEELING ➞ BEHAVIOR

Everything we experience in life is an event. Let's use the example above as an illustration—the woman who had her first argument with her husband. The argument was the

[3]Albert Ellis and Robert A. Harper, *A Guide to Rational Living*, 3d ed., (North Hollywood, Calif.: Wilshire Book, Co., 1975).

event. Her *thought* related to that event was, *This is horrible; it's the beginning of the end of our relationship.* This, of course, led to a *feeling* of anxiety. Because she felt as if she were in danger, her body responded as though she were in danger, and she panicked. Her *behavior* then was hopeless tears.

Suppose the woman had gone through this same event and had responded with a thought something like this: *I must be making progress because I am learning to have conflict.* This would have led to a very different feeling—one of accomplishment and pride—which in turn would have brought on very different behavior.

David Burns, M.D., in *Feeling Good*, describes a cute but poignant analogy about how the way we interpret the events in our lives leads to feelings: "Emotions follow your thoughts like baby ducks follow their mothers. That doesn't prove the mother knows where she's going."

Because we are always thinking, all of us base our feelings and behavior on what we think in response to events. My experience in working with people who are excessively anxious is that they often think negatively. So part of our anxious behavior results from our negative thoughts.

> *The significant problems we face today*
> *cannot be solved at the same level of thinking*
> *we were at when we created them.*
>
> —Albert Einstein

Realistic Goals in Therapy

I suggest to my clients that the goal of their treatment would be shortsighted if they simply tried to get back to the way they were before their anxiety symptoms began. The way they were then is what led them to misinterpret their bodies' signals and ultimately brought them to my office. Instead, I suggest they learn to listen to their bodies' symptoms, to understand the messages their bodies are trying to convey and to become healthier than they have ever been before. In doing so, they learn to put a distance between the stimulus and their response. In that gap, they recognize choices and options they never knew before, which can lead to a very different outcome.

When we approach recovery with this attitude, we don't have to be looking over our shoulders wondering if and when the symptoms will "get us" again. We can then recognize that the symptoms don't have a life of their own. We give them life. And we have the ability to end that life.

Research has been done comparing highly anxious and nonanxious people. The researchers found that, while both groups initially showed an increase in anxiety and physiological responses when in an unfamiliar situation, the nonanxious group's responses diminished with time. Those of the anxious group actually increased. My work with clients over the years agrees with those findings. With repeated exposure to a threatening situation, the "normal" person shows greater confidence and less anxiety, while a highly anxious person often simply becomes more anxious.

There are several possible explanations for this finding. After working with over a thousand people, I have consistently found one factor that affects clients' thinking, colors their attitudes and shades their beliefs. That factor is shame.

When I first begin seeing clients with excessive anxiety, their language is filled with "I can't," "I should" and "I ought to."

Their typical mode of operation is to avoid uncomfortable situations if at all possible. They often worry a great deal, and they may be plagued with physical symptoms. All of these characteristics grow out of shame.

Shame is a significant factor in the development of excessive anxiety. It is essential to deal with your shame if you want to eliminate excessive anxiety from your life. We will discuss shame more fully in the next chapter.

Suggested Exercises

1. List the physical symptoms you experience when you are faced with uncomfortable situations.
2. Write in your journal about the possible connections between your thoughts and the physical symptoms.
3. Use Dr. Ellis's EVENT —➤ THOUGHT —➤ FEELING —➤ BEHAVIOR diagram. Once you recognize the thoughts you have in an uncomfortable situation, what feelings (bodily or emotional) do they lead to? What behavior might those feelings lead to?
4. List some beliefs that govern your behavior. (For example: *If I'm not nice, people won't like me. I should be able to manage my life without any outside help. If I don't do something perfectly, the consequences will be terrible.*) Think about the list. Are there any other ways you might look at those beliefs? What impact do you think the beliefs have had on your life?
5. In your journaling, you might use the terms I described earlier in this chapter—*minimization, selective abstraction, magnification, catastrophization*—to help identify your methods of thinking.

Understanding, Coping with and Healing from Shame

All of us suffer with shame to some extent or another. Those with excessive anxiety struggle with more than their fair share. Shame is a dynamic that we have just begun to fully appreciate in the last ten or fifteen years in terms of its practical application to compulsive and addictive behavior. I believe that excessive anxiety is a shame-based disorder—not a disease—created by the way we think because of our shame.

The purpose of this chapter is to provide some background information on shame: what it is, where it comes from and how it affects us. I encourage you to apply the information to your own life as you read. In what ways have you been shamed? What coping skills have you learned that helped you survive the shame but that are now causing you problems? Understanding some of the ways we are affected by shame can be a useful first step in recovery from excessive anxiety.

Shame is often confused with guilt, but they are not the same. Guilt is generally a healthy emotion. It helps us realize when we have violated our own morals or ethics, and it leads us to apologize and change our ways. Guilt can bring us closer to other people. It is a developmentally more mature emotion than shame. To better illustrate the difference between shame and guilt, let me describe some significant things we learn at the beginning of our lives.

> *With guilt the person's values are reaffirmed.*
> *The possibility of repair exists.*
> *Learning and growth are promoted.*
> —Merle Fossum and Marilyn Mason

The Roots of Shame

Shame is rooted in the second stage of psychological development, which begins for a child between ages one and three. Erik Erickson, a psychologist known for his research in child development, describes the developmental stages and tasks a child needs to conquer at each stage.

Birth to Fifteen Months:
Trust vs. Mistrust

The main task for children from birth to fifteen months has to do with trust. As infants, we have our first experience of the world, most of which is determined by our caregivers. We are totally dependent upon those caregivers for all of our needs. The way we are touched, fed, talked to and treated determines our view of the world as either a safe and trust-worthy place or a place we need to guard ourselves against.

Ideally, through our primary caregivers, we are given the message that someone wants a relationship with us. This conveys to us as infants that we are loved in our own right, that we have value and are special. Our sense of trust evolves from expecting and being able to rely upon a consistent type of response from our parents.

Fifteen Months to Three Years:
Shame vs. Autonomy

Erickson says this is when children first begin to either develop autonomy or succumb to shame. Those of us who have been around children recognize that this stage includes the "terrible twos."

During this stage children begin to develop physical inde-pendence and can experiment with the balance between hang-ing on and letting go. They also begin to experiment with the word "no." If parents can recognize the importance of children's beginning attempts at autonomy, their independence and separateness can be encouraged. If, on the other hand, that autonomy is perceived by the parents as a threat, then they will attempt to quash their children's independence and bring them back under control.

Children need caregivers who are firm but understanding and, ideally, who are getting their own needs met; then the caregivers can be emotionally available to the children instead of making the children take care of them. If caregivers are not getting their own needs met, children may become confused about caretaking boundaries. They won't develop a clear sense of where their needs end and their caregivers' needs begin.

Children need to know that their budding independence and their urge to "do it myself!" won't destroy the bonds with their caregivers. If children can explore, test and have tantrums without having love withdrawn from them, then healthy shame can develop. An example of healthy shame may be moments of timidity, embarrassment or shyness as children become aware that they are not omnipotent.

If love is withdrawn or caregivers are threatened by children's outbursts, children begin to believe that their feelings are wrong or their need for autonomy is misguided.

Three Years to Six Years: Internalizing Right and Wrong

Guilt is learned in this stage of development. At this age children begin to understand the difference between right and wrong and how their behavior might hurt both themselves and other people. Guilt is the feeling they have when they have done something wrong or have gone against their own developing moral values.

Guilt helps us realize when we have hurt someone. It leads us to apologize and mend the fence. Guilt affirms our values. It is developmentally more mature than shame. While guilt helps us to reconnect with others, shame leaves us feeling separated. When we feel shame, we feel broken or different from others, as though we don't fit in or are never good enough.

> *Guilt is about making a mistake.*
> *Shame is about feeling as if we are a mistake.*
> —John Bradshaw

Guilt is a feeling. Shame is an identity. For example, it is one thing to steal something—that is a behavior about which it is appropriate to feel guilt. It is quite another thing to begin to perceive oneself as a thief. That is creating an identity as a thief, and that is shame—toxic shame. When we look at shame from this perspective, it sounds like something we want to avoid at all costs. However, that's not entirely true. There is such a thing as healthy shame.

What Is Healthy Shame?

Healthy shame has to do with realizing our own limits as human beings, accepting our limitations—or accepting our own humanness.

John Bradshaw, in one of his PBS shows on shame, talked about healthy shame as the beginning of our spirituality because it is the beginning of our acceptance of ourselves as simply human. We who suffer with excessive anxiety are usually trying to do it all by ourselves. Typically, the people I see in my office are ambivalent or even resistant about being there. "I should be able to handle this on my own," they say. But our attempts at dealing with our anxiety alone have only led to more frustration and more feelings of shame. We shame-based people maintain a distance from others; we are often forced to try to be more than human, to play God. Healthy shame helps us recognize that we are human, that we aren't God and that we need other people.

Unhealthy shame leads us to one of two extremes. Either we try to be "more than human," or we feel "less than human." In fact, it is often because we feel "less than human" that we compensate by trying to be "more than human." But what is missing in either case is a sense of belonging, of being equal to others.

This feeling that we are insignificant is a core cause of excessive anxiety. We are never quite comfortable in the world. We are always trying to fit in, to measure up, to find a place for ourselves. We live in a constant state of stress.

Beginning Our Recovery from Toxic Shame

Part of our recovery from unhealthy shame, then, is learning to feel more spiritually connected to the people around us and realizing that there is a power greater than ourselves. The beginning of our spiritual journey has to do with accepting our own limitations as human beings.

For this reason, Twelve-Step groups based on the recovery program of Alcoholics Anonymous are powerful resources for people recovering from all types of compulsive behavior, including excessive anxiety. The first step of the Twelve-Step recovery program—one of the most valuable, but also one of the more difficult ones to accept—says that "We admitted we were powerless over [our compulsive behavior]—that our lives had become unmanageable."

A lot of people don't want to give up the illusion of power. They want to keep trying. They think, *If I work just a little harder, I can make it happen.* It doesn't matter that the job is impossible; they just keep trying. It doesn't matter that the other person isn't participating in the relationship; they try to make it happen themselves. They are like the woman married to an alcoholic who told the members of her Al-Anon group (a Twelve-Step recovery program for those living with alcoholics), "I'm going to have a good marriage if I have to do it all by myself."

Healthy shame, then, is the beginning of our spirituality because we come to accept our human limitations, to acknowledge our need for help from other human beings in our journey through life and to believe that there is a power greater than ourselves on whom we can rely. Unhealthy shame is generally characterized by trying to be "more than human" (even as we feel "less than human"), trying to be beyond error and never admitting to our faults.

We Don't Usually Shame Each Other on Purpose

People don't intentionally damage one another with shame. Shame is simply such an effective method of controlling people that it has become an inherent part of our society. But shame severs a relationship between two persons, and behaviors like stubbornness, or feelings like fear and false pride, help maintain the break. We probably all have experience with people who have hurt us, then denied it or blamed us when we finally got up the courage to tell them how we felt. That separates us. On the other hand, if that person would say to us "I am sorry" or "I know I blew up, and I apologize," the relationship would be connected once again.

Shame originates in our interactions with others, usually in our most significant human relationships. But after years of being shamed, we can get to a point where we shame ourselves. When we do this, we can literally sever our relationship with ourselves, meaning that we lose touch with what we are feeling in an attempt to escape that feeling. We begin to perceive feelings as right or wrong instead of simply as feelings.

Many of my clients have been shamed and have shamed themselves to the point where they are trying not to feel their feelings. Those repressed feelings come out in the form of anxiety or depression.

Anxiety and depression, then, are not so much what we are feeling, but what we aren't feeling.

Warning

Before I go any further discussing and describing shame, I want to warn you about something. Shame is an inherent part of our society. We have all been shamed, and we all shame others intentionally and unintentionally. The first time I heard a presentation on shame, I felt awful. I felt as if the speaker had stripped me of my clothes in front of the group, exposed me and left me vulnerable.

As you read this section, you may identify with some of the examples and descriptions. Please do not take this as an indictment or a diagnosis of something wrong with you. The last thing I want is for you to feel shamed by my discussion of shame! The point of describing shame is to help people recognize their own wounds and begin to mend the relationships in which those wounds were suffered.

How Do We Develop Shame?

We can incorporate a sense of shame into our lives in many different ways. These five are among the most significant: modeling, verbal messages, abandonment, neglect and abuse.

Modeling

Until I learned about modeling, I could never understand why I felt so terrible about myself. After all, I was the first-born in my family, the first son in my family and the first grandchild on both sides. I continually got the message "Rex, you are the best thing since sliced bread." But even though I got verbal messages that I was the greatest, my mother and father struggled with their own self-confidence, and as a result they modeled shame. Both tried to deal with their shame in different ways.

I couldn't begin to count the number of times I heard my mother say after guests had left our home, "Oh, I wish I could be like them." She was constantly doing wonderful things for people in the hopes that they would like her. This is part of what Bradshaw refers to as "becoming a human doing." We are doing, doing, doing all the time for people, hoping someday they will accept us.

My father has a heart of gold; he was my baseball coach and my Boy Scout leader. He taught me my love of the outdoors. I remember many times as a child falling asleep in the car and having him carry me gently inside to bed. At the same time, he could be quite abrasive and sarcastic with people when he felt threatened. As a result of this mixed modeling, I was confused about how to relate to people as equals.

The modeling my father had received from his parents must have been even more confusing. From conversations we've had, my understanding is that they provided little guidance for him; he essentially raised himself. His father especially could be abusive. I remember as a child fishing with my dad and his father, and my grandfather making kites by hand for his grandkids. I also remember leaving my grandparents' house in tears because they had yelled at me for some minor offense. Coming from this background, my father deserves a great deal of credit for finding his own way to become a better parent than his parents were. Certainly he gave me far more than he had received himself as a child. Yet the shaming messages, however reduced, were still there. In this way, shame is passed along from generation to generation.

Verbal Messages

Verbal messages aren't nearly as powerful as the nonverbal ones we receive. Yet they can be devastating. Children who are told constantly that they are stupid, foolish or inadequate really have no other option than to feel "less than." They learn that being who they are is simply not enough. One common method of shaming in this way is comparing: "Why can't you be more like your cousin?" Through verbal messages, we may be criticized, humiliated or otherwise hurt intentionally or unintentionally.

Regardless of the intention, words can hurt, particularly if they are coupled with nonverbal messages that convey we are not valuable or that we are valuable only if we meet certain conditions. Usually, nonverbal and verbal messages happen simultaneously.

Abandonment

Abandonment happens frequently for all of us. But for children, it is particularly difficult. As children are growing up, they need a sense of security. That sense of security can be threatened in many different ways. People may move away. People may die. Parents may go through divorce, or the family may need to move away from what is familiar. These abandonments are difficult because children are egocentric. Everything from a death to an argument is "because of them." In blaming themselves they think things like, *Maybe if I behaved just a little better, this would not have happened.*

The worst kind of abandonment is not physical, it is emotional. Emotional abandonment happens when somebody who is significant and may be there physically is emotionally unavailable. This is devastating because a child can't help but personalize that kind of experience. Messages like the following are implied: *Maybe if I were just a little cuter, Daddy would pay more attention to me. Maybe if I were just a little nicer, Mommy wouldn't drink so much. Maybe if I were just a little more interesting, Daddy would talk to me.*

Ironically, children can also be abandoned when there is an overly close relationship with a parent. If parents didn't get their needs met from their own families growing up, they may try to meet those needs through their own children. Children sense this need in their parents and will try to fulfill it. In this way, they feel important and needed. But this is the opposite of what children should experience. Instead of being taken care of by their parents, they instead have to take care of their parents' needs. This is a form of abandonment referred to as "emotional incest."[1]

Children who are emotionally abandoned often blame themselves. They begin to feel insignificant or unimportant; they may feel invisible. The greatest thing we can give our children is a sense of being valued. We do that by being emotionally available to them, which means getting our own emotional needs met elsewhere.

Neglect

Neglect is a form of abandonment. Neglect is passive, while abuse is active. As a result, neglect is harder to pinpoint and prove than abuse, but the results are the same. In my practice I work with people who have been neglected and with people who have been abused. In some ways the person who is abused has an easier time of it in therapy because the

[1]Patricia Love, *Emotional Incest Syndrome* (New York: Bantam Doubleday Dell, 1991).

abuse is obvious. But the person who suffers from neglect often wonders, *Maybe I am just making this up* or *Maybe I am just making a mountain out of a molehill.*

In the following paragraphs I will describe physical, emotional, mental, sexual or gender, and spiritual neglect just to acquaint you with some of the many ways people can be neglected. Keep in mind that there are others.

Physical Neglect

The most dramatic example of physical neglect is "failure to thrive syndrome," where children die as infants because they don't get enough physical cuddling. They may be as organically healthy as any other child, but because they don't get any physical attention, they can die due to lack of touch, of physical and sensual stimulation.

I end up seeing a lot of clients who were raised in well-to-do homes. Many of these people had everything money could buy, but their mothers and fathers were so preoccupied that they didn't get the physical attention they needed. We don't need money to feel good. We don't need money in the family to get what we need emotionally. What we really need in the family is someone who will listen to us, who will care about us, who will hold us and leave us feeling valuable. I often ask my clients if they can remember sitting on their mother's or father's lap getting their back scratched, neck rubbed, hair combed or just being held while being read to. Too often they have not been touched. To appropriately touch is to convey value.

Emotional Neglect

To ask children, "How are you feeling today?" or to notice and say, "You look sad," gives them a sense that their feelings are important and that they matter to someone. If a child can go through a day and feel hurt or sad and nobody even notices, it conveys a message that can make the child think, *I must be invisible* or *I must not be very significant. Nobody even notices me.*

I often ask clients, "When you were upset as a child, who did you go to?" Often they will say, "Nobody, I guess. I guess I just learned to deal with it on my own." They learned very early in life that there was nobody to whom they could turn; they needed to learn to take care of themselves. These people then have a difficult time as adults asking for help of any type, let alone professional help. I was already a practicing therapist when I started my own therapy. I had to overcome some of the messages I had learned early in life that said I should be able to do things on my own. Instead, I realized, *If I am going to do this work, then I had better darn well understand what it feels like to be in the other chair.* Once I began therapy, I experienced the healing that comes with being listened to.

Mental Neglect

Just as it is important to ask our children how they are feeling, we need to ask, "What are you thinking about?" We can convey to children in many ways that what they think is important. We can encourage children as they grow up to pick out their own clothes. We can ask them questions as we watch a television program with them. On Friday nights in our house, the children get to pick out the meal, which tells them their preferences are important.

Children who aren't encouraged to learn and explore are also being neglected mentally. It's important for children to receive answers to their questions, to get help and encouragement with schoolwork, and to have access to learning tools, such as crayons, paper, books and toys.

Unfortunately, many children get the message that they are in the way or that there is only one right way to think. This can be conveyed either through obvious comments like "You shouldn't think that way," or in a more subtle fashion through disgusted looks, sighs or silence.

Sexual or Gender Neglect

The most obvious illustration of sexual or gender neglect is when we don't hear about the "birds and the bees." But there is much more to convey about sexuality than merely making this standard sermon. I remember my parents coming to talk to me about the birds and the bees. My father was not comfortable talking about this type of thing, and he walked behind my mother. They sat down, and my mother began by saying, "We want to talk to you about the way babies are born." She got red, my father got red, and they got up and left. That was the extent of my overt education about sexuality.

But I heard a lot of messages indirectly about sexuality. Much is conveyed by the way parents deal with each other. If people are kind to their spouses, then they convey a certain amount of respect. As parents interact with friends, kids receive a multitude of messages about what males are like and what females are like and how they relate to each other.

As they work and interact at home, either in traditional or nontraditional male and female roles, parents pass along a sense of what it means to be male or female.

Unfortunately, many of us get negative messages about being male or female. We may hear bitter comments from one parent about the other. We may be told directly or indirectly, "You can't trust women" or "Men are only interested in one thing." From birth to about age ten, children generally relate more closely with the parent of the opposite sex. Once we reach those prepubescent years, however, it becomes more and more important for us to model ourselves after the same-sex parent. That type of gender identity is important. Ideally, the parent of the same sex is both emotionally and physically available for that child to model. Parents' modeling, whether good or bad, has a huge impact on how children feel about themselves as young men and women.

Spiritual Neglect

Children need to have answers about why things happen as they do. Many of the clients who come into my office are struggling in some way or another with questions like "What is the meaning of life?" or "Where do I fit in?"

These are important spiritual questions that may never have been adequately explored in growing up. Or perhaps they were portrayed in a rigid and hurtful way. Even if children grow up and no longer believe what they were taught, they have had something to start from. Giving children a spiritual orientation or context for life is not necessarily conveyed through a formal religious belief system. Nonetheless, it is important that people have some sort of belief system, some coherent spiritual package, that helps tie together the meaning of life and helps explain why things happen.

Abuse

Abuse is an active behavior that hurts or controls another person. Abuse conveys some of the same messages that neglect does. The difference is that abuse is more overt. Neglect is passive, while abuse is active. The following sections describe some of the different types of abuse and their effects on people.

Physical Abuse

When children are physically abused, they are told nonverbally, "You have no boundaries. You have no rights over your own body." People who were born and raised in physically abusive homes end up as adults living in homes where there is also abuse or where conflict is avoided at all costs. Either extreme is easiest to practice as an adult because the rules are clearer. Living in the middle, or in a moderate position, where conflict can be constructive, is more challenging and takes a great deal more effort and communication skills.

Emotional Abuse

Emotional abuse conveys the message that there are certain right ways and certain wrong ways to feel. The truth is that while some emotions may be more pleasant than others, none are necessarily right or wrong.

In an emotionally abusive home, people's feelings are criticized, ridiculed or quashed in some way or another. After a while, the abuse victims don't even need the abuser around; they begin to ridicule and judge their own feelings.

In extreme cases, people may get to the point where they successfully do not feel any longer. Most persons who suffer with anxiety and depression have come from homes of emotional neglect or abuse or from families where emotions are bottled up. Their feelings then come out indirectly in the form of excessive anxiety and depression.

Mental Abuse

One of the most dramatic examples I can remember of mental abuse involved a client I worked with years ago. At the time, he was about thirty-five years old. Each time he would write his check at the end of the session, he would employ painstaking efforts to write his name perfectly. It looked like he was writing it with a ruler. After I had gotten to know him a bit, I asked him what that was about.

He said, "I think I know where it comes from. I remember being about ten years old, and I was drawing the inside of rabbit burrows at home. I was thoroughly enjoying it and looking forward to showing it to my father when he came home. But when I excitedly showed him the pictures, he said, 'That's ridiculous; let me show you how to draw!' He sat me down and started to show me how to draw a car with perfect circles and straight lines."

This man had become a draftsman, entering a creative profession where people draw by rules. In his family, there was only one right way to think about drawing. Any other way of thinking was rejected.

Sexual Abuse

Statistics indicate that one out of every three women has been violated in the process of growing up. I suspect that the percentages for men are high as well, but somehow things are translated differently. Remember the movie *Summer of '42*? An older woman took advantage of the desires of a young boy to meet her own needs. This was sexual abuse. But boys in similar situations get the message that they are "lucky," instead of recognizing that they were used.

When people are sexually abused, they are given the message that they don't have any rights over their own body. They feel as though they were to blame in some way or other for the violation. Sexual abuse is not about sex; it is about power and the misuse of power. Much of what gets hurt through sexual violation is a person's sense of trust. Someone who should have been trustworthy used another person for his or her own needs.

Victims of sexual abuse may be confused throughout their lives about appropriate ways to express themselves through touch and affection. Often they move from one extreme to another. Either they develop a sexual addiction, or they withdraw from people and remain aloof. They often suffer with a myriad of physical symptoms, ranging from headaches to gastrointestinal difficulties to chemical addictions.

Spiritual Abuse

Using religion to control people is spiritually abusive. Messages like "If you do that, you will go to hell" or "God will know" set up an incredible fear in our relationship with our Higher Power. It is one thing to hide from people, but how can you hide from God? Religious organizations are composed of human beings who, because of their own shame, may use religion to control or hurt people. Any religious experience that gets in the way of a personal and loving relationship with our Higher Power is spiritually abusive. Rigid thinking can happen in any arena of life, but in religious settings, where people attempt to conceptualize an open and nurturing relationship with their God, it can be particularly destructive.

Eight Rules
of Shame-Based Families

Merle Fossum and Marilyn Mason, in their book *Facing Shame: Families in Recovery*, list eight rules that represent a recurring pattern in shame-based families:

1. **Control:** Be in control of all behavior and interactions.
2. **Perfection:** Always be "right." Do the "right" thing.
3. **Blame:** If something doesn't happen as you planned, blame someone (yourself or others).
4. **Denial:** Deny feelings, especially the negative or vulnerable ones like anxiety, fear, loneliness, grief, rejection or need.
5. **Unreliability:** Don't expect reliability or constancy in relationships. Watch for the unpredictable.
6. **Incompleteness:** Don't bring intentions to completion or resolution.
7. **No Talk:** Don't talk openly or directly about shameful, abusive or compulsive behavior.
8. **Disqualification:** When disrespectful, shameful, abusive or compulsive behavior occurs, disqualify it, deny it or disguise it.[2]

[2]Merle A. Fossum and Marilyn J. Mason, *Facing Shame: Families in Recovery* (New York: W. W. Norton & Co., 1989), 86.

Strategies of Defense
Against the Pain of Toxic Shame

Because shame is an inherent part of our society, we learn many ways to protect ourselves against it. One is to attempt to transcend shame or to try to be more than human. These attempts to compensate for our internal emptiness and feeling of inadequacy show up in nonconstructive behaviors such as rage, contempt or arrogance, perfectionism, power, blaming, withdrawal, people-pleasing or caretaking, and compulsive-addictive behaviors.

Rage

Rage often gets confused with anger because they sometimes look alike. I used to think rage was just anger out of control, but I have since learned that rage usually has very little to do with anger. Rage is actually a protective mechanism. When we feel scared, lonely, hurt or threatened in some way, we blow up in order to push a threat or a person away from us.

Anger, as I will discuss in chapter 6, is an essential prerequisite in a loving relationship. Anger draws us together with people; rage separates us. Usually people who rage are also people who typically bottle things up. After a while there is no more room to bottle things up, and they blow up. Ironically, it is generally the people who have had the worst experiences with rage as children who want to avoid raging themselves. But in their greatest attempts to avoid that possibility, they only set themselves up to repeat it by repressing their emotions. They stuff their feelings until there's no more room, and finally they explode. Then they feel so guilty about blowing up that they try even harder to repress the emotions, and the cycle continues.

People can learn to recognize the more vulnerable feeling they may be experiencing beneath their rage. An example is a man who was in one of my therapy groups. He was six foot five and weighed approximately 250 pounds. Week after week, as we would check in with each other at the beginning of our session, he would slam his fist down on the side of the chair and exclaim, "I am pissed off!" As time went on, people would wait to see where he was going to sit and would sit apart from him. As this man persisted in his personal growth efforts, he came in one day and said, "I realize that I'm not pissed off—I'm lonely." Now people knew how to approach him. He had learned to communicate at a deeper level than the rage that had kept them away.

Contempt or Arrogance

People who come across as contemptuous or arrogant have generally been raised that way. Arrogant people deal with their feelings of shame by judging other people before they are judged, but their apparent self-confidence is very brittle. Healthy people can admit their mistakes and feel comfortable with their own human vulnerability. They can talk about their humanness. They can own their errors and just say, "Yes, that's me. I know sometimes I can be just like that."

Perfectionism

Perfectionism is probably one of the most prevalent ways that people deal with their shame in our society. As I indicated earlier, people who are shamed generally take one of two extreme positions. Either they put themselves above other people and become judgmental, sarcastic or arrogant, or they feel less than other people and come across as withdrawn or terribly shy. The latter has to do with feeling less than human; the former has to do with trying to be more than human. Both types of people are compensating for feeling as though there is something missing inside. Many people are a mixture of the two extremes; they have some awareness of their inadequacies and compensate by trying to be a perfectionist, or more than human.

The problem with perfectionism is that, because we are our own worst critics, the results are never enough. It used to be that if people would compliment something that I did, I couldn't accept the compliment because I knew I could have done better.

Perfectionism is a dead end. Recovery from perfectionism and shame is always relative. We may fear that we will move from being a perfectionist to becoming a slob. The point is to stop allowing perfectionism to control us and get to a point where we control our own perfectionism. When we recognize our unreasonable expectations of ourselves, we can say, "That's good enough, and I can feel good about that."

Power

Another way that we compensate for our feelings of shame and inadequacy is through the exertion of power. Some people develop an illusion of power by compulsively accruing money. Others try to control those around them in order to appear important.

Years ago a couple came to see me. Dave had been raised in a severely dysfunctional home. On numerous occasions he had come home to find his mother with her head in the oven, threatening suicide. His father was an alcoholic. Dave was in recovery from alcoholism himself. He had begun a business in his garage that had evolved into a multi-million-dollar operation. As Dave and his wife sat in my office, Dave's wife told him, "I want more from you." He blew up and screamed back at her, "What more could you want from me!" Her answer was, "I don't want money, and I don't want things—I want you." That was the one thing Dave did not know how to give.

Dave was most comfortable when he was on the road selling his product, flying from city to city with first-class accommodations. He was very generous with his money but had a very difficult time accepting generosity from others. By acquiring lots of money and lots of influence, he had tried to insulate himself against ever feeling vulnerable again—the way he had as a child.

Blaming

One of the easiest ways of dealing with the vulnerability inherent in shame is by never taking any responsibility for the things that go wrong: "If it weren't for my wife, I wouldn't feel this way." "If it weren't for the job, I would be fine." "If it weren't for financial difficulties, I wouldn't drink." "If it weren't for the kids, I wouldn't rage." For such people, there is never any personal ownership of mistakes or acceptance of one's own humanity. How close can you get to people who never own their mistakes? How close are blamers to themselves? People who blame hold others at arm's length. People can't even get close to themselves until they take personal responsibility for some of the inevitable calamities that befall us as human beings.

Withdrawal

One of the more acceptable ways of dealing with our shame is through social withdrawal. This can be either internal or external, and it seems rather painless to others. But it is unnecessary. When I was suffering with my greatest pain, I appeared to be the life of the party. As long as I could keep people laughing, I felt in control. But while I had a lot of people with whom I was friendly, I had no friends. Nobody knew me. I felt that I needed to "keep dancing" or else people would abandon me. I appeared to be anything but withdrawn—in fact, I was obsessed with being with people all the time. But I realized later that my compulsive need only kept me distracted from my fear of abandonment.

Others withdraw more literally from other people. In the saddest cases, people become convinced that they really don't need other people in their lives. Often they get so good at their own delusion that they don't even feel lonely anymore. However, they are making themselves their own Higher Power, and their front is as brittle as my social facade when I was entertaining people.

People-Pleasing or Caretaking

People-pleasing can be an example of repressing feelings in order to cover up shame. We can expend a lot of energy being nice to people to ensure that we won't be perceived as self-centered or selfish.

In caretaking or people-pleasing, the goal is the caretaking or the image, not necessarily a genuine desire to help the other person. Sometimes, because we are driven to this form of compensation, we may be helping people who don't want to be helped, or who need to learn the consequences of their own behavior. Therapists refer to this behavior as "enabling."

Compulsive-Addictive Behaviors

The word "addiction" for most people conjures up an image of drug or alcohol dependency. However, these are only a few of the substances or behaviors to which we can become addicted. Therapist and author Pia Melody has defined addiction as "any process used to avoid or take away intolerable reality." Unfortunately, addictions draw time and energy from other parts of our lives and thus become life-damaging. We pay a huge price for our relief from pain.

Some common addictions include:

- **Eating Disorders.** Eating disorders, which include obesity, anorexia nervosa and bulimia, are all attempts to self-medicate.
- **Activity Addiction.** Workaholism is an attempt to compensate. Running on adrenaline, going until you drop and constant busyness are conscious or unconscious attempts to numb parts of life that may be difficult. Finding balance between work and fun takes practice, discipline and examining one's priorities. Other activity addictions may include buying, hoarding, sex, reading,

gambling, exercising, television, computer games or anything done to excess.

- **Feeling Addictions.** Feeling addictions are another way to alter one's mood. Undesirable feelings are replaced by "family-authorized" feelings. Rage helps a shame-based person, who feels weak and split, to feel powerful. Often, raging gets us what we want, and that encourages us to use the method again and again. Unfortunately, we do it at the risk of severing relationships and ostracizing those who are important to us. Righteousness can be mood altering for religion-addicted people. Excitement addicts may look for a constant adrenaline rush to fill an otherwise empty feeling inside. For others, fear becomes an obsession rather like a bad but familiar friend. Guilt addiction leads some to a constant self-evaluation of failure. They may perceive life as a problem to be borne, rather than a mystery to be lived.

- **Thought Addictions.** By focusing on a recurring thought, one can avoid painful feelings. By obsessing about one thing, one can avoid something more painful underneath. Addiction to detail, however pointless it may seem, can provide distraction. Mental obsessing is a way to stay in your head and out of your feelings.

- **Life Re-Enactments.** Repeatedly entering into destructive and shaming relationships seems pointless. Yet we often see people born into alcoholic homes who marry alcoholics. Often a battered woman finds another man who will abuse her. Unconscious re-enactments of life events give people the chance to repeat events they are not "done" with. It also permits them, over and over, to express feelings that may not have been allowed in the earliest abuse. For instance, a man who was abandoned early by his mother may end up marrying a woman who is emotionally unavailable. The rage and self-righteousness that his marriage conjures up may give release, however unproductive, to feelings he was never allowed as a child.

What Must We Do to Heal Our Shame?

Fortunately, there is a way to heal our shame. The process of healing is specific and defined. Unfortunately, it is also one of the most difficult things to do for those of us who suffer with shame.

There is one thing, and one thing only, that heals our sense of shame—healthy, intimate human relationships.

As I explained in the beginning of the chapter, shame severs our relationships with people and can even sever our relationship with ourselves. Healing from shame involves learning new skills: either the skills to establish and maintain intimate relationships for the first time, or the skills to rebuild our bridges with other people and ourselves.

One way to learn and practice such skills is through therapy, either individual or group. Twelve-Step programs are also available throughout the country and have provided structured support to thousands of people who are interested in becoming healthier.

We need to become involved in healthy relationships where we can experiment with trust and learn that other people feel the same way we do. Then we begin to feel accepted by others and ultimately by ourselves.

Healthy human relationships affirm and free us. Healthy human relationships help us feel spiritually connected. They encourage us to be less judgmental of our own internal experiences as we realize that others feel the same way.

The remainder of this book will help you recognize how shame has damaged your ability to establish and maintain healthy relationships with yourself and others. I will point out ways to listen to yourself and recognize your needs as a prerequisite to having healthy relationships with others. I will describe how shame affects your ability to share healthy conflict and blocks your need to grieve your losses.

We have all heard the saying "You can't love anybody else until you love yourself." That's true! But we can't love ourselves until we feel loved. As we begin to recognize how we were subtly or not so subtly shamed in growing up, we can begin to see the connection between the ways we were treated and the ways we treat ourselves.

When we are shamed, we are given misinformation about our rights and feelings. As we approach adulthood with faulty belief systems and a perceived lack of choices, we may naturally feel anxiety and depression.

I will use the dynamic of shame to weave together the multitude of issues and attitudes that we need to learn in order to become healthy. We begin by learning to relate to anxiety and depression as the messengers and friends they really are. Then we can begin to eliminate excessive anxiety from our lives and replace it with confidence and a sense of empowerment.

Suggested Exercises

1. Think about or list ways you acquired some of your shame. What impact has shame had on your approach to life? What are your typical ways of coping with shame (rage, perfectionism, drinking, overeating, working, blaming, withdrawing, etc.)?

2. Describe the connection between shame and your anxiety symptoms.

3. Think about or list people (friends, family, therapist, minister) with whom you might consider sharing the parts of your life you have previously kept hidden. How might you begin to develop closer relationships with those people?

4. Pay attention to, and write in your journal about, the way you think of yourself when you are with other people.

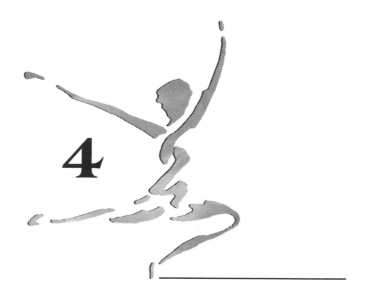

LEARNING TO WALK
BEFORE WE RUN

Seeing Symptoms as Messengers

When my excessive anxiety symptoms were at their
worst, I perceived them as a curse. At the earliest sign of

discomfort, I would tighten up my body and "hang on." Little did I know that the symptoms were only my body's way of tapping me on the shoulder and saying, "Rex, listen to me. Something needs to change."

Early on, my symptoms would come and go depending on the stress level in my life. During the good times I would think, *Whew! I guess I'm all right.* And then the stress would increase and, *Wham! Here we go again.* Later, my symptoms became chronic. I hadn't wanted to listen to my body when my symptoms were milder and would come and go. I didn't even know how to listen to my body. I wanted to believe these symptoms were transient and insignificant. As a result, my body had to "turn it up a notch" before I would pay attention.

At the beginning of therapy, most of my clients tell me either directly or indirectly, "Just help me get back to where I was before these symptoms started." The symptoms are scary. Some people fear the symptoms are an indication that something is seriously wrong. Others fear they are losing control, are going crazy or are dying. As a therapist, it is my job to help people learn to listen to what their bodies are trying to tell them. I try to help them realize that "just getting back to where I was before" is not enough. "Where I was before" is what generated the symptoms.

My goal in working with clients is to help them become healthier than they have ever been before. Once people develop healthier attitudes about life and learn to think differently, they don't need to be looking over their shoulders wondering when "IT" is going to get them again. They realize there is no "IT." "IT" was created by their thinking, so "IT" ceases to exist once their thinking changes. If symptoms arise again in the future, we can recognize them as our body's way of telling us to pay attention, that there may be something new we have to learn.

But while you are learning to think of your symptoms as well-meaning friends instead of enemies, you need to learn how to manage them. The symptoms aren't going to disappear like magic just because you start to recognize that they are only messengers. You need to find ways to live with them more comfortably until you have heeded their messages and are able to make lasting changes.

Losing Our Fear of the Symptoms

One of the first steps in recovery is to lose our fear of the symptoms. Once we understand how our thinking creates our symptoms, we have a greater sense of control. This gives us the sense of safety we need. Then we can begin taking small steps toward recovery, learning to walk before we run.

People with excessive anxiety are generally control freaks. We do a lot to protect the illusion that we are in control. We plan, worry and anticipate in hopes that we won't get caught off guard. And yet, try as we might, we can't plan for everything. So, often, in order to avoid feeling vulnerable or out of control, we stop taking risks. And every time we decide not to take a risk, our world gets a little smaller. Every time we fail to reach out or try something new, our lives become a little more limited.

The more we limit ourselves with "I can't," the more experiences we avoid. The longer we avoid, the more we come to think of "I can't" as a fact instead of a belief. Sometimes people even develop magical rituals to help control their lives: *If that sales call is within five miles of the hospital, I'll be fine. If I can drive to work without having to stop at any red lights, I'll have a good day.*

One of the first things we must begin to understand is how our thinking affects our bodies. Let's take another look at Dr. Albert Ellis's event-behavior continuum, which I first discussed in chapter 2:

EVENT ➤ THOUGHT ➤ FEELING ➤ BEHAVIOR

We are going through "events" constantly in our lives. An event can be anything from getting up in the morning to giving a major presentation.

Every event is colored by our thought or interpretation of that event. For most people, getting into the car to drive across town is a mechanical habit. But suppose a woman has had a panic attack in her car. She could begin to use her creative mind to interpret driving as a test. The event of driving would take on greater-than-normal significance: *Maybe I'll have a panic attack if I try driving again. Maybe driving caused my anxiety.*

This thought or interpretation may lead to a feeling of anxious anticipation: *What if . . . ? This could happen. . . .* This feeling in turn can lead to the behavior of avoidance: *Maybe I'll just call my husband and ask him to drive me to work.*

In reality, an event is just an event. It is our interpretation of the event that leads to our problems.

Remember: The body does not know the difference between real and imagined danger. If we constantly fill our minds with frightening possibilities, our body will respond as though it's in real danger. That is the source of many of our physical symptoms.

Research tells us that those who suffer with anxiety tend to be very bright, emotional, creative, intuitive people. But when I first meet clients at my office, they are not using those capabilities to enhance their lives. Instead, they are using their creative intelligence to scare the heck out of themselves.

Over time, as we react to events, we develop belief systems. These are ways of seeing and reacting to the world. They are based more on our thoughts and feelings about the events in our lives than on the events themselves. One person's experiences in relationships may have led that person to develop a belief system of "You can't trust people. If you let people get close, you'll just get hurt." Another person's belief system about relationships might be "I need the support and stimulation I get from the friends in my life." Obviously, if these two people have just moved to a new town, they are going to approach the challenge of making new friends very differently.

Shame-based experiences early in life can lead to self-defeating beliefs later in life. We may question our adequacy when it comes to developing relationships or approaching the other challenges that life inevitably offers us. Our early shaming experiences may be strong enough to override our natural, healthy, life-affirming responses.

Having seen how our thinking can affect both our bodies and our behavior, it becomes important for those seeking recovery to spend time tracing the roots of their own belief systems.

Fallacious Beliefs

Many of us have been told by our doctors, friends or spouses that this whole problem with anxiety is "in our head." That remark certainly doesn't make us feel understood or supported. But ironically, in a way, those people are right. Anxiety is caused by the way we think or by the way we believe things are.

Our thinking sometimes leads us to perceive situations in our lives as we believe them to be, not as they are. To use a familiar example, for many years people thought the world was flat; they believed they would fall over the edge of the earth if they sailed far enough. Now we all know that's not true. But how about our own beliefs that tell us if we do such and such a thing, this or that may happen? Many of us know logically that the consequences we fear are not realistic or likely to actually happen. But the shame that has shaped our thinking has also helped us create belief systems that have very little to do with logic. Because of that shame and those belief systems, we exaggerate the "what ifs" in our lives until we become afraid to attempt anything.

Dr. Arthur Hardy, who offered an anxiety treatment program, wrote a manual for his clients. In it he listed some fallacious beliefs common to most phobic or anxious people:

1. **Fallacious Belief:** "If I try harder, I could be perfect." **Reality:** Perfection isn't possible. I'm human and I make mistakes. What I would like is to be less demanding and have others be less demanding of me.
2. **Fallacious Belief:** "People won't like me if I'm nervous, so I must hide my nervousness because I want everybody to like me."

Reality: First, people won't necessarily dislike us if we're nervous; they're just as likely to be sympathetic and encouraging. Second, nobody likes everybody else. I don't like everyone I meet. I don't really need everyone to like me; I need a few people to really like and care for me and accept me even if I'm nervous.

3. **Fallacious Belief:** "If I succeed, people will hate me."
Reality: Some people will be jealous and some people will admire me for being a winner.

4. **Fallacious Belief:** "I can't tolerate failure because it means I won't be perfect and no one will like me."
Reality: I'm not perfect. Neither is anyone else, and we all learn by making mistakes. Everyone else makes mistakes, and they will understand if I do.[1]

In my program for recovery from excessive anxiety, we begin to look more and more at the fallacious beliefs that leave us feeling as if we can't possibly accomplish what we expect of ourselves. These unrealistic expectations have to do with our perfectionistic tendencies. We need to come to grips with the fact that sometimes we cannot change what happens to us, but *we can change our attitude about it*. So, as we are racing across town in the car with our knuckles white on the wheel, we can either continue to push ourselves and create emotional havoc, or we can relax and learn to leave a little earlier the next time.

Dr. Albert Ellis identifies a series of ideas or values that he believes are irrational, superstitious or senseless and that "would seem inevitably to lead to widespread neurosis":

1. It is essential that one be loved or approved of by virtually everyone in the community.

---

[1] Arthur Hardy, Terrap Foundation Manual (Menlo Park, Calif., 1981).

2. One must be perfectly competent, adequate and achieving to consider oneself worthwhile.
3. It is a terrible catastrophe when things are not as one wants them to be.
4. Unhappiness is caused by outside circumstances, and the individual has no control over it.
5. Dangerous or fearsome things are causes for great concern, and their possibility must be continually dwelt upon.
6. It is easier to avoid certain difficulties and self-responsibilities than to face them.
7. One should be dependent on others and must have someone stronger on whom to rely.
8. Past experiences and events are the determiners of present behavior; the influence of the past cannot be eradicated.
9. One should be quite upset over other people's problems and disturbances.
10. There is always a right or perfect solution to every problem, and it must be found or the results will be catastrophic.[2]

Spend some time thinking about this list of beliefs. How many of them do you subscribe to? It doesn't matter whether you agree or disagree with most of the items on the list. Use it as a starting point to identify some of your own fallacious beliefs. You might find it helpful to make your own personal list.

---

[2]Albert Ellis and Robert A. Harper, *A Guide to Rational Living*, 3d ed., (North Hollywood, Calif.: Wilshire Book Co., 1975).

Common Denominators That Lead to Fear

Most people's anxieties have one or two common denominators. Whether their specific fear is of flying, meeting new people or being alone, people with anxiety have a couple of basic things about which they are uncomfortable or fearful. One is "What will people think?" Another is the fear of being trapped or out of control. The bottom line is that we just don't feel we have what it takes to deal with certain situations. But as we face those situations and learn we have more choices and alternatives than we previously believed, our confidence increases and our anxieties are reduced.

Thought-Sorting

As anxious people, many of us find it difficult to sort and separate the jumble of thoughts whirling around in our minds. As we think about different issues and concerns, we never quite manage to come to any conclusions about them. Just as we are grappling with a particular concern and considering all its negative possibilities, along comes a new concern or issue to collide with the first one, and we are off in a new direction.

I find journaling a useful tool for breaking this cycle. Writing things down helps me to discipline myself. When I list my concerns, I can distinguish them from one another, and I am able to finish my thoughts about them. Even if I encounter negative or difficult possibilities, journaling helps me brainstorm and find effective responses. Then my mind can come to rest, instead of just obsessing and spinning.

Another valuable way to sort out your thinking is through counseling. It's often useful to spend some time reviewing your history to understand how your current reactions grow out of past experiences.

The realization that excessive anxiety grows out of our own thinking can be a double-edged sword. On the one hand, it can be extremely helpful to understand the relationship between thoughts and behaviors. On the other hand, we can waste a lot of energy trying to figure out what unconscious thought led to what anxious response. It's like asking a man with a long beard whether he sleeps with the beard inside or outside the covers. The poor man is likely to spend a few sleepless nights as he tries to pay attention to something he had been doing automatically. In the same way, we can drive ourselves crazy trying to figure out how our current anxiety symptoms may be related to specific thoughts. Often it's a better idea to simply work on changing the thought to something more constructive.

Every bit of our anxiety happens when we are either worrying about the future or beating ourselves up about a perceived failure in the past. We have absolutely no anxiety if we can discipline ourselves to live in the now.

Learning to Relax

An awareness of the way our thinking leads to our symptoms is only one step toward recovery. We also need to learn how to manage those symptoms and reduce their effects on our bodies. Learning to relax instead of tightening up and sending more adrenaline into our systems is an important part of getting better. Physical relaxation and anxiety are mutually exclusive.

I remember sitting in a physician's waiting room one day and hearing him in his office talking with another patient. "You need to learn how to relax," he told her. In a few minutes she came out with a prescription in her hand and went on her way. If that patient had known how to relax, she probably wouldn't have come to the doctor in the first place. Many of us have never had role models for relaxing, so we never have learned how. But relaxing is a very specific process that we can easily master with a little practice.

Goals for Relaxation

When people begin treatment for anxiety, they are often stuck in a cycle of fear that has left them more and more sensitive to stimuli in their lives. Stressors happen in everyone's lives, but because people with anxiety have a difficult time relaxing, they never fully allow their bodies to relax after each stimulus. With time, they become more and more guarded, and it takes less and less to set off unnecessary anxiety.

One goal of my work with people is to teach them what it feels like to be fully relaxed. The aim is, ideally, for them to be able to relax fully between each stimulus in life so they have all of their strength available when a new stimulus appears. The key word here is "ideally," because in all likelihood they will often not get themselves fully relaxed before the next challenge in life comes along. But once they do learn how to relax, once they recognize the need to have all of their strength available, they can practice relaxing more fully after each successive challenge.

Learning to Breathe Properly

When I ask my clients to take a deep breath for me, as we first begin our work together, most of them take a breath that raises the shoulders and fills the upper chest. This is known as "shallow breathing," and most excessive anxiety sufferers breathe very shallowly much of the time, periodically taking deep breaths, or sighing or yawning to "catch up."

This breathing pattern sets the body up for oxygen starvation and can create symptoms such as blurred vision, ringing in the ears, headaches, muscle tension, nausea, chest pain, hot and cold flashes or numbness in the extremities. Anxiety sufferers, being the creative and rather suggestible people they are, tend to interpret these symptoms catastrophically: *Oh no, here we go again. Maybe I'm having a heart attack. I wonder if I could have a tumor?* This kind of thinking leads to greater fear, which leads to more breathing problems, which leads to more symptoms. This continuing cycle builds on itself and intensifies, and our anxiety escalates.

Learning to breathe more deeply is a first step in alleviating those symptoms. This simple physical technique is the basis for relaxation and can be instrumental in learning to get oneself "centered in the here and now."

The foundation of deep relaxation techniques is breathing from the diaphragm. This is "belly breathing," and it does not involve raising the shoulders or expanding the upper chest. To practice breathing from the diaphragm, lie down and place one hand on your lower stomach area, just about at your navel. Breathe slowly and regularly, letting your belly rise and fall with each breath. You'll notice that your shoulders and upper chest hardly move.

When people are breathing in this way, they typically take from fifteen to twenty breaths a minute. Some interesting research has shown that people who have a pattern of breathing more slowly and deeply tend to be more confident, emotionally stable, and physically and intellectually vibrant. Those with shallow, rapid breathing patterns tend to be more passive, dependent, fearful and shy. Many of my clients have speculated that perhaps they learned to breathe shallowly for a variety of reasons: so nobody would notice they were there; because nobody noticed they were there; or in response to the continual tension and frustration they lived with.

Learning Deep Relaxation

Once you have become comfortable with deep breathing, it's time to move on to learning relaxation. There are many ways to approach deep relaxation, and it is important to find the type of method that is most helpful to you. Some persons respond best to a progressive relaxation, using imagery to begin at the top of the head and allowing each muscle group to relax as the image moves down the body. Others find meditation helpful. There are many books available on the subject. You may also benefit from classes in yoga or meditation. Regardless of the technique you practice, you'll find it valuable to use deep relaxation to take a bodily inventory of what may be going on inside of you.

I generally find with my clients that those who are not making the kind of progress they would like have skipped over deep breathing and relaxation because they couldn't find time for it or found it boring. Because it is a skill that requires practice, and because it may be so different from what someone is used to, deep breathing and relaxation take commitment and discipline to learn. I suggest to my clients that they practice relaxation twice a day for at least four weeks. Usually that is long enough to begin to see positive results and to develop a new habit.

Here's the deep relaxation technique I teach to my clients. A good way to practice it is to record the exercise on a tape for yourself or have someone else record it for you. Read the exercise slowly, in a soothing voice, pausing as noted to allow time to follow the instructions at a relaxed pace.

The technique is intended to first teach you how to relax, then teach you how to understand the connection between your thoughts, emotions and physical responses. If this whole idea is quite new for you, you might want to start by recording only part I of the exercise, including the creation of your own "safe place." Don't include part II, with the remembered emotions, until you can vividly picture your safe place. You may have a powerful response to the emotional memories. If so, perhaps your body is suggesting the need to explore your memories with a therapist.

In order to practice relaxation, find a time and a place where you won't be interrupted. I recommend to my clients that they practice twice a day, once in the morning to help get ready for the day, and once in the evening to unwind from the day. Loosen or take off any tight, constricting clothing and settle yourself comfortably on a bed, the floor or a soft chair. Then play the tape and follow the directions. Don't worry if you don't succeed in relaxing fully the first few times. This is a skill like any other; it takes practice. And even if you don't "do it perfectly," whatever level of relaxation you do achieve will be helpful for you.

Part I

Let's just begin by listening to your own breathing. *(pause)* In ... and ... out. Like the waves of an ocean, taking it in and letting it go. Taking it in and letting it go. *(pause)* When you're feeling scared, or lonely, or hurt, or vulnerable in any way, your breathing generally goes up into your chest, or perhaps you hardly breathe at all. *(pause)* But for just a moment, allow your breathing to become deeper and deeper with each passing breath. *(pause)* When you're fully relaxed, your breathing is coming from the very bottom of your stomach, in one slow, smooth process. And the only thing you're thinking about is your breath and my voice. In ... and ... out. In ... and ... out.

Now, slowly and easily, allow yourself to notice a gentle light above your head. *(pause)* It's a soft, mellow color, and it feels warm and soothing. *(pause)* Perhaps it gives off a gentle, rhythmic sound, like the soothing lullaby of easy waves lapping slowly on a beach. *(pause)* Once you're aware of that soft, warm light, allow it to drift through the top of your head and to move gently back and forth inside your head. *(pause)* Let the light be aware of all the little things that you have on your mind that can consume so much energy. And for just this moment, with each passing breath, let them go, one by one. *(pause)* Until, for just a few moments, the only thing that you're thinking about is that light and my voice. *(pause)*

Allow the light to pay particular attention to the muscles around your eyes, your nose, your mouth, your jaw and around the back of your head, until the muscles relax, loosen and sag. *(pause)* Perhaps your mouth hangs just slightly open. Do this until your entire head feels relaxed, pleasantly heavy and firmly supported by the surface beneath it. *(pause)* Then allow that warmth and that light to slowly drift down your neck, massaging the muscles that connect your head to your neck, *(pause)* drifting slowly down, massaging the muscles that connect your neck to your shoulders, *(pause)* until your neck, too, feels relaxed, pleasantly heavy and firmly supported by the surface beneath it. *(pause)*

Then allow that light to pause at the bottom of your neck, slowly separating into two lights, equally as warm, equally as relaxing. *(pause)* Allow one light to drift across one shoulder and one light to drift across the other shoulder, relaxing and massaging the muscles along the tops of your shoulders, *(pause)* your upper back, *(pause)* your shoulder blades. *(pause)* Allow each light to slowly drift down each arm, massaging and relaxing the muscles in your upper arm, *(pause)* through your elbow, *(pause)* along your forearm, *(pause)* through your wrists and into your hands, *(pause)* to the very tips of your fingers, until they, too, feel warm and relaxed, *(pause)* pleasantly heavy *(pause)* and firmly supported by the surface beneath them. *(pause)*

Now allow the two lights to gently and slowly drift back together again into one light at the bottom of your neck. *(pause)* And then allow that light to drift back and forth inside your chest, massaging and relaxing the muscles in your lungs, your chest, your middle back, *(pause)* drifting slowing down through your internal organs, allowing them to slow down. *(pause)* Allow the light to move around your waist, *(pause)* across your buttocks and throughout your entire pelvic region, *(pause)* until the entire upper and lower portions of your body feel relaxed, pleasantly heavy and firmly supported by the surface beneath them. *(pause)*

And then, once again, allow that light to pause and to separate slowly into two warm, soft lights. *(pause)* Allow one light to drift down one leg *(pause)* and one light to drift down the other leg, *(pause)* relaxing and massaging the muscles in your upper thighs, *(pause)* the backs of your legs, *(pause)* the fronts of your legs, *(pause)* through your knees, *(pause)* along your shins and calves, *(pause)* through your ankles, *(pause)* and into your feet, to the very tips of your toes. *(pause)* Let that warm light rest gently and easily, as by now your entire body feels relaxed, warm, pleasantly heavy *(pause)* and firmly supported by the surface beneath it. *(pause)* And, for a few moments, allow yourself just to be and to stay in that warm relaxation. *(pause)*

Be aware in a gentle way that there may be places in your body that, even since you relaxed them, have tensed up again. *(pause)* Perhaps they never relaxed at all. *(pause)* And if that's true, just quietly notice where those areas are. *(pause)* With time and practice, your relaxation will become deeper and more complete. *(pause)* Just be aware of how relaxed your body can feel and how long it may have been since you felt this relaxed. *(pause)*

And then, easily and gently, what I'd like you to do is create a place in your mind that feels very, very safe. *(pause)* It may be a real place. *(pause)* It may be an imaginary place. *(pause)* There may be trees, *(pause)* there may be animals, *(pause)* there may be sand and water, *(pause)* or there may be nothing at all. *(pause)* There may be other people, *(pause)* or you may be alone. *(pause)* But begin to create that special place in your mind where you feel absolutely safe and relaxed. *(pause)* Where you can gather your strength, where you can let down your guard and feel safe. *(pause)* Be aware of the colors in that place. *(pause)* Be aware of the smells in that place. *(pause)* Be aware of the sounds in that place. *(pause)* Take as much time as you need to experience all of them, clearly and vividly, but in a peaceful, relaxed way. This is your very own place of refuge and security. *(pause)* And just know that, anytime you like, your safe place is within you. *(pause)* You can go there anytime you need to. *(pause)* No matter where you are or what's happening around you, you can escape to that place in your mind. *(pause)* It's always there for you whenever you need to relax, to regain your strength. *(pause)*

Part II

Once you are comfortable within your safe place, begin to allow yourself to picture a time when you felt very, very angry. *(pause)* Be aware of the people and the circumstances of that time. *(pause)* Be aware of the sounds, the colors and the objects in that place. *(pause)* And picture yourself in that time—*(pause)* your own posture, *(pause)* the way you looked—*(pause)* and then put yourself inside that memory. And be aware of what it feels like to be that angry, *(pause)* and what happens to your body and your muscles and your breathing as you're feeling that angry. *(pause)* And then once again remove yourself from that situation, *(pause)* block it out completely. Block it from your mind and return to your safe place—*(pause)* that place where you can relax, *(pause)* where you can let down, *(pause)* where you can be absolutely safe—*(pause)* to regain your strength. *(pause)* Take a deep breath, hold it, and let it go. *(pause)*

And then allow yourself to remember a time when you felt very, very sad. *(pause)* Remember the people in that place, *(pause)* the objects *(pause)* and the circumstances, *(pause)* the colors, *(pause)* the sounds, *(pause)* the smells. *(pause)* And then remember yourself in that place. *(pause)* Perhaps you can picture the way your body looked when you were very, very sad. *(pause)* And then put yourself inside that memory, back in that place and time, *(pause)* and allow yourself to feel what it felt like to be that sad. *(pause)* Be aware of what happens to your body, what happens to your muscles as you feel that sadness. *(pause)* But before you get too terribly uncomfortable, allow yourself to return to your safe place. *(pause)* Go back to your refuge, and block out that picture in your mind where you felt sad, and instead just feel relaxed. *(pause)* Forget about that sad time, *(pause)* block it out and just regain your strength. *(pause)* Take a deep breath, hold it, *(pause)* and let it go. *(pause)* Take as much time as you need to feel safe and relaxed again in this place where you can let go and be yourself. *(pause)*

And then allow yourself to picture a time when you felt a lot of love and joy. *(pause)* Remember the time, the circumstances, the people. *(pause)* Remember the sounds, *(pause)* the smells, *(pause)* the colors. *(pause)* Picture yourself as you're feeling that kind of love and joy. *(pause)* Then put yourself inside that picture. *(pause)* Feel what happens to your body as you feel that kind of joy and love. *(pause)* Feel how it affects your muscles and your breathing. And then, once again, remove yourself from that memory and allow yourself to go back to your safe place. *(pause)* Return to that spot where you can gather your strength, where you can feel absolutely safe. Take a deep breath, hold it, and let it go. *(pause)*

Be aware of just how relaxed your body can feel. And know that, regardless of the circumstances in which you find yourself, you can allow yourself to escape to that safe place. *(pause)* That refuge is there for you whenever you need to back up, *(pause)* to remove yourself for a few moments from a difficult situation, *(pause)* to take a deep breath, *(pause)* to regain your strength and go on. With time and practice, the relaxation becomes easier and deeper. *(pause)* Be aware of how relaxed your body can feel. *(pause)* Allow yourself to fully experience and savor that feeling. *(pause)*

And then slowly allow yourself to come back to your physical surroundings. *(pause)* Become aware of the feeling of the surface you're sitting or lying on, *(pause)* any sounds in the room, *(pause)* the space that surrounds you. *(pause)* And when you finally feel ready, very slowly open your eyes, *(pause)* unfocused, *(pause)* and then gradually open them, *(pause)* fully aware. *(pause)* Come back into the present, fully awake and refreshed.

Deep Relaxation: The Value of Including Emotional Experiences

When I first teach people deep relaxation, I also use the opportunity to help them see the connection between their body's ability to relax and some of the thoughts that run through their head. When I ask people to think of angry, sad and happy times, they often notice how just recalling those memories leads to a change in their muscle tension and their breathing. As people recognize this connection, they become more able to recognize when their internal context is leading to some of their physical symptoms.

When you do the relaxation exercise, stay with the emotional memories only long enough to see the connection between them and your body's reactions. This might be only ten or fifteen seconds. If your emotions begin to feel overwhelming and scary, go immediately to your safe place. Depending on the severity of your reaction, you might consider discontinuing this part of the exercise for a time. Or you might begin with less powerful memories that evoke more subdued responses. And again, please remember that professional help is available and can be valuable as you work with strong emotional memories.

Once you have had the chance to do this exercise and see the connection between your emotional experiences and your body's ability to relax, you can record your relaxation tape again without including the emotional experiences at the end. Then you can use it simply as an aid to deep relaxation.

The Importance of Creating a Safe Place

The ability to create a safe place in our mind is of vital importance. Most people are able to construct or remember a place where they felt safe at some point in their lives. Realizing that they can take that place with them wherever they go, that they can enjoy the benefits of deep, relaxation by simply going there in their mind and taking a deep, cleansing breath, can be an important way for some people to learn the process of self-soothing.

Others in my practice have had a more difficult time remembering or constructing a safe place. Some of these people came from homes where they never felt safe, and they have known little happiness in their lives. If you are in a situation like this, it's important to take as much time as you need to create that safe place in your mind. You may need to repeat the relaxation exercise several times before you have a place that feels like a refuge for you. In creating that place, you can take advantage of the opportunity to include favorite colors, comfortable furniture and environments (real or imagined) that you find appealing. Make sure you pick a setting that actually feels safe to you, rather than one that you think ought to be relaxing. If you're uncomfortable in the water, for example, you might not feel safe in a beach setting.

Please take the time to do this exercise thoroughly, even if you need several sessions to complete it. It can be another way of becoming acquainted with yourself. Once constructed, the safe place becomes a very important technique you can use to see yourself in ways you may never have before.

Putting It All Together: Desensitizing

Once you understand how your thinking can affect your body and how you can relax your body instead of tightening it up, you can begin to use these techniques in your daily living. You can help yourself relax as you approach things in your life that you may have been avoiding or doing fearfully. The process of learning a relaxed and methodical way to face the things you are uncomfortable doing is called "desensitization."

Desensitization sounds very complicated, but it is actually

very simple. Basically it means taking things a little bit at a time. It's the same technique physicians use when they give allergic patients a series of allergy shots; they build up their patients' tolerance to an allergen by gradually increasing the dosage.

Desensitizing by taking a little at a time is important for a couple of reasons. At first, you will have to be thinking about what makes you uncomfortable and relaxing at the same time. It will take a while before relaxation becomes a practiced habit. Second, you have frightened yourself before in this situation, and you will have to rebuild your confidence slowly. Taking "too big a bite" will leave you feeling overwhelmed.

It is often helpful to start desensitizing by imagining yourself in a situation, rather than actually experiencing it. After a few trial runs this way, you are more prepared for the real event. It also can be useful to start with situations that are not the most stressful ones you have to face. If you can work your way successfully through a moderately stressful event, you help build your confidence to tackle a more stressful one.

As you begin desensitizing, study the following scale of physical symptoms. It will help you gain more and more awareness about your level of anxiety and ultimately give you more of a sense of control.

Scale of Physical Anxiety Symptoms

1. Butterflies in stomach	
2. Sweaty or clammy palms; feeling warm all over	AREA OF CONTINUED
3. Rapid or strong heartbeat; tremor; muscle tension	ABILITY TO FUNCTION
4. Shaky legs; feeling wobbly	
5. Dry mouth; feeling a need to escape or hide	
6. Lump in throat; strong muscle tension	AREA OF DECREASED
7. Tight chest; hyperventilation	ABILITY TO FUNCTION
8. Stiff neck; headache; feeling of doom	
9. Dizziness; nausea; diarrhea; visual distortion; numbness	
10. Panic (feeling disoriented; spacey; detached; nonfunctional)	AREA OF NON-FUNCTION

SOURCE: Arthur Hardy, Terrap Foundation Manual (Menlo Park, Calif., 1981). TABLE 4.1

Beginning to desensitize means taking on the frightening situation or the anxious thought in whatever way that lets you maintain your ability to function (items 1 through 3 or 4 on the scale). This may be through images in your mind as you are relaxing yourself in a chair, or it may be actually entering a circumstance that is difficult for you. Stay in the situation or with the thought, either in your mind or in reality, until your anxiety symptoms begin to rise above the level of item 3. Then retreat.

Retreating is leaving a situation with the intention of returning, and there is nothing wrong with retreating. In fact, all of us need to know that we have that option. Running, on the other hand, is leaving with the intent of never returning. Running leads to immediate, short-term relief but also leads to a loss of self-confidence and the belief that "I can't" in the future.

Express any feelings that may have been stirred up by being in the circumstance. Then keep practicing desensitization until your confidence in that situation is at the level you would like it to be.

Keep in mind that the technique of desensitization is much more effective if you practice it when there is little pressure on you to perform. For instance, if you are anxious about shopping and you must go to the store to buy groceries, using desensitization and deep relaxation can help. But your best time for developing even greater confidence is going to the store at a time when it isn't busy and when you don't have to buy anything. Then you are free to retreat as necessary.

If you want to try desensitizing on your own, read through the following examples from Dr. Hardy's manual.[3] Then adapt the process to fit your own needs. You might want to write out your own specific, step-by-step process. In some cases, the process is much easier if you ask a trusted friend or family member to work with you as a partner and support person. Some especially stressful circumstances are difficult to desensitize without help. It might be valuable to discuss these kinds of situations with a therapist for help in breaking them down into small, manageable steps.

[3]Arthur Hardy, Terrap Foundation Manual (Menlo Park, Calif., 1981).

Desensitizing Process for the Fear of Being Alone

1. Leave the house for 1–5 minutes; partner remains in the house.
2. Leave the house for 10–15 minutes; partner remains in the house.
3. Leave the house for increasing 10-minute intervals, up to 60 minutes; partner remains in the house.
4. Leave the house for 10–30 minutes; partner available by phone.
5. Leave the house for 30–60 minutes; partner's whereabouts unknown.
6. Leave the house for 2–3 hours; partner's whereabouts unknown.
7. Have partner leave you alone in the house for 1–5 minutes.
8. Have partner leave you alone in the house for 10–30 minutes.
9. Have partner leave you alone in the house for up to 60 minutes.
10. Have partner leave you alone in the house for 2–4 hours, calling you at half-hour intervals.
11. Have partner leave you alone in the house for 2–4 hours; partner's whereabouts unknown.

Desensitizing Process for Fear of Dentists

1. With partner, walk in and out of dentist's office.
2. With partner, sit in waiting room for 2–5 minutes.
3. With partner, sit in waiting room for 10–15 minutes.
4. Make appointment with dentist just to talk for 5–10

minutes. Explain your problem and the fact that you are trying to desensitize yourself; ask for dentist's cooperation.

5. With partner, sit in dental chair for 5–10 minutes without dentist in attendance, then leave.
6. With partner, sit in dental chair for 10–20 minutes without dentist in attendance, then leave.
7. With partner, make appointment with dentist to just look in your mouth and not do any work.
8. With partner, make appointment with dentist to do a small amount of work—10-15 minutes worth.
9. With partner, make a longer appointment with the dentist.
10. Without partner, make a longer appointment with the dentist.

(This process may also be applied to a fear of doctors.)

Desensitizing Process for Fear of Flying and Airports

1. Approach airport with partner and drive around it.
2. Park in airport garage or lot; remain, observing people, for 5 minutes.
3. Park in airport garage or lot, enter terminal with partner and remain 1–5 minutes.
4. Enter terminal alone and remain 5 minutes, browsing and observing.
5. Arrange to visit a grounded plane; enter with partner.
6. Enter a grounded plane alone and remain for 5 minutes.
7. Enter a grounded plane with partner and get buckled into a seat.

8. Enter a grounded plane alone, browse and then stay buckled into a seat for 10–15 minutes.
9. Schedule a short flight (10–30 minutes) and go with partner.
10. Schedule a short flight (10–30 minutes) and go alone.
11. Schedule a longer flight and go with partner.
12. Schedule a longer flight and go alone.

[Because of the prevalence of flying anxiety, some airports have actually set up programs to help people reduce their anxieties. If an airport near you hasn't done so, they may be willing to set up such a program or to help you individually if you ask.]

Other Ways to Manage Anxiety and Stress

There are many situations over which we have no control. All we can control is our attitude toward those circumstances, learning to do our best to approach them with increased confidence, using the tools and practices described in this chapter. There are also some other fundamental ways to help ourselves manage anxiety and stress during the recovery process. These include diet, exercise and sleep.

Diet

I worked with a client once for over six months before she inadvertently shared with me that each night she would go home, fix herself a pan of brownies and proceed to eat them all. No wonder she felt a little jittery in the evening and her sleep pattern was disturbed.

Even with busy schedules, we can take care of ourselves with a healthy diet. Getting ourselves going in the morning with a good breakfast and possibly some vitamin and mineral supplements can help with some of the metabolic fluctuations that make it harder for us to manage stress. We can also choose to avoid caffeine, sugars, nicotine and alcohol—all of which can lower our thresholds for stress.

Unfortunately, most traditional physicians are not trained in nutrition. You might need to contact a nutritionist at your local hospital or someone you trust at a health food store to learn some facts about how nutrition affects your emotional state.

Exercise

Most of my clients groan as we begin to explore this facet of their lives. Shame-based people often take a radical approach to exercise. Either they show their lack of concern for themselves by not taking care of their bodies, or else they compulsively exercise in an attempt to compensate for their feelings of inadequacy.

A healthy exercise program is important for many reasons:

1. Exercise releases endorphins in the brain, which are natural antidepressants and muscle relaxants.
2. Exercise helps people develop a more disciplined approach to life.
3. As people become more disciplined and see results from their exercise, it increases their self-esteem.

The Japanese have shown us that when they ask their workers to stop and exercise during the middle portion of the workday, workers become more efficient and actually accomplish more work in less time.

Sleep

If you find you are not sleeping well, or you want to sleep all the time, this may be an indication of excessive anxiety or depression. It may require specific attention in order to make your recovery more efficient. Many of us might see an increase in our ability to cope with stress if we would simply get into the habit of sleeping seven or eight hours per night.

I had a client recently who was going to school while mothering two children as a single parent and working part-time. The only time that seemed available to her for study was between 10:00 P.M. and 2:00 A.M. By the time I met with her, she was exhausted and her physical condition had deteriorated tremendously. Obviously, my first priority was to help her adjust her life so she was getting enough rest. Only after that change had taken place was it even reasonable to address the shame and anxiety that were causing her to drive herself to unreasonable limits and try to be "more than human."

Not many of my clients push themselves quite this hard, but many of them try to get by with less rest than they need. I encourage them to pay attention to this aspect of their lives. Even now, when I find my life temporarily difficult, I have found that taking care of myself with a little extra sleep can give me a boost to get through the challenging period.

The Role of Medications in Recovery

The role of medications in recovery from excessive anxiety is a controversial one. I once attended a hospital training session for the treatment of anxiety disorders. The seminar was directed primarily toward physicians. I was appalled to hear the psychiatrist who was leading the training say that, for most people diagnosed with anxiety disorders, medication was usually a lifelong necessity.

Fortunately, not all physicians share this view. The psychiatrist with whom I work agrees with me that, for most people, medication is something to be considered temporarily and only under the following circumstances:

1. A person's sleep pattern has been affected; the person is sleeping either too much or too little.
2. A person's eating habits have been significantly affected over a period of weeks, either through loss of interest in eating or through overeating.
3. There are indications of serious depression.
4. A person is unable to function on a daily basis in an efficient manner.

Medications under these circumstances can sometimes help people get back to a more normal routine. Then they have the strength to make better use of the information learned in their recovery process. Once people have developed healthier attitudes and belief systems in their approach to life, then generally the medication is no longer necessary.

I was never on medications during treatment for my own anxiety, but frankly, I think that they would have made my treatment more efficient. On the other hand, I have only seen a need for medications in about 40 to 50 percent of my clients.

Some clients, even when medications are appropriate, do not want to use them for various reasons. Their recovery may be slower, but it is certainly not impossible. It is important to remember that medications are a tool to facilitate recovery, not a cure in themselves. My ultimate goal in working with people is to help them reach a point where they feel they have the choice to reduce or eliminate the need for medications.

Conclusion

If you teach yourself the relaxation techniques and desensitizing processes described in this chapter, you may see a significant reduction in the physical symptoms of your anxiety. But please don't stop there. Keep in mind that this chapter is an interim one, intended to help you manage your symptoms and deal more comfortably with events in your life. It is an important step toward the larger goal of full recovery from your anxiety, but it is only a beginning. You don't want to remain at this stage, still looking over your shoulder as you try to stay one step ahead of your symptoms. Instead, you want to learn to live life fully and joyfully. In the next chapter, I begin to describe the skills you'll need to do exactly that.

Suggested Exercises

1. Practice the relaxation exercise described in this chapter. Make a commitment to yourself to practice relaxing twice a day for four weeks.
2. Use the desensitization processes described in this chapter to reduce your anxiety about one or more stressful situations in your life.

KNOWING YOUR RIGHTS AND SETTING YOUR BOUNDARIES

Seeing Yourself as a Person with Value Instead of a Passive Victim

I answered the phone at my office one Monday morning and heard a frightened voice pleading, "I've got to see you right away." Vicky explained that she had just been hospitalized over the weekend for her panic attacks. The psychiatrist there had referred her to me, and she wanted to get help as soon as possible.

My schedule was full with therapy sessions and classes. I talked with Vicky on the phone long enough to give her some reassurance and suggestions to help her cope with her immediate stress. By then she realized that, in spite of her feeling of urgency and panic, this was not an emergency. We set up an appointment for her on Thursday.

She called me on Wednesday to say, "I can't come in for my appointment. My son has asked me to come with him on a school field trip, and I guess I have to go." Then she sighed deeply and added, "I wonder when life's going to stop doing this to me."

Of course, "life" wasn't doing anything to Vicky. Vicky was doing something to Vicky. Her son's field trip wasn't an emergency. She didn't have to go; she chose to go instead of keeping an appointment that meant taking steps toward her own recovery. She didn't realize she was making a choice, because she felt like a victim who had no choices.

It may be easy to see the irony in Vicky's situation because it's so blatant. But many of us have learned to view life in the same way. Because of our shame, we feel powerless. We feel choiceless. We feel like victims. And we blame our families or our finances or our circumstances: "If I didn't have three kids to take care of, I could go back to school." "If I didn't have to work so hard, I could find time to exercise." "If I'd been able to go to college like my brother did, I'd have a better job." "If I had more skills and could get a job, I wouldn't have to stay in this abusive relationship."

An important step in recovery from excessive anxiety is

accepting the reality that we have many choices. That isn't to say those choices are easy. It's hard to juggle families and jobs to go back to school. It's hard to say "no." It's hard to change our priorities. But, difficult or not, the choices are always there.

Life continually challenges us with the need to make choices, none of which may be right or wrong, leaving us with a great deal of responsibility to determine our choice at the time. But most people who suffer with excessive anxiety see themselves as powerless or victims in one way or another in their lives. They don't recognize their choices, and they don't recognize their rights.

Excessive-Anxiety Sufferers Feel Powerless and Set Unreasonable Boundaries

Because of their history, people who suffer with excessive anxiety often have a hard time recognizing their rights. Perhaps their controlling families gave them no rights. Or perhaps their parents never knew they themselves had rights and modeled a powerless lifestyle for their children. People can come from many different backgrounds and still be confused about appropriate boundaries in their lives. Those who have been overly protected or overly close with their parents often learn to feel responsible for their parents' feelings. They then take that same habit into their adult lives, feeling overly responsible for their children, their spouses or their friends. People who have been violated as children—

physically, sexually or emotionally–have obvious gaps in their knowledge about setting reasonable boundaries for themselves.

Regardless of the source of our confusion over appropriate boundaries, it is very helpful to discuss and begin to understand what constitutes reasonable boundaries. In my program for people who suffer with excessive anxiety, I spend one session discussing assertiveness. Becoming assertive involves learning what we want and what to ask for. When we become assertive, we learn to express how we feel, regardless of whether that feeling is love, hurt, anger or simple confusion.

Many anxious people keep their feelings to themselves for various reasons. Some of them don't know what they feel after they have been shamed for so long. They are literally out of touch with themselves. Some people fear how others will respond to them. Still other people don't think that what they have to say is important. And there are some people who don't give themselves permission to speak their minds because they weren't allowed to express themselves when they were younger; they don't feel they have the right.

The purpose of assertiveness is not to bowl the world over, but simply to begin to understand that you are equal to those around you–that you have needs, wants, desires and feelings like everyone else. In *Your Perfect Right: A Guide to Assertive Living*, Robert E. Alberti and Michael L. Emmons sum up assertive behavior in these words:

> *To act in one's own best interests refers to the capacity to make life decisions (career, relationships, lifestyle, time schedule), to take initiative (start conversations, organize activities), to trust one's*

own judgment, to set goals and work to achieve them, to ask for help from others, to comfortably participate socially.

To stand up for oneself includes such behaviors as saying "no," setting limits on one's time and energy, responding to criticism or put-downs or anger, expressing or supporting or defending one's opinion.

To express honest feelings comfortably means the ability to disagree, to show anger, to show affection or friendship, to admit fear or anxiety, to express agreement or support, to be spontaneous, all without painful anxiety.

To exercise personal rights relates to one's competency (as a citizen, as a consumer, as a member of an organization or school or work group, as a participant in public events) to express opinions, to work for change, to respond to violations of one's own rights or those of others.

To not deny the rights of others is to accomplish the above personal expressions without unfair criticism of others, without hurtful behavior toward others, without name calling, without intimidation, without manipulation, without controlling others.

Thus, assertive behavior is a positive self-affirmation which also values the other persons in your life.[1]

Notice that last sentence. It underscores the differences between three basic ways of responding to people and situations: passively, aggressively or assertively.

Passive behavior avoids "making waves." Passive people don't value themselves much and are, in essence, saying, "I don't want to bother anyone with my needs. I'm not important anyway." Passive people often feel hurt, dissatisfied,

[1]Robert E. Alberti and Michael L. Emmons, *Your Perfect Right: A Guide to Assertive Living.* (New York: Impact Publishing) 1970, 1995.

depressed and anxious. Passive behavior encourages pouting or "silent wars." Anger is expressed, but not directly. Often the only option passive people give themselves is, "I don't get mad, I just get even." But the ones who suffer worst from passive behavior are the passive people themselves.

Aggressive people seek to get whatever they want and don't care who gets hurt in the process. Their behavior gets across the message, "I am important and nobody else is." Aggressive behavior may be full of put-downs, criticisms, sarcasm and "chin-out" behavior. Aggressive people seek to "win" arguments, never realizing that when the other person loses, both participants lose.

Passive people aren't necessarily powerless. In a conflict between a passive person and an aggressive one, the passive person generally becomes more passive and drives the aggressive person crazy. It's kind of like the war between the clam and the hammer. The more the hammer pounds, the tighter the clam clamps down. Some may feel that the passive person then "wins," because of the ability to silently control the aggressive person. But again, if someone has to lose, then both participants lose.

Assertive people seek only to express their viewpoints or needs. They understand that their opinion or desire is important, but they also understand that other people have needs, too. The goal is to find a way for both people to win. This can involve compromise, looking for creative new options or agreeing to disagree.

Passive Behavior	Assertive Behavior	Aggressive Behavior
1. Actual feelings are not expressed.	1. Feelings are expressed while respecting the feelings of others.	1. May get you what you want, but at the expense of hurting others.
2. Will achieve no satisfaction.	2. Will usually result in a satisfied feeling.	2. Will usually result in retaliation of some kind.
3. Results in guilt and self-denial.	3. Results in a situation where no one is a loser.	3. Will usually not achieve a satisfied feeling.
4. Chance of getting what you want is zero.	4. Chance of getting what you want is 50 percent.	4. Chance of getting what you want is 15 percent.

SOURCE: Arthur Hardy, Terrap Foundation Manual (Mcnlo Park, Calif., 1981).
TABLE 5.1

Assertive people understand that the point of assertive behavior is not simply to get everything that you want. As long as all humans have different needs, we realize that getting all we want is not possible. But we can guarantee we won't get what we want if we don't ask for it. (And if we do get it by passive or aggressive means, it won't feel good.) At best, we will only get what we want half of the time. But even that is not the point. The point is that we tried! We expressed what we had to say, and for that reason we can be proud.

If you have been passive for years, don't expect your first attempts at assertiveness to be smooth and certainly don't expect them to be comfortable. You are likely to be awkward and hesitant, and your first efforts may be only slightly more assertive than your usual pattern.

Alex, a member of one of my groups, had led his life passively, with as low a profile as possible. The price he paid was severe anxiety and terrible self-esteem. A turning point for him came at one session when he asked for some time to express himself. He shared that two weeks earlier another group member had made a comment that left him uncomfortable.

He had gone home that night not knowing exactly why he felt uncomfortable, but instead of trying to "forget it" as he had done in the past, he tried to remain curious about his discomfort. As the days passed, he journaled about the incident and talked with a friend about it. Now, two weeks later, he felt clear about why he was upset. Since he had seen so many others in the group risk sharing vulnerable feelings with each other that had led to greater closeness, he took the risk and spoke up.

For many people an incident like this would have been minor. For Alex, it was a significant step in recovery. It took him several days to figure out what he was feeling using the techniques he had learned in order to listen to his own body. Next, he needed to gather up his courage to speak up. It's not important how long it took him. What is important is that Alex *did* figure out his feelings and speak up. With practice, his future recognition happened sooner and he learned to speak up earlier.

The other thing that can happen for passive people when they start trying to be assertive is a pendulum swing to aggressiveness. Once you finally gather the courage to speak up, you may find yourself shouting. This can be a shock for yourself as well as those around you. But going from one extreme to the other, before you can come back to the middle, is completely normal. Again, it's just a step along the way to learning how to be aware of your feelings and reasonable in your method of sharing them.

Remember, if at first you sometimes go to extremes in expressing your new assertiveness, you can (and certainly should) always make amends to people with whom you have overreacted. But don't abuse yourself because you are awkward and make some mistakes. Remember that you're learning a new skill—and as with any other skill, becoming competent takes time and practice.

Indirect Ways of Getting What We Want

Manipulation

Manipulation works! If I want to get my wife to rake the leaves, I might promise to take her turn cooking supper. There's nothing wrong with this form of positive manipulation. It's a straightforward form of negotiation or give-and-take: "If you do this for me, I'll do that for you." Negative manipulation, though, is negotiation with guilt attached: "Because I've always done so much for you (and if you really cared about me), you'd do that for me." Anxious people might use this method occasionally. We don't know much about making straight and direct requests. Most of us, though, tend to be on the receiving end of manipulation. Our built-in sense of shame and our view of ourselves as "less than" means we have a hard time saying "no."

Hinting

This is another way we get others to do things. Slamming pots and pans may be a message that someone wants some help in the kitchen. Pouting may be a hint that we didn't get what we wanted. But while hinting can be fun and humorous at times, it can also be a way to avoid giving a straight and honest, "I want. . . ."

When you try to get what you want by hinting, you are placing the burden of the exchange on other people. It puts them into mind-reading mode and makes them responsible for figuring out what you want. This paves the way for all sorts of miscommunication on both sides. This is especially true if the person with excessive anxiety is on the receiving end of the hinting. After all, we're very creative and good at assuming the worst. We can mind-read ourselves and the other person into a dramatic and horrible conflict, when maybe all the other person is thinking about is what to have for dinner. Even if we mind-read the other person's thoughts accurately, the whole process is exhausting and produces unnecessary anxiety.

Let's face it: Telling people what you want is tough! You may get rejected. But it is your request that is rejected, not you as a person. Perhaps you've discounted your needs for so long that it's hard to know what you really want anyway. This new behavior will take practice and awareness of healthier alternatives.

Your Assertive Rights

The following list of assertive rights is taken from *Your Perfect Right: A Guide to Assertive Living* by Robert E. Alberti and Michael L. Emmons.[2] The examples following each one come from my work with clients. As you read these, think of specific ways each one might apply to your own life. How many of these rights do you currently believe you have? How many of them do you routinely exercise? How many of them have never occurred to you? Give yourself permission to consider these rights for yourself in the future.

1. **You have the right to become the judge of your own behavior, thoughts and emotions, and to take responsibility for them.**
   EXAMPLE: I had a client recently who read this statement and said, "Yeah, I do that. I take the blame for all my screwups." She had concentrated on the last few words and missed most of the point. Do you exercise your right to judge your own behavior, thoughts and emotions? Or do you end up justifying what you do, feeling guilty about your thoughts and inhibiting your emotions because they might upset other people?

2. **You have the right to give no reasons or excuses for your behavior.**
   EXAMPLE: If someone calls and invites you to go out for

[2] Alberti and Emmons, 59.

coffee, and you don't feel like going, the only thing you need to say is, "No thanks, not this time." Any explanation you give is optional. Too often we give some excuse or try to rationalize why we can't do something so we don't hurt other people's feelings. It's fine if you choose to give a reason, but remember that it's optional.

3. **You have the right to decide whether you are responsible for other people's problems.**
EXAMPLE: Anxious, phobic people chronically take responsibility for whatever goes wrong. Either they are constantly apologizing for anything that might cause discomfort to someone else, or they allow other people's problems to become their own. Those who suffer from excessive anxiety are sensitive and emotional. Too often they pick up on others' discomfort and begin to respond to the emotional level of the other person. They become angry, sad, hurt, lonely or embarrassed along with the other person. The other person may satisfy the need to "get it off their chest" so they can relax, but the anxious person stays stuck with the feelings.

I often have clients who call because they're having trouble keeping appointments. Maybe a friend is in trouble and needs someone to talk to; maybe a relative needs a ride to work; maybe the boss has a last-minute project and needs someone to work overtime. The clients immediately feel the need to put that other person's problems ahead of their own and put off their own need to help themselves.

Helping others without considering the consequences is similar to walking down a street with a friend and having that friend fall into a deep pit. Some of us may think that the most helpful thing to do would be to jump down into the pit with our friend, but that would just leave two people stuck instead of one. Instead, a healthy person realizes that the most helpful thing they can do is stand at the top of the pit and offer a hand to help the friend out.

Helping others is great and has rewards of its own, but we also need to learn a balance between taking care of others and taking care of ourselves. Ironically, sometimes in our helping we actually do more harm than good. Not only might our own needs or our family's needs be neglected as we get really involved in someone else's problems, but our intervention may deprive others of the chance to learn from their mistakes. Suppose little Johnny comes home from school crying that the teacher is picking on him, the kids are teasing him and that's why his grades are suffering. If you as parents immediately take his side against the teacher, Johnny may never feel the need to look at how he provoked her, how he needs to learn to get along better with his friends or how irresponsible his study habits are.

The next time you're tempted to get overly involved in someone else's problems, try this:

- Listen to the problems and try to understand.
- Ask questions only for information.
- Ask the person to analyze and define the problem, stating the need clearly.
- Decide whether there is anything you can do about the problem.
- If you can't help, say so.

- Ask the person to list all the possible solutions that person can think of; do not offer yours.
- Ask which solution seems most helpful or appropriate.
- Encourage the person to try that solution.
- If the person's possible solutions don't work and the situation is causing a lot of difficulty, perhaps you could suggest that the person see a professional for help instead of taking on the load yourself.

4. **You have the right to be illogical in making decisions.**
   EXAMPLE: Sometimes what we feel the need for makes no practical sense; it's just what we need. Suppose you are tired; the kids or your job really have you exhausted. You have the need for a vacation, but you only have one hundred dollars in the bank. As you learn to take care of yourself, you may find a creative way to get away in spite of the lack of funds. It makes no sense, but you may even choose to borrow the money and go on vacation anyway. You may come to realize in looking back on the vacation that you'll only remember the good times—not the money spent.

5. **You have the right to make mistakes and be responsible for them.**
   EXAMPLE: People who are anxious tend to make a big deal out of everything—from choosing a movie, to deciding where to go on vacation, to saying "the right thing." All these examples have the same assumption: that there is one "right choice."

   We cause a great deal of our anxieties when we live by "shoulds," "oughts" and "musts." In reality, the only thing that makes some things right is whether they are right for you. There is often no one right or wrong decision. You need only make a decision based on the information you have at the time. *It's what you do with the decision that makes it right or wrong.* If you get new information in the future, you then have the right to change your mind and make a new decision.

Issues that you decide are important may not be as critical as you think. Perhaps blowing things out of proportion keeps you from making decisions. But if you screw up, so what? You're human. Other people make mistakes, and the world doesn't fall apart. Learn to make a decision as best you can at the time; then deal with the consequences if and when they happen.

Anxious people feel the need to have control of everything, and that's what makes so much of our lives a big deal. But that just leaves us walking on eggshells and uptight much of the time. How can we have fun if we can't relax and just enjoy whatever happens? Sometimes we can't control the situation, but we can control our attitude toward it. If we've planned a picnic and it rains, we can either be upset over missing the picnic or take advantage of the time to catch up on our reading.

6. **You have the right to change your mind.**

EXAMPLE: One of the ways we trap ourselves is to lock ourselves into decisions. Very few decisions have to be permanent, even such big ones as career choices. Just because I get my education and choose a field doesn't mean I can't change jobs later on. Just because I said I'd go to a movie this weekend doesn't mean I can't change my mind. Take a look at all the things you might believe you have to do. Do those "have to's" still fit for you, or could some of them change?

A member of one of my classes who had volunteered to become the president of his club after his friend left town described feeling very trapped and anxious. He explained that, when he took on the job, he didn't fully understand the extensive expectations that this national club would have for its president. He would be expected to travel to national meetings and to promote programs that he did not necessarily have any interest in. "When I became a member of this local chapter, I just thought I was helping out my friend. I didn't realize it was such a big deal."

This young man didn't have the money or the time to travel to these meetings. The only alternative he saw for himself was to quit. Some of the class members began to brainstorm and helped him to realize that, while he did have the right to quit, he also had alternatives. He could remain the president but delegate the travel to other members who might enjoy doing it. Or perhaps the local club members could discuss not participating in all of the national events. After these alternatives were discussed and he realized he had more choices than he had thought before, he reported feeling noticeably more relaxed.

7. **You have the right to say, "I don't know."**

EXAMPLE: No matter what your boss, teacher or client asks you—whether it's your boss wanting to know if you understand the most basic instructions or your child wanting to know why frogs are green—you have the right not to be perfect. Here again, we tend to think we should know or understand. That's a lot of pressure to put on ourselves. Learn to say, "I don't know" or "I'll try my best to find out," and leave it at that.

8. **You have the right to say, "I don't understand."**
EXAMPLE: Anxious people generally don't feel that they quite measure up to others' standards. They often feel queasy about saying, "I don't get it." They expect themselves to always understand, always listen and always know.

9. **You have the right to say, "I don't care."**
EXAMPLE: If a friend calls with a problem or a child bombards us with questions the minute we come in the door, we expect ourselves to care. People who don't like themselves much want so badly to be liked that they never give themselves permission not to care about others just long enough to recharge their own batteries. It's okay to call the friend back after you finish watching a TV program. It's okay to lock the door and take a bath for an hour before devoting yourself to the kids. We can't always care.

When people begin treatment for anxiety, everybody else's feelings are paramount, and their own are mired in obscurity. The goal of recovery is not to turn you into a selfish, aggressive, noncaring person. Instead, the goal is to help you learn to balance others' needs with your own and to at least consult with yourself before you choose to jump in and help.

10. **You have the right to say, "No."**
EXAMPLE: No matter what you want to do, it always gets screwed up! You'd like to stay at home and relax, but a friend needs to talk. Your boss has a great promotion for you, but it's not what you want.

You have the right to say no. If you don't, nobody else will take care of you. If you don't feel you have the right to set your own boundaries, you're constantly placing yourself at the mercy of those around you. Naturally, you're going to feel out of control and therefore anxious.

11. **You have the right to express how you feel.**
EXAMPLE: "I wish you'd stop your crying." "You don't have to get so angry." "You shouldn't feel that way." When you express feelings, it stirs up other people's similar feelings, which they may not feel comfortable expressing. Is that a reason for you to bottle up what you need to express? Don't your desires or opinions count? Yes, they do, but only if you give yourself that right.

12. **You have the right to ask for what you want.**
EXAMPLE: Not only do you have the right, but you have the responsibility to ask for what you want. Otherwise, how can you expect others to know what you need? Each of us has the responsibility to teach others what we need instead of expecting them to know by reading our minds. You have the need for certain things in life like everyone else, but you've got to begin to believe you're worth it.

These are your rights. Review them often. Many people who go through my program hang these rights up on their mirror or refrigerator as reminders. Learn to hear these rights in the back of your mind when you find yourself in difficult circumstances.

Learning to Balance
Other People's Rights and Your Own

A stumbling block for many anxious people is the fear that, as they begin to assert their rights, they will begin trampling on the rights of others. They have learned to be caretakers. They believe they have to take care of everyone's needs except their own. Everybody else's needs are important, and their own are consigned to oblivion (see figure 5.1).

Others' Needs Are More Important

FIGURE 5.1

Their fear is that they will move from sensitive and caring people to becoming selfish and insensitive. They fear that their needs will become the only ones that are important, and nobody else's will matter.

One's Own Needs Are More Important

FIGURE 5.2

I explain to clients that it's normal for them to be uncomfortable when they first begin to exercise their rights. They have been motivated by their guilt and shame into being caretakers. As shown in figure 5.1, feeling guilty at the thought of letting others down, anxious people have been overbalanced in the direction of others' needs. As they start to change, at first that guilt only shifts in another direction. Now they feel guilty when they let themselves down, so for a while they might overbalance toward their own needs, as displayed in figure 5.2. The goal, of course, is to learn to balance the importance of other people's needs with your own needs.

Everybody's Needs Are Important

FIGURE 5.3

Figure 5.3 illustrates the importance of considering both yourself and the other person's needs. Before you react automatically and take care of other people's needs, you begin to learn to consult with yourself first. Is taking care of the other's need really in your best interest, or even in the best interest of the other person? Once you believe you can make a choice, you are no longer operating out of guilt, and your decisions are usually appropriate.

Being Aware of Your Intentions

An even bigger stumbling block to becoming more assertive is other people's reactions. If you have always been a care-taker—the one who always said yes to working overtime, the one who always did what your spouse wanted to do on Friday nights, the one who always gave in to your kids—it will come as a surprise to those around you when you start to change. Some of the people in your life might support you, but others are likely to resist. They've been used to your caving in and doing whatever they wanted, and most of them probably liked it.

You give your power away when you judge whether you have the right to express yourself based on the reaction you get from others. If you can determine what your intentions are before you express yourself, you end up feeling much less confused. Even if the other person reacts poorly to what you have to say, as long as your intention was to set your own boundary and have the potential for an open conversation with the other person, then you may have to just accept a negative reaction. Sometimes people react because the shoe fits, and you need to let them wear it. Asserting yourself is not necessarily about getting what you want, but feeling good about expressing yourself.

Changing your behavior in the face of opposition from those around you isn't easy. Chapter 10 will offer some suggestions for helping you cope with this challenge.

Conclusion

Clients continually tell me that reviewing their rights as human beings is incredibly helpful in the recovery process. Because of their shame-based histories, they have felt disempowered and discouraged from trying new things and stretching themselves. They struggle with feeling less important than others. As a result, they often keep a low profile and try not to rock the boat. Obviously, feeling insignificant and powerless contributes heavily to a feeling of anxiety. Learning your rights as a human being is one big step in beginning to feel empowered and important.

Suggested Exercises

1. Spend some time reviewing the twelve assertive rights. Write down specific examples of each one in your own life.
2. Think about your typical style. Would you consider yourself passive, aggressive or assertive?
3. As you begin to take your rights more seriously, consider your intentions before you assert yourself. If you're reacting with anger to protect yourself, you're probably being aggressive, not assertive. If you're stating your point of view so you can "be known," in hopes of encouraging open communication in the future, your intention is to be assertive.
4. Thinking back on a time you asserted yourself—and didn't get the response you wanted—did you question whether your efforts were worthwhile? Remember, the point of asserting yourself is not so much to get what you want, but to feel good about your efforts. If you get a positive response, that's gravy.
5. In your journaling include times when you have asserted yourself. Write about how it felt to take your own thoughts and feelings seriously enough to express them.

HEALTHY ANGER:
A PREREQUISITE IN INTIMATE
RELATIONSHIPS

I remember, as a young teenager, going to a church camp
in the mountains of Southern California. I was a very good

boy. I was polite, a good student and generally the kind of kid that people could easily be around. As we were playing outside in the snow one day, somebody came up behind me and threw a whole bucketful of snow down my back. I exploded with profanity I had never used before. Once I recovered, I felt acutely embarrassed and exposed. People had seen something that "just wasn't me." The anger and swearing didn't fit my image of myself.

> *During their fourteen-year marriage, Sandy and Rick almost never argued. Rick was an alcoholic who got quietly drunk every night after work. Sandy was sick a lot with stomach problems and irritable bowel syndrome. When Sandy finally filed for a divorce, Rick exploded in rage. He made an attempt at suicide and threatened several times to kill Sandy. Several years later, even after extensive therapy, his rage was still as fresh and strong as it had been the day the divorce decree was granted.*

> *Dee was working full time at a job she didn't like because her husband, who had just received his master's degree, had been unable to find work. Their plans had been for her to work while he finished his degree, and then for her to quit so they could start a family as soon as he found a job. Dee never complained overtly or expressed any anger over the delay in their plans. However, her voice was a constant whine, she went about her work listlessly and made careless mistakes, and she developed a habit of making "joking" verbal digs about her husband behind his back.*

The above are examples of some of the ways we anxiety sufferers handle our anger. Most of us have not had much experience with healthy anger. Instead, what we learned growing up was that when people got angry, they would withdraw, pout, silently punish each other, pretend nothing happened or explode in rage that sometimes resulted in threatened or actual physical violence. This taught us that anger was to be avoided at all costs. We came to see anger as something that drove people apart. The challenge in recovery is to understand that anger actually can bring people together and is an essential skill in maintaining a healthy lifestyle.

Those of us who suffer from anxiety and phobias tend to be "people pleasers." Because of our anxiety and lack of confidence in our ability to soothe ourselves, we often become dependent on others for reassurance. Expressing overt anger seems risky because we're convinced it might alienate the people we depend on. Moreover, research tells us that anxiety sufferers have a high need for control. Since anger seems like a very unpredictable and uncontrollable emotion, once it begins to leak out, we fear anger.

We need to remember that anxiety is not so much what we are feeling, but rather, what we are not feeling. When we suppress any feeling, it can have several different results. First of all, feelings that are chronically repressed lead to muscle tension. Back in chapter 4, at the end of the relaxation exercise, I had you remember different emotional experiences so that you could see the connection between the memories you have, the emotions that were present during those experiences and the resulting muscle tension. Different feelings are held in by tightening different muscle groups.

Second, when people suppress their feelings, the result can be psychosomatic symptoms, such as headaches, breathing problems, high blood pressure, stomach problems, dizziness, blurred vision, heart palpitations, chest pain and various other symptoms. When those symptoms are interpreted as dangerous, that can lead in turn to more fear and more symptoms.

Third, people who suppress their feelings often experience depression. Recognizing your feelings and then expressing them can often make the difference between a depressing day and an enjoyable one.

Confusing Anger with Rage

One of the reasons we learned to avoid anger is that we confused it with rage. I used to think that rage was anger out of control, but I have since learned that they are significantly different. Anger is something that, when shared, can help a person understand how strongly somebody else feels about something. Anger can bring people closer together. Anger is a response and is usually premeditated before being expressed.

Rage, on the other hand, is a reaction. It is a protective mechanism that tries to stop a person from feeling vulnerable. Rage often has nothing to do with anger. It is more often a result of fear, loneliness or hurt. By raging out, we try to keep the other person from hurting us further or from making us feel any more vulnerable. By lashing out, we try to stop the other person's behavior, which threatens or hurts us. Unfortunately, in the process we also separate ourselves from the other person.

Sometimes people are surprised to learn that most people who rage actually tend to stuff their feelings, burying them inside rather than expressing them. They stuff and they stuff and they stuff, and finally when there is no more room, they blow up. Most of the time they feel so bad about blowing up that the only thing they know how to do is return to stuffing, which just sets them up for the next explosion. Others who suffer with anxiety rarely rage and seem to have an incredible tolerance for misery. If we just keep stuffing our feelings and never allow for their expression, it's easy to understand how this can lead to anxiety. Suppressed emotion is energy, and when suppressed energy finally comes out, it often comes out in the form of anxiety.

Hate is another example of protecting ourselves. Personal, individual hate is what we feel for people who are important to us but who have disappointed or hurt us. Bitter ex-spouses might fall into this category. Impersonal hate, such as racism or bigotry, is based on fear and ignorance. "Those people" are different and might hurt us, so we'd better hurt them first. In either case, hate is a protective wall that attempts to keep us from getting hurt further. To live with continual hate is exhausting—like driving a car down the highway at sixty miles an hour with the brakes on. We're using a lot of energy against ourselves. Hate, while it can protect us from getting hurt, also leaves us lonely.

Anger Is a Prerequisite in a Loving Relationship

I discuss anger in this chapter before I discuss love in the next one. There is a reason for that. Healthy anger is a prerequisite to love and an important component of love. Until two people have enough commitment in their relationship with each other to lock horns and disagree, they are not going to get to know each other very deeply. As a result, they will not share an intimate relationship.

Relationships that avoid anger and confrontation may feel secure and safe, but they are not intimate. Intimacy, as Frank Pittman defines it in his book *Private Lies*, is about "being known." If we avoid conflict or disagreement, if we hesitate to share something that might upset another person or if we choose not to share something because we feel as though the other person has "enough to worry about," we aren't being known and we aren't being intimate. From being shamed growing up, we learned to go into hiding, which is the opposite of letting ourselves be known. This keeps us separate from others and from ourselves.

Anger is not a sin, a failing or a weakness. It is a tool. Anger is a way that we define our boundaries and show that we value ourselves. As we grow healthier, we realize we are the only ones who can set the boundaries in our relationships with others. Anger protects us from giving something away when it would not be in our best interest to do so. Healthy anger, then, is something we become skillful at and comfortable with as we learn to love ourselves.

Perhaps one of the most practical books I have ever read on anger is Harriet Lerner's *The Dance of Anger*. In it the author points out how anger helps us to define who we are. It helps us to find our own boundaries. Going into a relationship without feeling comfortable with our anger means going into a relationship with nothing to help us protect our boundaries. It's like learning downhill skiing and not knowing how to stop. When I first began to ski, even the beginner hill seemed frightening because of the possibility of being out of control. Once I learned how to stop, I could go anyplace on the mountain and know that I was safe. In relationships, the anger that helps us protect our boundaries can provide the same sense of safety and control. Without the ability to stop or slow down when we need to, the whole notion of getting involved in relationships is frightening.

Many of us grew up thinking that we were not supposed to be angry. We then entered into relationships living behind a mask or relating to another in fantasy fashion. We may have believed we should always be understanding, patient, warm, humorous and easygoing. However, that isn't humanly possible, especially when we share our lives with other human beings who make mistakes, hurt us, disagree with us or have needs different from our own. We are going to be angry from time to time. Trying to pretend we don't feel that anger is a source of tremendous anxiety.

Anger can take many forms, from mild wishful thoughts against another person to violent destructive rage. Obviously, as we become more adept at recognizing our anger when it's at a much lower level, our chances of making constructive use of that anger and suffering with the more frightening forms of anger are reduced.

Levels of Anger	
1. Held-in Irritations	
2. Angry Feelings	SUPPRESSION LEVEL
3. Sarcasm	
4. Hurtful Fantasies	BEGINNING EXPRESSION OF AGGRESSION
5. Critical Remarks	
6. Prejudice and Rejection	PLOTTING FOR A DESTRUCTIVE OUTLET FOR ANGER OR HATRED
7. Destructive Fantasies	
8. Hate	ORGANIZED, HURTFUL AGGRESSION
9. War	
10. Random Violence	DISORGANIZED, OUT-OF-CONTROL AGGRESSION

SOURCE: Arthur Hardy, Terrap Foundation Manual (Menlo Park, Calif., 1981).

TABLE 6.1

Recognizing Our "Dark Side"

All of us have a "dark side." All of us have the capacity to be angry, jealous, insecure, vicious, judgmental and resentful. Because of our shame, we try to deny that dark side, thus using up huge amounts of energy.

As we become more knowledgeable and aware of that dark side of ourselves, we can spend less energy trying to protect our "good little boy" or "good little girl" image. As we become more comfortable with ourselves as whole people with flaws and failings, we no longer have such a strong need to defend ourselves when people give us feedback about ourselves. Acknowledging our own dark side means that it isn't devastating when someone criticizes us, because we already know and accept that we aren't perfect.

One indication of personal wellness is when our insides are consistent with our outsides. When our insides are in conflict with our outsides, we can expect to feel anxiety.

Learning to Express Anger in Healthy Ways

It may make sense to us to think of anger as a tool that protects us and helps us become closer to others. We may understand that it's important to express anger and deal with it. But that doesn't mean it's easy.

We've called anger a tool. Think of it as a powerful and somewhat frightening tool that can be damaging if uncontrolled—like a chainsaw. You wouldn't expect to use a chainsaw skillfully and safely without some instruction and some practice. In the same way, it's unreasonable to expect to suddenly know how to use anger in a healthy way. Here are some suggestions that might help as you practice:

1. Start small.

   Don't immediately rush out to confront your former spouse or your intimidating boss. Practice in situations that aren't as threatening. If you're waiting in line at McDonald's and someone cuts in front of you, don't let it slide. Say, "Excuse me, I was here first." If a telemarketer calls you at dinnertime, don't continue to listen while your food gets cold. Say, "I'm really not interested" or "I never buy from companies who call at mealtimes" and hang up.

2. Express anger while it's fresh.

   If we hold in our anger, we can become depressed and withdrawn. This makes us "hard to read" and also separates us from others. And held-in anger can have serious consequences. It comes out sideways, like Dee's passive-aggressive jabs at her husband. It shows up in physical symptoms, like Sandy's stomach problems. Practice speaking up when you first feel irritated or have a sense that your boundaries are being violated. Deal with the anger while it's still small and doesn't have a bunch of old resentments piled onto it.

   If we recognize our angry feelings when they are fairly mild, our chances of dealing with those feelings rationally are greatly increased. As the intensity of our anger increases, the ability to deal with it rationally is decreased. The following diagram shows how, as feelings build up, there is less rationality to our display of anger.

Options for Dealing with Emotions

Extreme	Subjective Thinking	Level 1	Irrational, hysterical outburst of feeling
	FEELINGS	Level 2	Act out feelings
Best Combination		Level 3	Talk out feelings
	RATIONAL		
	THINKING	Level 4	
Extreme	Objective Thinking	Level 5	Feelings avoided by intellectualizing

SOURCE: Arthur Hardy, Terrap Foundation Manual (Menlo Park, Calif., 1981).
TABLE 6.2

3. Remember that you don't have to be right to be angry.
   A counselor used to remind me, "Sometimes anger is just what opens the door so an issue can be resolved. You don't have to be right or on the winning side before it's okay to be angry." Anger is a feeling that doesn't always have to be justified. Think of it instead as a feeling that gives you the energy to do what needs to be done.

4. For old or intense anger, find a safe place to "take the top off the volcano."
   Anger that has been festering for a long time can be destructive when it finally "blows." Instead of confronting

the person you're angry with right away, consider talking with someone else about it first—a friend, a pastor or a counselor. With that person, you can "take the top off the volcano." You can be irrational, swear, threaten and call names so that when you do actually go talk to the person you want to confront, you can be more rational.

5. Ask yourself, *How would I react if this were directed at someone else?*

For many of us, our first reaction to a violation of our boundaries is, "Oh, it isn't worth getting upset about." Maybe it's not. But maybe it is. Too often we try to convince ourselves that something doesn't matter because we're afraid to confront it. One way to decide whether you're pretending is to see if you would get angry if this offense were against someone else. If it's worth getting angry about for another person, it's worth getting angry about for yourself.

People who suffer with anxiety often want to eliminate the guilt that they feel because they don't believe they should have angry feelings. The bad news is that we never get rid of guilt. As people become healthier and learn to express their anger more openly, the guilt shifts. Previous to recovery, people feet guilty about hurting others with their anger. As their recovery proceeds, they experience guilt when they have let themselves down and not expressed justifiable anger.

Another interesting thing happens when people recover. Previously, they used to rationalize about not asserting themselves because "the relationship was not that important." With recovery, and regardless of the importance of the relationship, people begin to assert themselves because they would feel bad about their lack of honesty and integrity if they didn't.

6. Remember that you can manage your physical symptoms.

The relaxation and breathing techniques described in chapter 4 are intended to be helpful in stressful situations. Practice them before you express your anger. Remind yourself to breathe. Stay in the now instead of catastrophizing. Visualize yourself beginning the discussion in a way that you'd feel proud of. Remember that sweaty palms or a fluttering stomach don't mean you can't handle an issue; they're just indications that what you have to say is important.

7. Ask yourself, *What do I want and need?*

Before you start to express your anger, think for a minute about your goal. You might want to feel heard, be respected, or accomplish something specific, like working out who does the dishes or getting the other person to change a behavior that bothers you. Keeping your goal in mind can help you stay focused on the outcome of the conflict instead of getting bogged down in accusations or old issues.

8. Pay attention to your intention.

Healthy people ask themselves the question, *What is my intention in sharing my anger?* If someone has hurt you and you want to hurt that person back, expressing your anger with that intention will sever your relationship with the person. If, on the other hand, your intention is to heal the relationship and to be known, then your motivation is pure. You can't always be assured that, even with the best of intentions, the other person will meet you halfway and that you will become closer. But at least you will know you have tried.

Remember the saying "Honesty without compassion is abusive." This particularly applies when we are tempted to lash out and "let them have it for their own good."

9. Don't take it personally.

The other thing we often do with anger is personalize the attack. We assume that, just because a person is angry, it has something to do with us. One of my therapy groups once included Dale, a physician, and Renee, a nurse. This group had been together for over a year, knew each other and knew how to work as a group. One evening Renee was talking, when out of the blue (and out of character) Dale interrupted with, "You controlling bitch!"

The group got so quiet you could hear people breathing. Renee started to cry. My impulse was to jump in and explain it away, but because this group knew how to work together, I bit my tongue and waited. After what seemed to be forever, Dale said, "You know, my mom is visiting this week, and what I just gave you is what I have been wanting to give her. I'm sorry."

This incident gave Dale a chance to learn how suppressed anger can come out indirectly. It was also a strong learning experience for Renee. First of all, she learned she had previously assumed that, just because somebody else said something, it must be right. She realized that she ultimately needed to weigh her own reaction to determine whether an accusation was true. Furthermore, she learned that, regardless of the truth or falsity of a statement, she had the choice of responding in any number of ways, instead of reacting with tears or self-protective rage.

During the rest of the group, there were several encounters like this between these two. Renee learned to look at Dale and say, "I'm not so sure that this is true or even my problem." She learned not to personalize other people's anger or to assume that it was her fault. And Dale learned to recognize his anger when it was at a much more manageable level, where his chances of constructive resolution were much greater.

10. Don't expect to be comfortable.

If you picked up a chainsaw and turned it on for the first time, you almost certainly wouldn't be comfortable. And even after you got used to using this powerful tool, you probably wouldn't treat it casually. Why expect anything different when learning to use that equally powerful tool, anger? Your stomach will lurch, your palms will sweat, your heart will beat faster, and you will wish you didn't have to do this. All of those reactions are absolutely normal. Anger is a powerful emotion that deserves our respect. Using it is probably always going to be uncomfortable. That's just fine—go ahead and use it anyway.

Three Stages in Healthy Conflict

Once you begin to practice expressing anger and dealing with conflict, you can start working toward resolving conflict in a win-win way. It is helpful to realize that there are three stages in a healthy conflict: (1) the air-clearing stage; (2) the cooling-off stage; (3) the learning and resolution stage.

Stage One: Air Clearing

All human beings have different thresholds for absorbing angry feelings, and each has a particular disposition from birth about sharing their frustrations. But whatever their temperament, it is important that people "clear the air." Some can do this very easily and gently, while others steam, sputter, rant and rave.

Some of my clients have watched their parents abuse and punish each other with their rage. Others never saw their parents fight at all. Both types of people flounder when trying to share frustration appropriately with those they care about.

People who are more overt with their anger may need to learn diplomacy, patience and appropriateness before they can share their anger constructively. Violence is never acceptable as a means of clearing the air. On the other hand, there is no virtue in holding all those feelings inside.

Actually, I have found it easier to help people who may be more outward in their display of anger because at least I know where they stand. However, since I specialize in working with those who suffer from excessive anxiety, I work more often with "emotion stuffers." Working with stuffers is a lot like pulling hens' teeth. But whichever type you are, you can become more skillful in expressing your anger.

Once a conflict has been brought out into the open by one or both parties' clearing the air, there is often a sense of "now what?" Either or both might feel guilty, confused or bewildered after the initial feelings have been shared. It is then time to cool off.

Stage Two: Cooling Off

During the cooling-off stage, the two persons who are in conflict agree to take a break for a predetermined period of time. They may take a walk to gather their personal thoughts. They may choose to journal. Or they may just choose to ponder separately what has happened up to that point. The important element is *mutually agreeing* to the cooling-off break. Usually one person in a relationship wants to withdraw, while the other takes the position that "You're not leaving here until this is settled." Mutually agreeing to take a break is already moving toward a respectful resolution for both parties.

The unfortunate thing that many people do during this period is to review the argument in their mind and to create good comebacks for any points where they felt vulnerable in the air-clearing session. This tendency to try to create an airtight argument and "win" will only lead to more frustration. As long as one person feels the need to win an argument, then nobody wins. The intimacy in the relationship suffers.

Instead, I suggest that you use the cooling-off time to ask yourself these questions:

- What is it that I really want to convey to the other person?
- What do I think the other person is trying to convey to me?
- What would I like to see come out of this discussion?

This type of internal questioning is going to encourage a

posture of real listening in the next stage of conflict resolution. If you say to yourself, *I really want to understand what that
other person is trying to tell me, and I want them to understand me as
a result of this conflict,* then constructive use of conflict is a real
possibility. If we move into the third stage of conflict resolution with this type of listening attitude, we have a good
chance of developing a greater closeness.

Stage Three: Learning and Resolution

Once two people have had a chance to clear the air and
have then moved away from each other to cool down and
determine what they are feeling and what they want to convey, it's time to come back to the conflict. Ideally, each person will come back with the goal of understanding and being
understood.

The third stage of conflict resolution is sharing what you
learned during that cooling-off period. Oftentimes, during
the air-clearing sessions, things are said that may intentionally or unintentionally be hurtful. During the third stage of
resolution, we may apologize for some of our statements, but
we can also recognize that there may have been a grain of
truth in what we expressed. This time, when we express our
feelings, we can do so in a diplomatic and thoughtful way.
While we may have raged in the first stage of clearing the air,
we now have a chance to look underneath that rageful reaction and share what we are really feeling.

For example: "I told you I was really pissed about how
often you have come home late recently. Now I realize that
I feel insecure and scared. I am afraid you don't enjoy my
company anymore." Looking underneath our rageful

accusations to the more vulnerable feelings there allows two people to "become known to each other."

After the two spend some time sharing what they learned during their cooling-off period, then they might go on to ask for what they would like in the future. During this stage, the art of compromise is vital. Coming to agreement at this stage can build a foundation of cooperation that reduces future conflicts and thus reduces anxiety.

Constructive Anger
Is a Skill to Be Proud Of

Finding a way to resolve situations where both people have a chance to win is reason for celebration. Once we see how valuable healthy anger can be in creating closeness in a relationship, we want to share that closeness with others.

I have had many couples who said with a certain pride, "We never argue in front of the kids." In some ways, that is unfortunate. Children need to see that people not only have a right to their feelings, but that those feelings can lead to greater closeness when shared in a healthy manner.

As children, most of us didn't have good experiences with anger. I'm not talking about the kind of anger where you start throwing things and saying whatever you can to hurt the other person. That is certainly not good for a child to watch. But it is good for children to have some experience with seeing Mom or Dad angry and seeing that it doesn't mean raging or hurting or the end of the relationship. It's also healthy for children to see parents admit a mistake and say, "I'm sorry" or "That was uncalled for."

The point of anger is to let us know how important something is to ourselves or someone else. There is no right or wrong way to be; there are just different perceptions. If we can remember that in an argument one of us doesn't have to come out losing, we've made a huge step.

The challenge is that the only way to learn to deal with anger is by experiencing it. We can't wait until we're comfortable. That is never going to happen. We probably never will feel comfortable sharing our anger. The only thing that changes is our realization that the gain is well worth the effort and discomfort. When we learn to express anger in such a way that it gets us somewhere and helps us become closer to one another, we can finally feel at peace with it.

It Takes Two

You might be able to polish your skills in sharing anger to a fine art. You might feel sure that you've done all you can do to express yourself clearly with the best of intentions. Unfortunately, that isn't going to automatically take care of all your conflicts. Resolving a conflict requires the willingness of two or more people to meet halfway. Interpersonal anger cannot be solved unilaterally. Both persons must accept ownership of their part in the conflict: their perceptions, assumptions and reactions. A genuine mutual desire for agreement must exist.

Once an attitude of seeking a win-win resolution exists, and two people recognize the importance of sharing anger so the relationship can improve in the long run, both of them can enjoy the benefits of being in a fully committed relationship. Behavior such as threats to end the relationship every time conflict arises no longer seems necessary. People who threaten to end a relationship when there is conflict are protecting themselves from being abandoned by jumping ship first. But as long as those types of threats continue, real closeness and intimacy are not possible.

The best time to mutually develop the capacity to grow closer from constructive conflict is obviously when we're not in conflict. It is after the initial getting-acquainted stage—when we sense that this relationship might be an important one—that we should talk about what our hopes and needs are whenever there is a disagreement.

It's important to realize that seeing things differently is inevitable in a close relationship. It's not a question of whether conflict is going to happen. Rather, the question is, How are we going to handle it when it happens? Each of us has the responsibility to teach those we care about what we need when things are emotional, tense or in conflict.

One major myth that complicates loving relationships is exemplified by the statement "If you loved me, you'd know what I need." That's simply not true. No matter how much they may love you, people don't know what you need until you teach them. In fact, many of the hurts and disappointments between people arise because one person *assumes* what the other wants or needs—because those wants and needs have never been expressed.

When there is conflict in a relationship, many people tend to feel more vulnerable, more lost and more in need of protecting themselves. Two people who have taken the time to teach each other what they need—if a conflict should arise—have given each other a real gift. If you and your spouse, or others who are close to you, haven't done this for each other, don't assume it's too late. It certainly is still possible to change the way you deal with conflict.

One strategy for dealing with conflict that might be useful to share with family members is a specific plan for fighting fairly. You might base your plan on the following steps:

1. If you are upset or have a problem, it's your responsibility to bring it up; don't wait for your spouse or family members to read your mind.

2. When you bring up the problem, state it clearly and briefly: "I am feeling _____ because _____."

3. If your spouse or family members don't understand the problem, it's their responsibility to ask for clarification.

4. Don't discuss the problem until everyone is clear just what the problem is.

5. When you bring up a problem, it is your responsibility to suggest a solution.

6. The solution isn't an ultimatum, but an opening for negotiation and compromise.

7. When you discuss options, concentrate on finding something that is practical and likely to work. Then discuss specific changes that each person involved will make—and make a commitment to those changes.

8. Discuss ways all the parties involved might sabotage the agreement; then agree that no one will do that.

9. Congratulate yourselves for working together to solve a problem.

10. Agree on a time to check in and decide whether the plan is working or whether you need to agree on more changes.

If two people aren't willing to try to use anger produc-
tively, their relationship may not survive. One danger sign is
what Daniel Goleman, in his book *Emotional Intelligence*, calls
"toxic thoughts." These are assumptions someone makes
over time about a friend or partner, such as: "I've given up
talking with him. He's a selfish jerk and never listens." These
toxic thoughts make it impossible to really listen to each
other. They are signs that one person has basically written
off the other as hopeless. Recognizing and changing these
toxic thoughts are important steps in revitalizing a damaged
relationship.

Of course, there are times when people attempt to teach
what they need during conflict, and the other persons
involved are too fearful, too angry or too indifferent to
respond. If this happens, it may be necessary to stand back
and evaluate what this means about the relationship. The
prerequisites for sharing a loving relationship that I discuss
in the next chapter will shed further light on this issue.

Conclusion

Healthy people recognize the need for listening to and
expressing their anger. Listening to ourselves when we're
angry can direct us toward the actions we may need to take.
Listening to others' anger, without personalizing it or assuming it is correct, allows us to see our impact on people.

Learning to express ourselves when we're angry, then
cooling down while we rethink what we're trying to accomplish, and finally coming back together to discuss what we
recognized during the cooling-off period, increases our odds

of growing closer and learning more about each other.

Expressing our anger assertively empowers us, leaving us feeling alive, potent and worthwhile. It reduces the anxiety that results when we discount ourselves and trap ourselves in a pattern of avoidance. Taking our anger and ourselves seriously leads to a sense of integrity.

Suggested Exercises

1. Since anger and rage are so often confused, try writing down in your own words how they differ. Check your definitions against those given at the beginning of this chapter.
2. Write down how the sharing of anger was modeled in your family. How does that compare with your typical mode of operation around anger?
3. What are the "dark sides" of yourself that you rarely show others or would be uncomfortable sharing because of your fears about how you would be perceived?
4. Compare how you feel when you share your irritations and frustrations with how you feel when you don't.
5. List some of the people you care about. How much time have you spent teaching each of them about what you need and want if the two of you are in conflict with each other?
6. Try the three-step method of constructive anger resolution the next time you're upset. Then consider the following questions: How did it work? What was the biggest challenge for you?
7. Write in your journal about any new thoughts you had concerning anger as you read this chapter.

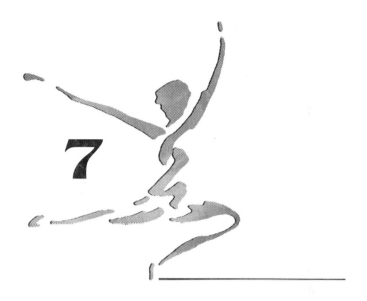

Coming Out of Hiding: Allowing Yourself to Love and Be Loved

This chapter on love is particularly important for those who suffer from excessive anxiety. I have found that anxious people, because of their shame-based experiences, have developed flawed belief systems about love. As a result, they tend to be socially isolated in one of two basic ways. Some are literally withdrawn from other people, having learned early in life that connecting with others only leads to hurt and disappointment. They may be totally alone, or they may find one person upon whom they depend heavily. Others may have an active social life and a lot of acquaintances, but no real friends who know them intimately.

The Withdrawn/Dependent Type

When I first met Helen, she had just moved to the United States from Austria with her husband, who was in the military. Her husband had been at home with her for the past three weeks because she felt absolutely incapable of staying home by herself due to panic attacks and a constant state of anxiety.

Helen had no friends locally. She talked periodically on the phone with her sisters, who were scattered across the United States. She had no driver's license. She did not even feel comfortable sitting in my office alone.

As I got to know Helen, I learned that she had been born and raised in a small community in Austria. Her parents had been farmers. Her father was a man who was filled with rage and constantly critical. He had sexually molested Helen and several of her sisters when they were small. Helen's mother was very superstitious and felt incapable of standing up to her husband's abuse, which was directed at her and the children. She was in and out of the hospital with periods of severe depression and virtual incapacitation.

Helen was a very intelligent woman, responding rather dramatically to therapy. She became more comfortable quite quickly, once I taught her some techniques to relax and explained how she created her anxiety. We also explored some of the superstitious beliefs she had learned from her mother.

Shortly after I began working with Helen, she and her husband learned he was to be sent out of the state for a month for training. Helen initially felt paralyzed by the possibility of spending a month alone. As we talked, however, she and I developed a plan. First of all, we decided that this would be a great reason for Helen to get her driver's license. She passed her test several weeks later. Next, we helped her to look into resources on the military base for child care and social support. By the time her husband left for his training, Helen was reasonably comfortable with the idea of being alone. While he was gone, she gained a great deal of confidence in her ability to manage her life adequately.

Those Who Live Behind an Image

Those who live behind an image may have people that they refer to as "friends." They may also have one person, or a very small group of people, who see the "real them." But even those they trust most closely get a censored view. Dan epitomized this type of person.

He was a teacher who, at age thirty-eight, had recently gone through a divorce. As I tried to reach him for appointments,

I noticed that he was rarely home. He later shared with me that he was out almost every night with friends.

As I got to know Dan, it became clear that part of his reason for being out every night was his strong discomfort at the idea of being alone with a lot of unstructured time on his hands. He had few hobbies or areas of interest and very little in the way of inner resources.

I had a difficult time getting to know the details of Dan's life. He reported nothing traumatic or even difficult about his life growing up, but he did indicate that he didn't feel very close to his family. We began to explore his relationship with his friends, and Dan admitted that there was no one he felt he could tell about his therapy. Later he realized that there had been no one in his life with whom he shared his intimate hopes, dreams and concerns.

The Lack of Role Models

Excessive-anxiety sufferers have generally not had healthy love modeled in their families. While their parents tried their best to raise their children well—and generally did a better job than the generation who preceded them—they still weren't able to give their children what they needed in order to develop healthy relationships. As a result, those with excessive anxiety struggle with how to live in relationships with others. They do not know how to voice their needs, say "no" comfortably, have reasonable expectations for themselves and others, or use conflict constructively to get to know and share mutual respect with those around them.

Instead, anxious people tend to be rather black and white

about relationships. They either don't risk rocking the boat by asking for what they might need, or they take the opposite position of being insensitively or unrealistically demanding. They may either acquiesce to others' requests—believing they have to in order to keep the other person happy—or they don't let anyone close enough to consider making a request. They may chronically go the extra mile for others and expect little in return. They might avoid any chance of conflict with the significant people in their lives. They might see themselves as continual victims, whining and lamenting about how they are treated by the world and everyone in it.

As I described in chapter 3, these people may have been blatantly abused or neglected. Or they may have been overprotected, superresponsible or "model children"—all in an attempt to maintain their parents' approval. Research finds that excessive-anxiety sufferers are often the firstborn, the last born or the "responsible" children in their dysfunctional families.

Regardless of the circumstances, they share one characteristic—they don't have reasonable expectations of themselves in relationships. This leads to anxiety and confusion about how to relate to significant people in their lives. They want to love and be loved, but they don't know what genuine love is.

What Love Is Not

To try to come up with a definition of healthy love, let's start by taking a look at some of the things love is not.

Martyrdom

While true love may mean periodically choosing to put another person's needs ahead of your own, there are those who *chronically* put other people's needs ahead of their own. Much of their identity may be centered around notions of "being needed" and "look what I put up with."

The most dramatic example of the person who lives the life of a martyr may be the woman who lives in a physically abusive relationship. If you were to ask her why she stays, she might look at you with an incredulous expression. "Because I love him, of course. He's really a very good man when he's not raging or drinking." Time after time, this woman returns to her husband after being abused, contending that "He's learned his lesson this time. It's going to be much better now."

Dependency

We all have dependency needs, and we all need to know we can rely on someone else to be there for us emotionally. However, healthy people know they can generally manage life on their own. Those who are dependent feel as though they need someone else in order to survive. They hang onto the other person in their life almost like a leech, expecting that person to be not only their spouse, but their best friend and their only confidant and companion.

Dependent people often find others who need to be needed, and together they begin a relationship. At the beginning, the one person's dependency leaves the other partner feeling very important. But after a while, that continual neediness becomes a real drain on the relationship.

Lust

While physical attraction to another person is one of the gifts God gave us to help us start a relationship, it's simply not enough to sustain one. Our sexual attraction, or lust, might move us toward a person in the beginning, but we need to admire and respect other qualities in that person, as well as share similar values and dreams, if the relationship is going to flourish.

Intensity

People who were brought up in families where there was no emotional connection may perceive intensity in a relationship as proof of real love.

In working with those in recovery from alcoholism, for example, I have found that such people often struggle as they get involved in relationships that aren't in continual crisis. They wonder if it can really be love. Making up after periods of abuse, either physical or emotional, can feel extremely attractive. Usually, however, the periods between violent outbursts become shorter and shorter, until eventually they are not enough to make up for the chaos.

Emotional Incest

When I described different forms of abandonment in chapter 3, I discussed the concept of emotional incest—when the roles of the parent and child are reversed. While it feels as if the parent is there for the child, what may actually be happening is that the child is taking care of the adult.

I work frequently with clients in their thirties, forties, fifties and even sixties, whose anxiety is maintained in part by parents who continue to make extreme demands on them. They are expected to take care of, entertain and generally center their lives around their parents. People who are in this position feel both very important to their parents and absolutely overwhelmed. (For more on this topic, I refer you to Patricia Love's book *Emotional Incest Syndrome.*)

So What Is Healthy Love?

M. Scott Peck, in his popular book *The Road Less Traveled,* defines love as "the will to extend one's self for the purpose of nurturing one's own or another's spiritual growth." "Extending one's self" implies that there is effort involved in love. One of the myths in our society is that love is simply a feeling. While feeling is certainly a part of love, in any long-term relationship the "feeling" of love waxes and wanes. What we must be taught are the efforts two people can make to bring that feeling of love back into a relationship.

Love the feeling is a fruit of love the verb.

–Stephen Covey

Frank Pittman, in his book *Private Lies,* gives us a very practical definition of intimacy: "Intimacy is about being known." Blending Peck's thoughts about the effort involved in a loving relationship with Pittman's definition, we can begin to understand the efforts needed in sharing a loving relationship.

The Healthy Components
of a Loving Relationship

Attentiveness

What I mean by attentiveness is real listening—not just hearing the words. I really can hear everything my wife says, even when I'm watching TV or reading the newspaper. I can even repeat the words back to her. Is that real listening? No. Real listening is not only hearing her words, but trying to interpret the body language or being able to "read between the lines" and understand what she is communicating. It means really hearing how important something is to her.

When another person makes the effort to reach out to us in intimate communication, they are risking making themselves "known" to us. They are offering a gift of love. Responding with love, then, means that we make the effort to truly listen and understand.

We can't always do real listening. It's hard work that requires attention and energy. Sometimes at the end of the day you might get home tired and drained, and your spouse or your kids pounce on you. Here's a place to use the assertiveness skills you're learning and to set a boundary. It's perfectly okay to say, "I'm really tired right now. Give me an hour to change clothes and read the paper, and then I'll listen to you." Or, "Come help me get dinner started, and then we can sit down and talk." Mutually agree on a time to talk with the other person. Then make sure you keep your part of the agreement.

Having reasonable limits on your ability to really listen is being honest and respectful with both yourself and your family. It's far healthier to agree to talk later, when you can really listen, than to half-listen with irritation and resentment.

I used to get annoyed because it seemed that people always called me when I was in the middle of a TV show I really enjoyed watching. I would sit and listen with half an ear as I gave most of my attention to the TV; and of course the caller could tell I wasn't really listening. Finally I realized I had the right to say, "I'm watching this TV show that I really like, and I'll call you back right after it's over." The first time I said that, I felt terribly selfish. Then I realized that that particular form of selfishness was also honest. I was taking care of myself and being respectful of them—by calling back when I could genuinely be attentive.

Risking Loss and Rejection

If we're going to love people, it means we risk being hurt. Many of my clients have been hurt. One way some people cope with that hurt is by deciding they are never going to get close to anyone again. When people have gone through a serious loss, in future relationships they may be careful to keep one foot out the door. If there is trouble or if the relationship gets too intimate, then out they go. Well, keeping that distance does work. But it comes at a very high price. Because if we don't get close to people, we deny ourselves the warmth and connectedness that comes with love.

It helps to accept the fact that close relationships come at the price of some hurt and pain. People are going to hurt us, and we are going to hurt them. It's not a question of *whether* that will happen, but what we are going to do *when* it happens.

Commitment

This is probably the most important point in a loving relationship. Without commitment, there can be no love. Genuine love doesn't have "unless" attached to it—I will love you unless things get too hot, unless you hurt me, unless you tell me something I don't want to hear.

One of the things that impresses me most as I lead group therapy sessions is the way they give people the experience of commitment, often for the first time. No matter how angry, hurt, scared or lonely a group member becomes, the others in the group are going to come back, listen and talk it through.

All that really is required to work something out is being willing to meet each other halfway, to really listen, to hear each other out and come to some sort of compromise. It doesn't mean people will necessarily agree; they may agree to disagree. But they have a commitment to sticking it out, locking horns if necessary and getting something resolved.

My wife and I have been married for over twenty years now. It wasn't until perhaps ten or twelve years ago that we actually made a commitment to each other. Saying that confuses some people. "But you made a commitment at the altar." Wrong! We made a *promise* at the altar. It was kind of a naive promise to begin with, even though we both meant it at the time. People change and grow, and can move in opposite directions. A healthy relationship means changing together. We had enough commitment to stay together even through some rough times. But we really didn't have a sense of genuine intimacy until we said, "We are not going to keep threatening each other with divorce."

I once began working with a couple who had been married for seventeen years. They first came in during a crisis—they had had it and were going to get a divorce. After a few sessions things were smoothed over, and they got back together. A year or so later the same thing happened. And they were back again a few months later. Finally I said, "You have been married for almost twenty years now. Isn't it time to quit threatening each other and make a decision? Either commit to each other or get out, but stop threatening to leave simply to protect yourself." They told me later that that confrontation was a turning point in their therapy. They decided to commit to each other, which changed the focus of their therapy from crisis management to building a stronger long-term relationship.

We have to make a conscious decision for commitment. That means choosing not to have affairs, choosing not to make another person as important as our partner, choosing to talk to our partner rather than someone else when we're angry, choosing to listen, choosing not to threaten divorce when things get tough, choosing to see things through. That requires a very conscious decision and a strong verbal and emotional commitment.

Risking Independence and Separateness

In the beginning of our relationship, I thought my wife and I had gotten together because she needed me. (The truth was more that I needed her.) But all of a sudden she started developing a life of her own. She went back to school and got an advanced degree. She started having friends without my approving of them. She started having activities of her own that took up some of "our" evenings. It really pressured me. Was this what she needed? She didn't need me anymore.

It was a struggle, but eventually our relationship was no longer based on need. Now it is more "I love you, I want you, I am committed to you, but I don't need you." My life would be more difficult without her, and it's nice to share our lives; but I don't need her in order to be happy.

The issue of encouraging a person's separateness is a key point and a challenge in a relationship. Most of us have grown up with the idea of putting our own needs aside and attending to those of our mate. But genuine love requires risking that independence and separateness.

On the other hand, many people confuse true independence with a pseudo-independence or counterdependence. This is much like remaining distant from others as a way to protect against being hurt. These people may be convinced that they don't need other people. But they actually keep their distance because they know themselves so well. They realize that when they get involved with people, they tend to give their power away and get "swallowed up" in the relationship. Their distance is based on fear and insecurity. Truly independent people, however, have no fear of losing themselves in relationships. They have learned to think for themselves and are able to set healthy boundaries with others. Because they are secure within themselves, they can enjoy the synergy and stimulation that relationships can provide.

*Love is more a solvent than a glue, a freeing up of two
people to be truly who they are.*

–Source Unknown

Risking Confrontation

Part of what we must determine when we think we need
to be assertive is whether we really care about this relationship. If we do, then we really don't give ourselves another
choice—we need to confront issues. We can't wait until we're
comfortable to do it. We never get comfortable with confrontation. When I need to confront someone, my heart
starts beating fast, my head and hands start shaking, and my
throat gets so tight I feel as if I'm choking. But I know I've
got to do it. It's part of my commitment to keeping this relationship honest and aboveboard. It's part of my dedication
to "be known."

What would happen if I didn't confront issues? The relationship would remain superficial and become stale. Sometimes, if we know the other person isn't going to change or
we don't know whether the relationship has the capacity for
real closeness, the confrontation doesn't feel worth the effort.
But genuine love requires honesty and confrontation.

Don't misunderstand—I don't mean the kind of aggression
and arrogance that people sometimes use to abuse others.
When we do confront someone, it needs to be from a position of humility. It comes after a lot of thought and self-
exploration. I need to clarify my own thinking and decide
whether this is my own issue or the other person's. Then I
can confront someone because I value myself and intuitively

sense that I really do know what I'm talking about and can trust my instincts. Then I don't need to attack out of my own fear or defensiveness. I can share my observations and feelings in a way that says, "I value my thoughts, but I can't be positively sure. This is what I believe, and it's important for me to share it with you."

Discipline

The discipline involved in love takes two forms. The first one has to do with our commitment to the other person. Parents who love their children, for example, will set aside their own wants in order to meet the needs of the children. This involves such basic things as interrupting a television show in order to help a child with homework, setting aside time to take them to soccer practice or dance lessons, preparing nutritious meals instead of letting them have ice cream and soft drinks for dinner. All these are forms of giving and nurturing that are a part of parental love. They require self-discipline and maturity.

The other form of discipline that makes up genuine love involves limiting and focusing one's love. Because genuine love requires so much effort, a disciplined person doesn't waste it. This might mean choosing to concentrate your attention on your family and close friends, rather than trying to spread your love among so many people that it is too diluted to mean much.

This disciplined love also means a person who wants to share a loving relationship does not waste time trying to do so with someone who is incapable of responding. I meet many people in my practice who are trying frantically to maintain a marriage or other close relationship unilaterally. They just work harder and harder, trying to manipulate their partner into caring, even though the other person refuses to communicate openly or accept a fair share of responsibility in the relationship. Some people are willing to accept the illusion of a loving relationship because they are simply too afraid of being on their own. Or they don't believe they are capable or worthy of a more intimate relationship.

I see many clients in my anxiety program leave very quietly and thoughtfully after the presentation on love. Learning about disciplined love really challenges them to evaluate and consider whether their relationships are mutually loving ones. Part of what we may need to accept is that, while we can unilaterally love someone, we can't share a mutually nurturing relationship unless the other person is also willing to make an effort. Perhaps you might decide it's okay to maintain a few unilateral relationships for one reason or another, recognizing that if you stopped trying to maintain them, they would probably unravel. Perhaps you might choose to end most of these relationships. Either way, recognizing your choices and your own need to be disciplined helps you stop wasting energy trying to maintain relationships that are illusions. Then you can devote your efforts to building relationships that are mutually loving and based on equal partnership.

One of my therapy groups included a woman in her early thirties who was attractive, intelligent, and had a career and many other things going for her. But she had never been married. Abby didn't feel that her life was complete until she could "become one with somebody." So a great deal of her energy was spent in trying to find somebody she could love.

She found a lot of people who were willing to be loved, but they weren't willing to love her. She got hurt. She got used.

But in the group, Abby learned more about real love. She began requiring more honesty in her relationships in their early stages. As she came to value herself more, she came to realize she deserved more in relationships. Eventually she began dating a man and for several months enjoyed a relationship in which they communicated, shared their feelings, confronted each other and were beginning to see the possibility of commitment to each other. Then her lover got a letter from his ex-girlfriend blaming him for her suicide attempt. He just shut down.

At first Abby said, "I love you. I'll give you some time." Several weeks passed. She suggested that he go see a counselor. He refused. A few more weeks passed. Finally she said, "If you are not willing to talk to me, to see a counselor, to get some help with this issue, then I can't be with you. I require more. I'm worth more than that."

Once we get to the point of knowing and saying, "I'm worth more than I'm getting," we have a choice of confronting the other person or leaving. The relationship has a chance to grow, and if it won't grow, we know it's time to leave.

The Need for a Support Network

While it's true that you can't love anybody else until you love yourself, it's also true that you can't love yourself until you feel loved.

We are all reflections of the way we have been treated. If we were obviously or subtly criticized, put down, compared to others, or accepted only conditionally or with strings attached, that's the treatment we have learned to expect from others and the way we have learned to treat ourselves.

The only way we recover from this early shaming, which has damaged our sense of self, is by counteracting the beliefs we developed about ourselves. Some of these erroneous beliefs might be: *If you let people get close, you just get hurt. If people really knew me, they wouldn't like me. I've got to be good or perfect in order to be loved.* We need to learn to replace those beliefs by experiencing healthier, more intimate relationships.

Most of my clients have had very few people in their lives who have unequivocally supported or intimately known them. Due to their shame, anxiety sufferers have lived behind images or masks, reluctant to be genuine because of the negative experiences they have had in the past.

What I find in my practice is that many people, once they get the new information about how to encourage better relationships, immediately begin to apply that information and see improvement in their interactions with the people close to them. Others find that the information makes sense in their heads, but they are afraid to take risks or to rock the boat, so they continue acting in their old ways.

I encourage people to practice using this new information in several ways. One is to begin voicing their needs, asserting their rights and evaluating the reciprocity in their existing relationships. Exciting changes for the better often begin to happen. Just as often, the people in their lives react with discomfort or even hostility to this new behavior.

As a result, it's important for anyone trying to change their beliefs and behavior about love to have a support network. Sometimes my clients find new supporters in the treatment program. Other times I may suggest that they participate in various Twelve-Step programs or other therapy and support groups. All of these resources offer people a place to bond with others who have similar problems, histories and goals of recovery. Regardless of where clients go to build their networks, I provide support in ongoing counseling as they make their attempts, stub their toes or get confused and frustrated as they try to improve their relationships.

Becoming a confident person who is comfortable in loving relationships is important work, and it's certainly not easy. A support system is crucial for strong and lasting growth. I encourage you to build one for yourself with the resources you have available.

Conclusion

In this chapter, I've tried to encourage you to understand the difference between love the feeling and love the verb. Once you understand some of the effort involved in establishing and maintaining genuinely loving relationships, you can start to evaluate the relationships in your own life. Since developing intimate and healthy human relationships is a key way to heal our shame, it's important that we learn to do that.

Trying to keep ourselves safe by hiding from love doesn't work. We can't ever be safe by keeping people at arm's length or by burying ourselves in dependent relationships.

As long as we expect betrayal and abandonment, we will feel powerless, fearful and anxious. It's only through coming out of hiding that we can find healing and safety. The affirmation and support that come from loving relationships are empowering. They help us begin to live life with more creativity, spontaneity and self-confidence.

Suggested Exercises

1. Write down some of the things (martyrdom, lust, dependency, among others) that you may have confused with love in your own life.

2. Evaluate the relationships in your life you have always considered loving ones. How do they rate when you assess them using the six building blocks of a loving relationship described in this chapter? Are both people working equally hard at maintaining these relationships, or are you doing it all yourself? If you are doing most of the work and you stopped, would the relationship unravel?

3. Do you share any relationships in which you wouldn't worry about being abandoned if you showed the other person your "worst self"? Write down what you value and appreciate about the people in your life with whom you have such a relationship.

4. Do you have a group of people who know you "warts and all"? Write down some ways you could begin to enlarge your network of support.

REPAIRING YOUR
SHAME-PLAGUED SEXUALITY

Cliff and Maria came to me because their marriage was in trouble. Once I learned about their histories, it was no surprise that they struggled. Cliff came from an abusive home where he never got any affection or heard any affirmation

from either of his parents. Instead, he was constantly criticized. The one thing his parents could agree on was that
Cliff was a failure. Maria had grown up with little contact
with her father, who had abandoned his family for another
woman when Maria was small. Her mother never got a
divorce, but she constantly complained that men were bums
who couldn't be trusted.

Before she met Cliff, Maria had spent several years in an
abusive relationship with a controlling and critical man. Cliff
had been in a long-term dependent relationship with another
woman who had dumped him shortly before he met Maria.
He was still in pain over the end of that relationship when he
and Maria married.

Among the many problems in Cliff and Maria's marriage
was a lack of emotional and sexual intimacy. After five
years, their marriage had barely been consummated. Marital
frustration was the issue that finally drove them to seek help.

No aspect of human activity is more likely to be shamed
than sexuality. To fully understand human sexuality, we
need to realize that it is more than just sexual activity. Sex is
actually only a small part of sexuality—vital and potentially
enjoyable, but small. Sexuality is not just something we do
or have, it is who we are as males or females. Sometimes the
factors that shape our self-images as men or women leave us
with unrealistic expectations of ourselves and others, which
lead to unnecessary anxiety. This anxiety is especially likely
to affect our attempts to share affection through sexual activity with our partners.

Traditional Sexual Role Models

For most of us, our sexual role models were our parents. If, like many adults in their forties and fifties, you were raised in a traditional family, your father was probably not very emotionally expressive. He had probably learned from his father, who learned from his father, that a man's main function in life was to earn the money that the family needed to survive. His role was not to be heavily involved in the day-to-day activities of his children, except perhaps as a disciplinarian. He probably did not talk much about his early life or how he felt about things. His ways of expressing himself were most likely withdrawing emotionally, moody silence when he was upset, or raging. Since he likely did not learn how to be direct with his feelings, what emotions he did express may have been expressed indirectly, through sarcasm or teasing, keeping people around him at an emotional distance.

Traditionally, men were expected to be strong and self-sufficient, with their self-worth tied to how well they provided and how much money they made. Emotionally, they were taught to be tough: "Don't cry." "Be a man." "Don't let them know they hurt you." "Don't be afraid." Men often learned this toughness so well that they didn't even know what they felt. As a result, no matter whether they felt hurt, scared, lonely or frustrated, they either stayed withdrawn or vented with rage.

While men were being strong and stoic, feelings were a female prerogative. Emotional support for the family was the mother's job. She was expected to be her husband's helpmate and to sacrifice her needs in favor of her husband's and her children's. Women were expected to be "ladies" who were not openly angry or assertive, but who could deal indirectly with anger through tears, guilt and manipulation. In other words, ladies didn't get angry—they got even.

These traditional role models, while oversimplified here, were the basis for most male-female interactions for many years. The roles extended, of course, to sexuality. Men were expected to be the aggressors, while women were responsible for not letting anything go too far before marriage. Women were taught to provide sex out of obligation, perhaps faking sexual satisfaction so the man wouldn't feel like a failure. Men, as part of their protective role, were expected to be responsible for female satisfaction in life—including sexual satisfaction. The irony here is that both women and men were taught that, if their spouses were happy, they would be happy. Each one was responsible for the other's happiness instead of their own.

Neither of these rigid, traditional role models was very healthy for either men or women. They limited the choices available to sons and daughters as they grew into adults themselves. And, of course, the negative effects were much more severe when families were affected by alcoholism, physical abuse, sexual abuse or other types of dysfunction.

Changing Sexual Role Models

Obviously there have always been variations in families, but by and large in our society, the traditional roles we've just described were the norm for a little more than the first half of the twentieth century. Then along came the

1960s–with the pill, the sexual revolution and the feminist movement–and things really got confusing.

Now women were expected to have careers, while they continued to provide the emotional stability in their homes. They began to express themselves more openly and to put a higher priority on their own needs. Men, while still expected to provide financially for their families and do the heavy lifting, were suddenly supposed to know how to be sensitive and express emotions openly. The changes, necessary as they were, were confusing for both sexes as everything they had been taught to consider normal was turned upside down.

If you are in your twenties or thirties, you may have grown up in a family struggling with shifting sexual role models. Again, the challenge of these changing times would have been exacerbated for your family if you had an alcoholic, abusive or otherwise dysfunctional parent.

In recent years the confusion has continued, with changing social attitudes about divorce, out-of-wedlock births, sexual activity and parenting roles. We're now seeing some signs of a reaction against the sexual permissiveness of the last few decades, emphasized by the need for protection against AIDS and other sexually transmitted diseases. At the same time, the sexualizing of everything from television comedies to advertising puts tremendous pressure on children to be sexually active without giving them a healthy sense of what that really means. There are still many traditional shaming messages around sex. In some cases, however, the message also seems to suggest that it is shameful not to be sexually active.

The sixteen-year-old daughter of a friend of mine told me

about a recent conversation she had with a boy her own age, a casual acquaintance. First he told her that his girlfriend was pregnant. He was worried about how he was going to stay in school and hold down a full-time job to help provide for the baby. Then he asked her if she was still a virgin. When she said she was, his response was, "What a shame." She thought his reaction was bizarre, considering the difficulties he was facing as a result of his own sexual involvement. But this is a sample of the confused attitudes about sex that our society is transmitting. About the only thing we know for sure about sexuality is that we don't quite know what to do with it.

Sex Without Intimacy
Leads to Waning Sexual Interest

Many of the people I see in my practice report that their sexual interest is waning. David Schnarch, Ph.D., in the *Family Therapy Networker*, reports that "Sexual boredom, low sexual desire and lack of intimacy are so common as to be one of the major complaints among couples who seek marital counseling, and are probably considered inevitable and incurable by the legions of other bored couples who don't."[1]

Traditional role models do not teach us direct ways of communicating with our spouses. People mistakenly use the terms *sexual intercourse* and *intimacy* interchangeably. But intimacy, as we have discussed earlier, is about being known to your partner. When the natural sexual hunger that couples share upon first meeting begins to wane and they have not learned the skills to remain emotionally connected, sexual intercourse can become boring and monotonous.

[1]David Schnarch, "Inside the Sexual Crucible," *Family Therapy Networker* (March/April 1993), 42.

In his article, Dr. Schnarch further suggests that

People have boring, monotonous sex because intense sex and intimacy (and change itself) are far more threatening and fearful than they can imagine, and require more adult autonomy and ego strength than they can muster. Intimate sex is for most people a terrifying and utterly mysterious business. . . . Through sex, we can encounter—though usually we repress it—the fear of not being loved and the terror of losing what we love, the dread of exposing everything within us that is vulnerable and helpless, inadequate and impoverished or ugly and hateful. . . . To see inside each other during sex requires the courage, integrity and maturity to face oneself and, even more frightening, convey that self—all that one is capable of feeling and expressing—to the partner.

Cliff and Maria's relationship was an illustration of Dr. Schnarch's teaching that intimacy, in any relationship in general and during intercourse in particular, doesn't come naturally. As Dr. Schnarch goes on to say, intimacy is

a learned ability and an acquired taste. . . . Marriage forces us to see (if we have the courage to look) the worst, as well as the best, parts of ourselves; it reveals our capacity for sadism and hatred, our desire to punish and control our spouses, our secret neediness and insecurity, our shame-filled sexual fantasies, and, most of all, our usually unacknowledged terror of being left alone to our own inadequate selves, of being rejected, of losing someone we love.

Dr. Schnarch further describes the "paradox of intimacy" as "the acute awareness of our fundamental loneliness and separateness from other human beings that motivates intensely intimate contact." Unfortunately, most of us are not taught how to maintain that intimate contact.

(For anyone interested in further information about the connection between sexual and emotional intimacy, I would urge you to read David Schnarch's thought-provoking book *Passionate Marriage*, which deals more fully with the ideas mentioned here.)

How Comfortable
Are You with Being Touched?

Many anxious people were brought up in families where either they were not given much affection, or they were smothered by it. As a result, they are not comfortable with touching or being touched. Since touch invades a person's "private space," it leaves us vulnerable and open to possible rejection. We need to be comfortable with ourselves in order to be able to touch and be touched freely.

When I talk with clients about the importance of touch in our lives, I often use the analogy of vitamins in our diet. We can live for a long time if we don't have the proper vitamins, but without them we eventually start to decay from within. Our skin, fingernails and hair begin to lose their luster and glow. Long-term depletion of essential vitamins leads to illness and starvation. In the same way, we can survive without being touched. But inwardly we are dying or starving ourselves because of the lack of emotional nurturing that touch provides.

Many of the people I work with have convinced themselves that they don't need other people and don't need to be touched. Others seek the constant reassurance of someone else's touch and affection to compensate for their own internal emptiness. These people often get involved in inappropriate or hasty sexual relationships, using sex to try to satisfy their need to be touched.

Touch can convey many different things. Some of them are:

1. **Acknowledging One's Presence.** A parent in the middle of a conversation who is interrupted by a small child might put an arm around the child as a way of recognizing the child's presence but helping the child wait a moment before getting the needed attention. If you attempt to join a group where a conversation is already in progress, you receive a "don't bother us" message if people keep their backs to you as you approach. But if instead someone in the group reaches out and puts a hand on your shoulder or offers a handshake, you feel accepted, valued and welcomed.

2. **Invasion of Personal Space.** All of us have a different need for a certain amount of physical space around us to feel comfortable. People arrive at that boundary rather naturally as they speak with one another. If you ever want to experiment with that as you're talking with someone, take just half a step in their direction. You will probably find that they will immediately back up. In extreme cases, they may become absolutely hostile.

   I remember asking a woman who suffered with panic attacks and an inability to form long-term relationships whether she would like to join my anxiety program. I knew enough of her history to know that she had been molested by her father early in life and later had been raped by a stranger. I asked if she would have a problem working with me since I was male. She immediately said, "Of course not."

I asked her to humor me as I tried an exercise with her. I stood at the far end of my office and asked her to pay close attention to her own bodily reactions. I told her to let me know what her body was telling her as I slowly moved forward. After my first step, she said, "Stop!"

This woman wanted very badly to trust people, but because of her history she had an understandably difficult time in doing so. After this experiment, she realized that she had repeatedly attempted to ignore the messages that her body was giving her. She felt she "should" trust people, particularly men, before she was genuinely ready. This woman, like most victims of sexual violation, needed a large amount of personal space, and she had been trying to ignore that need.

3. **Nonverbal Communication.** Much of what we convey and interpret as we communicate with others is done nonverbally through body posture, gestures and facial expressions. Those of us who were brought up in homes where we were shamed tend to read the worst possible meaning into these exchanges. Our creativity and sensitivity help us turn a raised eyebrow or a shrug of the shoulders into a total rejection of us as human beings. Those same traits, of course, sometimes make us able to read body language extremely accurately. The way we are touched or not touched says a lot to us about our value as human beings. The challenge for anxious people is to keep those negative nonverbal

messages in perspective, rather than interpreting them as an accurate assessment of our own worth.

4. **Value and Security.** From the moment we are born, the care we receive conveys to us either that the world is a safe, nurturing and secure place to be, or that we are in the way, a bother or invisible. I ask clients how often they were held on their parents' laps as children, having their backs scratched, their hair combed or being snuggled as they were read to. Many of them received little or none of this kind of touching. Being touched in a loving way lets children know they are valued, and the lack of touch conveys just the opposite message.

5. **Vulnerability.** It is certainly possible to remain aloof and detached even during intercourse. People who have been shamed are likely to hold themselves back even then, unwilling or unable to trust their partner enough to open up fully to them. Then, like Cliff and Maria, couples struggle with an unsatisfying or almost non-existent sex life. Learning to let go and to become comfortable—first with ourselves and then with our partners—allows us to surrender to feeling vulnerable and open with each other. Recovery from shame and anxiety means learning to be naked emotionally as well as physically, resulting in a truly awesome sense of connectedness and affirmation during intercourse.

Talking Openly About Sexuality

It seems ironic to advocate talking about sexuality when sexual conversation surrounds us. All you have to do is turn on the television set or pick up a popular magazine, and you're bombarded with articles, stories and jokes about sex. But this overload of sexual information often has little to do with real openness. It tends to focus either on "how-to" physical details or sniggering innuendo. Either of these messages can just add to our sense of shame and anxiety around sex.

What I'm advocating instead is that you find a safe place to begin discussing your own feelings, fears and beliefs about sexuality. This might be in a support group, with a therapist, with a close friend or with your spouse. Since sexuality is such a personal subject, it takes a lot of courage to discuss it openly. What I am encouraging you to do, though, is consider the price you pay if you don't give yourself a chance to talk about your sexuality.

I spent years feeling as though my sexual thoughts and feelings were disgusting. The more I lived in hiding with those feelings, the more I was convinced that they needed to be hidden. This hiding out is the epitome of living in shame and suffering with anxiety, convinced we are different.

I encourage you to begin to look for relationships with people where you, very slowly, can begin to talk more and more about honest issues. You will begin to realize that the thoughts you believed made you different and disgusting are instead the same thoughts that make you human and just like everyone else. Many of my clients begin by broaching those subjects with me. Once they realize that the sky doesn't fall as a result of their sharing, and that those feelings are both normal and healthy, they can begin to share more intimately with other supportive people in their lives.

Other Messages That May Lead to Shame About Sexuality

There are many messages about sexuality in our society, both secular and religious, that lead to a great deal of ambivalence and shame. I don't want to press my value system on you in regard to sexuality. But I do want you to consider some of the messages that you have received around the following issues. You may have been left feeling dirty, sinful or shameful about issues such as masturbation, fantasy and sexual thoughts, contraception or sexual activity in general. Instead of just blindly accepting these messages as truth, think about them as honestly as you can, so you can decide for yourself what you believe as a thoughtful, responsible adult.

Masturbation

Messages about masturbation are conveyed both verbally and nonverbally. Perhaps the nonverbal message is the most powerful of all. Learning to give yourself pleasure or to provide pleasure to a partner in any way other than intercourse is often discouraged. This discomfort with providing self-stimulation can become exaggerated as people are led to feel uncomfortable even looking at their own bodies in an affirming way.

I once worked briefly with a couple in their sixties who had recently married and were on the point of divorcing when they came to see me. She had been widowed, and he had never been married before. She was shocked and horrified when she found him masturbating one day. She interpreted it as meaning two things: that she was inadequate sexually and that he was a pervert. In reality, this was a perfectly normal and rather practical activity for a man who had spent most of his life unmarried. A little education and communication was all it took to help this couple's marriage survive.

I have found that many of the sexual difficulties couples have are a result of each partner having a very limited idea of what their body needs to feel pleasure. Often the sensual experience is limited to the genitals, and they can literally experience little sensual enjoyment in other areas of their body.

Lonnie Barbach, author of *For Yourself,* helps women understand their own bodies. She contends that women who suffer with sexual dysfunction often do so because they don't know how their own body functions or don't experiment with what their body needs. When those same women get involved in sexual relationships, they can only hope their partner will stumble onto something that is pleasurable. The woman may enter the relationship with no "map" of where to go or what is necessary for her in experiencing sexual satisfaction. There are many excellent books to help both men and women better understand how their own bodies function; a few of them are listed in the bibliography.

Fantasy and Sexual Thoughts

Many of my clients have been brought up with a religious interpretation of fantasy and sexual thoughts that leads them to believe that "if they have thought it, they have already sinned." Since they believe that what they think is sinful, they are reluctant to share it with someone else because of fears of being judged or rejected.

I remember being in a men's group where we shared some of our sexual fantasies. This was very threatening for me since I believed that if people knew my inner thoughts and fantasies, they would think I was disgusting. The more I believed that, the more I kept them to myself and the more I was convinced I was right. When I finally took the risk of sharing, I found that many others had the same thoughts and fantasies. I realized these thoughts didn't make me different. Instead, they made me human. I also learned that while I was not in control of what I felt (in fact, the more I tried to control it, the more it persisted), I did need to be responsible for my behavior associated with those thoughts.

Contraception

Again, I do not feel comfortable in suggesting what a person ought to believe regarding contraception. However, I have seen what happens for many people who go into hiding as a result of covertly deciding to choose a form of birth control that their church or a significant person in their life firmly disapproves of. The damaging factor is not what the person or the church believes, but the process of deception that leads a person to feel unacceptable or judged. I strongly advise people in this position to find someone in their lives with whom they can share their choices so they don't suffer with the inevitable anxiety and shame that naturally come with deception.

This kind of conflict between a person's externally imposed belief system and internal needs can lead to harmful and sometimes tragic consequences. Theresa, who briefly attended one of my groups, was raised a "good Catholic girl." At the same time, she had received almost no attention or affirmation from her father, so sex became a way to get that missing affirmation from men. As a teenager, she became pregnant. Despite their church's beliefs, her mother (without consulting Theresa) decided Theresa would have an abortion to "protect the family image." Afterward, her doctor suggested she go on birth control pills. Theresa refused: she was convinced that she would never have sex again outside of marriage, and she meant it. But because she felt so empty, she repeatedly and shamefully acted out the same sexual pattern. Eventually she had four abortions. Each time the doctors were more judgmental and more aggressive about her need for birth control. Each time, she was serious about her commitment to abstinence. But because of her shame and her neediness, she was unable to keep that commitment. She was caught in a destructive cycle of deception, shame and anxiety.

Sexual Activity in General

I remember coming home from my first date. I was excited about having passed through this rite of passage and moving into a new era in my life. Unfortunately, instead of sharing my excitement and asking how my night had gone, my mother met me with accusation after accusation about what I had done on this date. Certainly the chance to be with my girlfriend had stirred natural feelings of yearning, but I immediately got the message that these feelings were wrong. This, added to other messages about my sexual feelings, led me into greater shame about my sexuality. Apparently my mother had been led to feel that her own sexuality was bad, and I became the recipient of her sexualized rage.

Experiences like this can lead people to keep their sexual and their personal relationships hidden and private. This adds to the sense of being different and reinforces our anxiety about our sexuality.

Sexual Dysfunction Sends the Message That Something Inside Needs to Change

I want to mention briefly some of the more common types of sexual dysfunction that people suffer with needlessly. I say needlessly because, while there are many diseases or medications that might lead to sexual dysfunction, the majority are caused by psychological factors. These disorders respond very quickly and efficiently to psychotherapy, but because people have such great embarrassment about ever sharing their frustrations, they are reluctant to seek help.

Let me list some of the more common forms of sexual dysfunction.

1. **Impotence.** Impotence can happen for both males and females. While women are slightly better at faking sexual satisfaction (which only leads them deeper into hiding), men cannot hide their inability to maintain an erection. I have found over the years that men who have a difficult time maintaining an erection have a

self-esteem that resembles their flaccid penis. Generally these men are both unassertive and lack confidence. They have a difficult time asking for what they want; they don't believe they have a right to happiness in life. As their confidence increases—which it begins to do immediately when they begin to talk about their frustration instead of hiding it—their sexual ability improves.

Female impotence, also known as frigidity, prevents the woman from lubricating properly. As a result, intercourse is uncomfortable or even painful. Like their male counterparts, impotent women generally feel powerless and are lacking in confidence. They often aren't fully aware of the choices they have available, including the right to be treated sensitively by their partners and the option to say no until the experience is a pleasurable one. As these women develop more assertiveness and confidence, learn to ask for what they want, and come to believe they have a right to pleasure, their capacity for sexual pleasure increases as well.

2. **Premature Ejaculation.** A man whose sexual experiences have been ambivalent at best may end up suffering with premature ejaculation. One situation that can lead to this difficulty is repeated involvement with women who shame and criticize his sexual performance or his desire for sexual expression. Another is excessive exposure to pornography, which leads him to make objects of women. Instead of making love with a person, he has sex with body parts. Men who suffer with premature ejaculation are often exclusively genitally oriented. It's helpful for them to learn the capacity for sensual

enjoyment in other parts of their body through massage, touching, licking or kissing. As they begin to broaden their sensual repertoire, they can learn to become less performance oriented. This helps them begin to be with their partner in a more loving and intimate way.

3. **Vaginismus.** Vaginismus is characterized by painful and spasmodic contractions of the vaginal muscles upon penetration by the penis; sexual intercourse is all but impossible. The vaginal muscles of women who suffer with vaginismus are trying to give these women "a message." On the outside, these women may very much want to trust, but their body is saying no. Vaginismus often happens to women who have been violated emotionally, physically or sexually. The woman I described earlier in the chapter, who had been molested by her father and later raped by a stranger, understandably suffered with vaginismus. As she began to accept her distrust instead of judging it, her body began to relax. She began to get involved in relationships at her own pace instead of trying to respond to her partner's pace.

Homosexuality

All the issues, anxieties and fears we've discussed in this chapter certainly apply to homosexuals as well as heterosexuals. Those anxieties have an added dimension, however, because society provides such confusing and shaming messages around homosexuality. People who are gay struggle with the difficulty of finding role models for healthy sexuality, with the fear of coming out, with the message from many segments of society that homosexuality is a sin and with the discomfort many heterosexual people have about homosexuality. This is in addition to the difficulties with relationships that may result from growing up in an abusive family, not learning to express emotions and all the other anxiety-producing factors I have been discussing throughout this book.

A few years ago, a friend of mine ended a long-term lesbian partnership. At the same time, one of her male coworkers was getting a divorce. She said bitterly one day, "You know, he and I are going through the exact same pain and loss. I hurt just as much as he does. The only difference is that it's okay for him to talk about it, and it's not okay for me."

If you are suffering with anxiety and are also homosexual, I strongly recommend that you form a support network of people, both gay and straight, who will accept your sexuality. If you choose to see a therapist, it's important to find someone who is comfortable with homosexuality. This doesn't necessarily mean you have to come out blatantly in public. In your particular situation, that may or may not be the best thing for you to do. But in order to recover from your anxiety, you need to have safe people and places in your life with whom and where you can be completely yourself. Full recovery simply isn't possible as long as such a significant part of yourself as your sexuality remains hidden.

Victims of Sexual Violation Often Develop Anxiety

I include this information in this chapter because I am describing things that are related to our body and our sexuality. On the other hand, *sexual violation is not about sex; it is about power or the abuse of power*. It is also about a violation of trust. When people take advantage of their power or their position of authority in a relationship to meet their own needs, it is a violation.

Sexual violation is not just rape or intercourse. Sexual violation can also happen when one person looks at another in a way that makes the person being looked at feel like an object; by inappropriate hugs or touching that is intended to meet the toucher's own physical needs; or through lewd or suggestive comments. Sexual violation does not just happen between adults and children, but in any relationship between two persons of unequal power or authority, such as teacher and student, pastor and congregational member, physician and patient, or mentor and protégé.

The following lists include some physical, social or emotional, and spiritual symptoms that are common results of sexual violation. Just because you may have one or more of these symptoms doesn't necessarily mean you have been sexually violated. However, if some of these symptoms do apply to you, consider the possibility that sexual violation might be one of the factors. I've included this information in hopes that people who have never recognized their violation can do so. Then they can begin to heal and put into perspective some of their symptoms and characteristics, including excessive anxiety and shame.

1. Physical Symptoms of Sexual Violation

- Severe headaches
- Irritable stomach
- Menstrual irregularity
- Severe menstrual cramping
- Vaginitis
- Sleep disorders
- Nightmares
- Anorexia or obesity
- Bed-wetting
- Generalized aches and pains

2. Social/Emotional Symptoms of Sexual Violation

- Lack of trust
- Difficulty expressing emotions
- Low self-esteem
- Feelings of being unworthy/unimportant, dirty, apologetic
- Assuming parental duties in home where a parent is sexually abusive
- Running away from home
- Chemical abuse
- Neurosis
- Few intimate friends
- Self-mutilation
- Depression
- Suicidal thoughts
- Competitive with family members

3. Spiritual Symptoms of Sexual Violation

- Detachment
- Isolation
- Aloofness
- Guardedness

If you suffer with any of these symptoms or know of times in your life you were involved in a sexual violation, I encourage you to seek professional help. To deny it or to remain in hiding can lead to the development of physical symptoms as your body keeps score. Anxiety and depression are often signals of unexamined violation of some sort.

Sexuality Is an Important Part of Being a Healthy Human Being

Since our sexuality is so often shamed, it is not surprising that the techniques and methods used in establishing or reestablishing a healthy human sexuality are the same ones needed for recovery from shame in general.

Slowly establishing healthy, intimate relationships with other human beings, where we can openly share and own our thoughts and feelings, is vitally important. Establishing relationships with both men and women is extremely helpful in filling in some of the gaps that resulted from our earlier lack of healthy sexual role models.

Journaling, in an effort to recognize and curiously explore our thoughts in general, and our sexual thoughts and feelings in particular, is extremely helpful.

Experiential techniques such as deep breathing, deep relaxation and Reikian body therapy (which teaches relaxed belly breathing, deep relaxation and emotional expression) allow us to become much more aware of how much energy it takes for our body to maintain a guarded, vigilant or tense posture in response to our shaming. As we learn to relax ourselves fully and let down our guard, unexpected feelings, emotions and thoughts often begin to surface. These are extremely important in helping us to reconnect with those parts of us that have been shut down and repressed for years.

Conclusion

One part of recovery from anxiety involves learning to understand and be aware of some of the roles, attitudes and behaviors we have soaked up by watching and listening to important men and women in our lives. Once we are aware of these, we can start to question whether they still fit for us. *Many of the frustrations and conflicts we have in relationships with others come from assuming instead of negotiating.* For example, a man may feel resentment for his wife, who is staying home with the children, because he feels trapped and unappreciated as he provides financially for the family. Ironically, his wife may be feeling limited and stuck at home. Both may have assumed their roles because that's the way it was done in their families. If the issue were discussed and negotiated, both might be surprised by alternatives they had never considered, and the partners would become more intimately connected in the process.

Another facet of recovery is coming to terms with your own previous sexual behavior. People who have grown up being abused or shamed often try to meet their needs in unhealthy ways. This might include inappropriate and painful sexual acting out like that of Theresa, with her guilt, her shame and her four abortions. In situations like these, recovery means more than just changing the sexual behavior. It also means exploring the reasons for the behavior, finding healthier ways to meet your needs and forgiving yourself for your past mistakes. Because of the burden of shame and anxiety that can be the consequence of such mistakes, the help of a therapist is often extremely valuable.

The question of who you are as a man or a woman is a crucial one, part of your core identity. Exploring the beliefs that helped shape your own sexuality is an important part of full recovery from anxiety. It can lead to greater self-awareness, more choices and a sense of empowerment and freedom.

Suggested Exercises

1. Write down some of the things your role models taught you about the way you could express yourself emotionally and the way you could get close to people.
2. Do you think your role models were excited about their lives?
3. What kinds of things do you expect of yourself simply because you are a man or a woman? Make one list of your beliefs about what men should be like and a second list of your beliefs about what women should be like.
4. Do you see any correlation between how intimately you share with a partner and the amount of passion you feel with that partner (both emotional and sexual passion)?
5. What would be the riskiest thing people could know about you sexually?
6. Do you feel comfortable with your own body and what it needs to be orgasmic?
7. Have you taught your partner what feels good to you sexually?
8. How does your religious history affect your sexuality?

LEARNING TO GRIEVE
OUR DAILY LOSSES

I remember some years ago getting a letter from the school district informing us that it was time to register our oldest son for kindergarten. And I remember the feeling of disbelief: *He's not that old yet, is he?*

We tend to think of such events in our lives as milestones to mark our progress, steps toward the future, which of course they are. But we don't pay as much attention to the fact that each of them also contains a loss. For me, realizing my firstborn was ready to start school came with a pang of grief. *He's growing up. Pretty soon he's not going to be there on those mornings when I'm home. I'm going to miss him.*

Both my sons are in middle school now. I'm proud of them, and I enjoy watching them become young men. But the losses continue to go hand in hand with the milestones, as they become more independent and no longer need me in the same ways they used to.

The words *grief* and *loss* evoke images of deaths and funerals, of the big losses that all of us will experience eventually in our lives. Those losses are traumatic and important, and we'll talk about them in this chapter. But it's also important to pay attention to the smaller losses that we deal with every day. Some of these are intensely personal but usually go unnoticed. I feel a sense of loss every evening when I see the sun go down: Another day is gone; time is slipping away. Any sort of hurt we experience is a kind of loss—of our self-respect, our confidence or our integrity. Some of these are significant. Many of them are tiny and easily repaired, but they are losses nevertheless.

In twenty-plus years of practice, I have found that the bulk of work in therapy is about loss and grief. Clients sometimes balk when I make that statement, as if they think of grief only as it relates to the death of a loved one. It makes more sense to them after we begin to explore other examples of losses in their lives. Some of those losses might include:

1. Separation or divorce
2. Losing a job
3. Loss of a dream, fantasy or long-term goal
4. The letdown after achieving a goal
5. Loss of health
6. A friend moving away
7. Robbery or rape (loss of privacy, sense of violation)
8. Loss of self-respect
9. Loss of youth or beauty
10. Menopause
11. Loss of privacy and freedom as children are born
12. Kids leaving home
13. Death

The Greatest Loss: Loss of Self

People who suffer with excessive anxiety often identify their greatest loss as a loss of self or self-alienation. This is a direct result of the shame they have lived with. When you are shamed, you are told that a part of yourself is not acceptable. "No, you shouldn't get mad at your brother. Good girls don't get angry." Children who constantly hear messages like this are learning that anger is wrong and should not be part of them. In reality, anger is a necessary and important feeling for a child's own protection; if they disown that feeling, they are disowning a part of themselves.

If you constantly receive shaming messages, more and more parts of yourself are labeled as unacceptable. Eventually you conclude that nothing about you is okay. You have internalized the shame until it takes over your sense of who you are. You believe you are a failure, fatally flawed and inferior. You are likely to feel that you don't belong, that you're always on the outside looking in. You may develop a sense of depression and passivity: *If I'm a loser anyway, why should I even bother to try?*

Underlying this pain is the knowledge, buried somewhere beneath all the shame, that the failure isn't the real you. There is still a part of you, smothered and stifled as it might be, that is authentic and vital. The shaming you received as a child caused you to abandon this authentic part of yourself. That is the core loss behind your fear and your anxiety. An important part of your recovery is reconnecting with this deep inner self.

Developing Excessive Anxiety Can Create a Loss in Itself

As I discussed in chapter 2, your excessive anxiety symptoms can actually be the first step toward breaking free of your fears and forging an exciting new way of life. However, when you first recognize the symptoms, they certainly don't feel like anything positive. Instead, they bring with them a sense of loss—the loss of a sense of control, the loss of image—and a feeling of hopelessness. Before the symptoms began, you may have been feeling "fine." (Later in therapy you may realize that "fine" merely meant you were numb and out of touch with your own feelings. But even that oblivion felt better than the anxiety symptoms.)

It's extremely important to allow yourself to grieve the

losses brought on by your anxiety symptoms. This grief has two components.

First of all, it's okay to be angry and sad over losing your sense of control. Your anxiety symptoms might be the beginning of a change for the better, but working your way through that change can involve tremendous pain. Surrendering, letting go and feeling the pain is necessary, but that doesn't mean you have to pretend you like it. Go ahead and grieve.

A second and even more important component of this grief is likely to come along later in your recovery. The fearful, shamed self that you have been is a part of you; the hiding and withdrawal have served to protect you. So when you begin to move on and leave those elements behind, you are losing something of yourself. It's crucial that you acknowledge and grieve that loss. This process helps you let go of the old you in order to make room for the new, stronger self you are growing into.

There is a saying in recovery: "We can heal what we can feel." Yes, the tears are painful, and the loss is tremendous. But wasn't that loss worth the tears?

Healing from Loss Is a Process

Regardless of the severity of a loss or whether it is tangible or intangible, there is a process of grieving that must unfold before healing can take place. Harold Bloomfield, in *Surviving the Loss of a Love*, describes this process as: shock/denial; anger/depression; and understanding/acceptance.

Let's take the example of divorce. Suppose I am a man

whose wife tells me she is desperately unhappy and is going to leave me. At first my reaction would be shock and denial: *She doesn't really mean it. I'll make some changes, and everything will be fine again. This will blow over.*

Later, after my wife has packed her bags and moved to Toledo, I may begin to recognize that this isn't going to blow over: *She really means it; she has left me.* Now the anger begins. I'll probably begin by blaming her: *She's being unreasonable; she never really loved me anyway; she's out to ruin my life.* I might also blame myself: *If only I hadn't spent so much time at work; if only I had been different; if only I had given her more of what she needed.* This anger may come out aggressively, with my wanting to hurt her the way she hurt me. I might rage, threaten her or call up her friends to tell them what a witch she is. If I keep the anger inside, I'll become depressed, apathetic and perhaps even suicidal.

Eventually I will probably get to a point of understanding and acceptance: *Yes, she is really gone. Yes, this marriage is really over. I made some mistakes, and so did she. Now it's time to make some changes and get on with rebuilding my life.*

Even in an amicable divorce, this process would apply. The grief might be less intense, but it is still there and still necessary. There are losses. You may have lost the dream of the life together you had once hoped for, your image of yourself as a good husband or wife, or the pattern of your life as a married couple.

This process of shock/denial, anger/depression and understanding/acceptance applies to all of the losses we go through. In some of the small daily losses we experience, the process may take only a few seconds. For a large loss, such as a death or a divorce, the process may take several years.

It's important to remember that, especially in major losses, the grief process isn't necessarily tidy and linear. We don't move neatly from one step to another. One day we may be angry, the next day we might have flashes of understanding and acceptance, and a week later we may be deep in depression. We need to accept where we are in the process and listen to whatever message our bodies need to express. It's also helpful to keep in mind that healthy grieving will eventually move us through the process.

It's also important to realize that understanding and acceptance are not the same thing as "getting over it." We don't really "get over" serious losses and forget them. Instead, we integrate them into ourselves as we rebuild our lives and go on. Ideally, the process will help us become more compassionate, empathetic and closer to the people we care about.

There Are No Time Limits on Grief

The idea of a formal one-year period of mourning after a death seems archaic to us now. We no longer wear black or observe the other social rituals that went with that practice. Yet people who have lost a family member sometimes tell me that there is a sense of ritual throughout that first year—going through all the holidays, the birthday, the anniversaries and the seasons for the first time without the loved one. There is a certain cycle and rhythm to mourning.

But at the same time, we can't put time limits on grief. *It's been a month now; I should start to feel better. I went to the funeral and cried a lot; I should be done crying. It's been a year now; it should be over.* Why should it? Who says so? The more major the loss, the greater the time to heal. And everyone goes through the process at their own pace and in their own way. The important thing is to give your grief the attention it deserves and to complete the process.

One woman was referred to me about three years after her husband had died. Her pastor referred her because she wasn't doing well. And as I began to talk with her, it became clear why she wasn't doing well. It was because she had never allowed herself to grieve. As I talked with her about her expectations, she said, "Well, I had to be strong for my kids." But when she finally started exploring beneath the surface, she discovered that her grief was as strong as if the loss had happened yesterday. And in a way it had—because she had never begun to explore those feelings.

Failing to Mourn
Only Compounds a Loss

Sadness and grief are symptoms that indicate you have been emotionally wounded. If you're pruning a tree in your backyard and you cut yourself with the saw, you have a physical wound that requires attention. If you just stick a bandage over a deep cut without cleaning it or stitching it together, it's likely to become infected. You avoid the intense short-term pain of dealing with the injury, but you end up with long-term discomfort as the injury festers and takes more time to heal.

Emotional wounds require attention in the same way. When you suffer a loss, one choice you have is to cover the injury with a bandage of pretense. "Oh, it's all right. I'm over

it. I'm fine." This protects you from the intense pain of grieving that loss. But beneath the bandage, the pain never really
goes away. If you try to avoid the deep pain by not mourning, you subject yourself instead to a less intense pain that
can haunt you for the rest of your life.

If you allow yourself to experience the pain and go through
the cycle of grieving, you can get to a stage of acceptance and
eventual integration. At that point, you may even begin to get
excited about doing something new, starting over and rein-
vesting yourself in life. If you don't allow yourself to go
through the anger and feelings in the grieving process, the
grief can remain just under the surface for years as though it
just happened yesterday. You can develop physical illnesses,
depression, anxiety and feelings of hopelessness.

The following list gives examples of some feelings and
behaviors that often follow a loss and are perfectly normal
responses. However, if the feelings and behaviors become
chronic, they are good indications that someone has not
been able to grieve and begin healing. A person with chronic
symptoms can often benefit from professional help or guidance to begin dealing with the unresolved loss.

- Anger or irritation
- Social withdrawal
- A severe change in sleeping or eating habits
- Increased smoking
- Increased alcohol or drug use
- A lack of energy, or a feeling of hopelessness or despair

While both men and women may have difficulty recognizing and grieving their losses, men are particularly trained
not to express grief. I worked recently with a young couple

who both had come from families where alcoholism had led to loss and abandonment. The young woman was openly tearful as she remembered her history. The young man, on the other hand, couldn't see that there was any connection between his past and the intense anxiety and perfectionism that were causing him problems in the present.

One day, as we were talking about how lonely he had felt as a boy and how much he had sought his dad's approval, the young man began to feel tears in his eyes. Eventually they overflowed and ran down his cheeks. He covered his face and tried his best to stem the tide. Later, as he walked out of my office, he expected his girlfriend to ridicule him. Instead, he got wholehearted support from her. She felt included in his life by his willingness to express his grief.

This incident was a breakthrough for the young man. He began to read books to help him understand his shame. Later he even joined a therapy group, making some exciting attitudinal and behavioral changes that improved the quality of his life remarkably. His tears had begun his healing.

Grieving the Small Losses Isn't Silly

Sometimes we are embarrassed or ashamed to acknowledge our minor losses. One of my clients told me about her experience when she traded in a car she had driven for twelve years. "I actually had tears in my eyes when I left it at the lot and drove off in my newer car," she said. "The salesman looked at me like I was nuts. But there were a lot of memories tied up with that old car; it was part of my life for a long time."

Another woman came into my therapy group one night apologizing because she was crying over the death of her dog. She had told herself, *You shouldn't feel that way; it was just a dog.* Where would she have heard that message before? What she ended up doing in group that night was grieving the loss of her dog. What she got from the group—and gave to the group—was the realization that every one of them had experienced certain losses they had discounted just as she had done. Her work helped all of them to realize, *Yes, that was an important loss. It mattered to me.*

Obviously there is a hierarchy of loss. We wouldn't expect someone to go into hysterics or depression over trading in an old car. By the next day, this woman was happily driving around town in her new car. Losing a pet is much more significant, but certainly not on the same level as the death of a family member. Within a couple of weeks, the woman whose dog had died still missed her pet but had essentially completed her grieving process.

However, just because some losses are far down on the scale doesn't mean we should ignore them. They are still losses that affect our lives. Acknowledging and feeling them actually helps us stay in the moment. Paying attention to our losses adds to our ability to appreciate and enjoy what we gain. Then, too, fully experiencing smaller losses is "practice." Going through the grief process for minor losses helps teach us how to deal with the major ones that will inevitably come along.

We also shouldn't discount ourselves by comparing losses. Suppose you lost a family member in a plane crash or car accident. Someone else lost three family members. Is your grief any less because of their loss? Of course not. But sometimes we feel as if we don't have a right to hurt because someone else's pain seems more important. If I am grieving because I'm going through a divorce, and a friend's wife dies, his loss may be greater than mine. That doesn't mean mine is unimportant or I shouldn't feel it. There may be times when, for one reason or another, it's appropriate to put our own grief "on hold" for a little while in order to support someone else. But it's important and necessary for our healing to get back to our own pain and go through the grieving process. Otherwise we're shaming ourselves with a message that our own pain doesn't matter.

Unfinished Business

One reason that we react to a loss with anger is that we weren't "finished" yet. This is most dramatically brought home to us with an unexpected and sudden death. There were things we wanted to say to, do with and share with that person. We didn't have a chance to say good-bye. We weren't ready for this.

This component of grief is present in other losses as well. Have you ever been fired from a job? You weren't able to take care of that unfinished project at the bottom of your "to do" pile. You never knew how a certain project came out.

If a friend is moving away, how often do we say something like, "I'm not going to say good-bye, because we'll stay in touch"? Yes, we'll stay in touch, but the relationship isn't going to be the same. There has been a death of sorts. Sometimes our unwillingness to say good-bye is just a reluctance to acknowledge that loss and hurt. We want to leave the door open. We want to have a chance to finish every-thing we need to do and say.

And yet, how often do we really do and say those things before it's too late? How long has it been since you've told your spouse how special he or she is to you? Or your children? Or your parents? Or a friend?

Losses in life can be reminders that we need to stay in the moment, appreciating and valuing the people in our lives and what we have. So take advantage of the opportunities you have to share your feelings. Tell the people you care about how special they are. Savor what is around you right now. You simply aren't going to have it forever; so appreciate it by staying focused and alive right here and now.

Pain Is a Part of Life

One message our society sends is that pain is unnecessary. If you have a headache, take some pain pills. If you can't sleep, take some sleeping pills. But in order to grow spiritu-ally, we need to hurt. It's an inevitable part of life.

About twenty years after my mother died, I was teaching about pain and grief in my anxiety program, and all of a sud-den I just started crying. When I got feedback at the end of the program, my clients pointed out that the most important experience of the whole sixteen weeks was the session when "Rex broke down and cried." They went on to say that "It's one thing for you to tell us about grief; it's another to see you go through it." I certainly didn't intend to grieve in class in order to be a good example; I just hurt. And the class seemed like a safe place to feel the pain. It was healing to share that experience with those people.

The other thing about pain is that it's okay to need comforting. But often, because of our reluctance to hurt any more, we don't want to set ourselves up for rejection, so we don't ask people for comfort. We feel too vulnerable. But we need to teach people what kind of comfort and support we need from them. After my mom died, and I came back to work, everybody kind of avoided me at first. I said to a close friend, "You know, I'm really hurt. Nobody's saying anything." And he said, "Well, Rex, give them a clue." People had been waiting for me to let them know what I needed from them.

Some people in pain want to be left alone; others want to talk about it. Nobody knows what you want; you need to give them a clue. We have to teach each other what we need during times of pain and grief.

I was working with a couple once, and during one session the husband started crying. The wife ran over to him with a tissue and said, "Don't cry; don't cry. It will go away." A couple of weeks later during a session, she started to cry. And he said, "Don't cry; don't cry. It will go away." She pushed him away. I said, "What's going on here?" She said, "What I want is just for somebody to hold me and let me cry." Then I asked him, "When this happened a couple of weeks ago, was that what you wanted?" And he said, "Yeah, that's what I wanted, too. It made me angry when she said I shouldn't cry."

Our natural tendency is to comfort someone, and what we think we need to do is help them not to cry. Perhaps the best thing we can do as a friend is put a hand on someone's shoulder and say, "It's okay to cry. It's okay to hurt." And if this, in turn, is what we need from others, we need to let them know that. It's our responsibility to train people, including our parents, how to give us love.

Losses Can Foster Closeness

Grief, sadness, anger, loss—all of those feelings are active and need to be shared. A lot of us deal with these feelings by going home and hiding in the closet to cry. And sometimes it's good to let out your feelings when you're alone. But if that's the only grieving you do, you are denying yourself one of the most important parts of the healing process. Because painful emotions, when shared, bring us closer. That's what life is all about—the sharing of emotion. We're human beings. We have feelings and go through losses, which only make sense to us because we have brains. And what pulls us together as people is the ability to share our losses. Unfortunately, many of us withdraw when we hurt. "Don't talk to me—just leave me alone." Of course we need to respect that person's need for withdrawal. But the alternative of sharing our grief can be a powerful aid to healing.

This is why funerals can be such moving and healing experiences. When my mother died, I did the eulogy at her funeral. It was the hardest thing and also the best thing I'd ever done in my life. This was on a Monday afternoon, and the whole church was full. There were hundreds of people there. It hurt me to see how a woman who had discounted herself so much had nevertheless had such an impact on her world. She had wasted so much energy wishing that "I could be like anybody else," when there were probably people in that church who wished they could have been like her. Being a part of that gathering and realizing how much people cared about my mother was intensely powerful for me. Now, many years later, there's a part of me that actually welcomes the possibility of something stirring up that grief again, because it feels good to remember that intensity.

A woman I worked with had lost her daughter five or six years earlier. One of the things that became clear as we talked is that she did not want to go through the grief. The pain she kept having after five years was because she had not allowed herself to let it go. But she couldn't let go, because it would have felt disloyal to the memory of her daughter. What would be left to connect them? She believed the pain was the only connection she had.

In fact, the truth is that once you are able to grieve and let go, you can have more of a connection—and one that is healing and enriching instead of hurtful. My mom is now a pleasant memory for me, instead of the painful memory she would have been if I had tried to hang onto my grief and pain.

The kind of unresolved grief experienced by the woman who lost her daughter results in not having anything to give to anyone else—either to the people already in one's life or to others who may come along. Of course you can't "replace" someone you have lost. That doesn't work, because people aren't the same. In my therapy groups, people periodically will leave. That's a real loss because people spend a year or more in this group, and they get close to one another. So when a new person comes in, there's a little resentment. There's often that sense that the new person is trying to replace the one who left. It's important for me to explain that I'm not bringing someone in to replace that former member—nobody will do that. The group needs to accept new people for themselves.

It is really important, after any kind of loss, to eventually open ourselves up to letting life in again. We can slowly start engaging in all sorts of activities that symbolize "I'm going on; life goes on." In the beginning, these actions might be as simple as buying a plant or a new piece of furniture. Slowly but surely, we will soon begin to open up again to new people, new activities and new rhythms in our life.

Conclusion

Grief is another one of those emotions that leads to anxiety when it is stuffed, denied, repressed or sidestepped. Remember, again, that *anxiety is not so much what we are feeling and expressing as what we are not feeling and expressing.*

Loss is part of our daily life, experienced in everything from divorce to aging, and not just related to death. Learning to deal with loss honestly and effectively is necessary to becoming an empowered, healthy, active human being. Keeping losses submerged only drains our energy. Healthy grieving can help us stay fully alive and become more compassionate, more empathetic and less judgmental.

Many people would like to avoid such pain. "Do I have to talk about that or think about this?" they ask. Well, no, you don't. You don't ever have to hurt again. But then you would never feel close to anyone again, either. That's the price you pay in order to avoid pain. And it's much too high a price.

Instead, if we accept pain and grief as inevitable parts of living, we can enrich our lives and open ourselves up to increased closeness to those around us.

Suggested Exercises

1. Look at the list of things that can result in a feeling of loss given at the beginning of this chapter and evaluate your own losses. Which seem resolved? Which are unfinished?
2. How was loss handled in your family? How do you handle loss?
3. Have you taught the people you care about what you need during periods of grief?
4. Can you think of times you felt closer to someone because one of you chose to share an experience of loss with the other?

10

Learning to Communicate with Yourself and Others

Years ago, if you would have asked me what I thought about something, I would have looked you in the eye and tried to figure out what you wanted to hear. If I began my response and you looked upset, I would have subtly changed the way I answered your question until you looked pleased. By the time we finished our conversation, you might have thought I was extremely intelligent and insightful because I agreed with you so closely. But you would have gotten nothing of what I really thought.

This was partly because I didn't have the confidence to express my own ideas, but it was also because I really didn't know what I thought. I was a people pleaser, trying my best to keep everybody happy. I had no clear sense of myself. I couldn't communicate effectively with you, because I didn't know how to communicate with myself first.

When clients begin therapy, they often ask, "What should I do?" about particular situations in their lives. Others ask at the end of their appointment times, "Now when should I come back?" But I can't answer those questions for them. My job is to help them find their own answers by learning to communicate with themselves.

These examples are typical for those of us who suffer with anxiety. Because of our shame, we tend to become either superficial people pleasers or isolated loners. For that reason, in this chapter I'll discuss two levels of communication: communication with oneself and communication with others.

Communication with Oneself

Our excessive-anxiety symptoms, whether they be headaches, panic attacks, obsessive worry, stomach problems or chest pain (to name just a few), are a clear indication that we are not communicating well with ourselves. The symptoms are our body's desperate attempt to communicate with us.

"Listen! There's something inside that needs to be attended to."

But anxiety sufferers have never learned to communicate with themselves. In fact, we have learned to ignore ourselves. We tend to take care of everybody else or to be constantly busy as an unconscious way of avoiding dealing with ourselves. My clients often tell me that the most difficult times for them are evenings and weekends. During the day we have jobs or other activities that dictate the way we use our time. Given that structure, we do fine. (In fact, we're usually great employees since we have such high standards for ourselves.) But when time is not structured, many anxiety sufferers are distressed by the existential responsibility that comes with "now *you* decide what to do with yourself and your time."

When I first met Ginny, she was a bright, creative, attractive and chronically busy woman who was suffering with obsessive thoughts that she might hurt her child. Those thoughts had begun when she was pregnant. She had gone to a doctor and begun medication for her condition, and the thoughts generally faded. She attributed them to the hormonal changes of the pregnancy.

After the birth, she decided to lose some weight. She began to have the same thoughts. This time she attributed them to body changes. As she was about to go back on medication, a friend suggested she consult with me.

When I explained to Ginny that her thoughts were just trying to get her attention, that made a great deal of sense to her. She was very unhappy, had always been horribly shy because of a shame-based childhood and was terribly ambivalent about her marriage.

Within weeks and without medication, Ginny's obsessive thoughts ceased. She continued to see me for a year while she dug deeply into some of the unfinished business in her life. While her progress was consistent and exciting, her chronic busyness remained. One day, when her son was ill, she took a day off from work to stay home and take care of him. As soon as she slowed down, the obsessive thoughts returned. This time she got the message about the role played by both her busyness and her obsessive thoughts. This time she began to see the need to slow down and start to communicate with herself more effectively.

What Does It Mean to Communicate with Oneself?

I realized as I began to write this portion of the chapter that self-communication has already been discussed, a piece at a time, in earlier chapters. This is such an important issue that it really can't be separated from other aspects of recovery. But because it's so important, it also deserves to be reviewed and summarized here.

As Carla sat on the ski slope in chapter 1, she was debating with herself. *Do I quit, tuck my tail between my legs and wonder as I carry my skis down the hill why everybody else can ski and I can't?* No. Instead, Carla compared herself with the internal image of the confident person she wanted to be. Her mission, or inner picture of herself, provided the incentive to draw her forward and help her work through her fear. Being able to communicate with herself was crucial.

In chapter 2, I described how the physical symptoms we've been interpreting so catastrophically are just the body's attempt to get our attention. Actually, they aren't dangerous at all. They're trying to let us know things have been brewing inside that need our attention. If we don't communicate with ourselves emotionally, eventually our bodies will take over and try to do it for us.

In chapter 3, we learned how shame contributes to our tendency to underestimate our adequacy and creatively worry about all the terrible things that could happen to us. Shame cuts off our self-confidence at the knees, shutting us down until we literally don't know how we feel or think.

Chapter 4 presents a skill that is crucial to reconnecting with our bodies and learning how to communicate with ourselves. Deep breathing and deep relaxation help us reverse our tendency to tighten up when we feel vulnerable. By relaxing, we allow ourselves to become aware of negative thoughts, pictures and sensory memories that are contributing to our anxious feelings. Then we can learn to concentrate instead on comforting and affirming thoughts. Disciplines such as journaling, yoga and meditation are valuable ways to encourage self-awareness and help us understand ourselves.

Chapter 5, with its discussion of our rights as human beings, is tied in closely with the issue of communication. Along with all of our rights comes the inescapable fact that communicating and asserting those rights is our responsibility. If we are to become powerful, assertive and competent people, we need to learn to communicate effectively.

Using Our Creativity to Hurt Ourselves or Help Ourselves

As human beings, we have two valuable gifts: self-awareness and imagination. Self-awareness is our ability to recognize our own thoughts. Imagination is the ability to see beyond our present realities. Anxious people, as I've said repeatedly in this book, have those abilities to the fullest. We tend to be intelligent and creative. There's nothing wrong with our minds except the fact that we tend to use them to scare ourselves half to death.

What we need to do in recovery is turn this weakness into one of our greatest strengths. Instead of using our creativity to worry and imagine horrible eventualities, we can learn to use it to visualize awesome, positive possibilities. We can change worrying to planning, begin looking at challenges as opportunities and start moving more confidently toward our goal.

Making these changes starts with paying attention to the ways we communicate with ourselves. We tend to be embarrassed or joke about talking to ourselves. "Well, at least that way I know someone intelligent is listening." Actually, we all talk to ourselves, whether we're aware of it or not. Inner self-talk is as common as getting up each morning and getting ready for the day. We have a much different feeling when we begin our day with *Good morning, God* than if we start it with *Good God, it's morning.*

Not only do we talk to ourselves, but we do so in more than one voice or personality. This doesn't mean we're crazy; it's just a way of labeling the various internal messages we give ourselves. Different authors have several ways of describing our various internal voices.

Edmund Bourne, in *The Anxiety and Phobia Workbook*, describes the Worrier (who uses "what-if" statements to creatively scare the heck out of you), the Critic (who points out your flaws and limitations, reminding you that you are a failure), the Victim (who creates depression by promoting hopeless and helpless statements) and the Perfectionist (who continually pushes because "you should be better").

Because of our shame, anxious people give these critical and negative voices a great deal of power. Part of our recovery is to learn to communicate more positively with ourselves, changing those negative internal messages to positive and supportive ones.

In *Don't Panic: Taking Control of Anxiety Attacks*, Reid Wilson suggests that we develop a supportive internal observer. This is a neutral voice or position that allows us to stand back and assess a situation objectively. This supportive observer can take the wind out of the sails of our catastrophic "what-iffing" and allow us to come to a reasonable alternative. Part of the observer's job is to help us objectively explore our thoughts to test for the truth.

There are times when it's awfully hard to "stop the train" when our negative creativity kicks in. This is particularly true if we let it stay in our heads. One of my clients once described this as having a hamster wheel inside her head, with a little creature running frantically around and around but never getting anywhere. Part of the reason we get stuck in these negative cycles is because we start obsessing and rarely finish our thoughts.

At times like that it's extremely helpful to discipline

yourself to pursue your thought, write it down on paper and check it against these questions:

1. What is the proof that this is true?
2. Is it always true?
3. What are the chances that this is really going to happen?
4. What's the worst that could happen? Would that really be so bad? If the worst did happen, what would I do?
5. Is there more to the picture than the piece I'm concentrating on?

If I take the time to write down and analyze my situation, it's rarely as unmanageable as it seems when it was just spinning around in my head.

Recognizing the Difference Between Anxiety and Excitement

What I realized after I began my recovery from anxiety is that anxiety feels the same as excitement in our bodies. We just interpret it differently.

One of my clients some years ago was a young woman who had just finished training as a teacher but was working at a job she disliked while she waited for a teaching position to open up. When she came in for her appointment one day, she asked me to help her prepare for an upcoming job interview. I asked her how she felt about it. "I'm really anxious and scared," she said. "I'm worried about it." "You know," I said, "you don't look anxious. You look excited."

As we talked further it was obvious that her primary reaction to the job interview was excitement. She was a little nervous, certainly, but she was also thrilled at the prospect of getting her first teaching job. But because she was used to thinking of herself as anxious, she assumed that her feeling was anxiety. She was trying to stifle the feeling because she felt it wasn't safe to go into a job interview and show that much emotion. I finally suggested, "What if you just went in there and let them see your excitement? They'd probably love to see someone show that much enthusiasm."

That's exactly what she did, and she promptly got the job. She's been teaching ever since, and one of the things her kids love about her is her enthusiasm and the excitement she brings to her work.

Those of us who are excessively anxious are accustomed to using our creativity in negative ways. We worry, we visualize horrible possibilities, we frighten ourselves like children telling ghost stories in the dark. Part of recovery, as we've discussed previously in this book, is learning instead to use that creativity in positive ways. We also need to practice noticing and appreciating our positive emotions. Some of us have such long histories of not feeling that we tend to label any feeling as anxiety.

Different Ways of Processing Information

I once arranged to see Jennifer and Mark, a couple who were having difficulty in their marriage. Jennifer's primary complaint was that her husband never listened to her. At our first session, I could understand why. She came in with a virtual flood of language, talking rapidly and repeating herself as she tried to explain how she felt. Anytime she appeared to be running out of words, she would look at Mark, who had his head down and his eyes half closed, and start over again.

The problem this couple had wasn't simply that she talked too much or that he didn't listen. Instead, they were virtually communicating in two different languages.

There are three primary ways people process information internally: visually, auditorily and kinesthetically. Everyone uses all three of these methods to some degree, but we usually are most comfortable using one mode most of the time. You can identify which mode someone is using by watching their posture and gestures, and by noticing the way their eyes move and what words they choose.

Visual Processing

Some people literally see pictures or movies in their minds as they learn something new, access a memory or consider different possibilities. They might say, "I get the picture" or "I see." Their eye movements will be up, usually to the left for a remembered picture and to the right for a picture they are creating. Or they may stare straight ahead with their eyes unfocused, seeing their internal image instead of what is in front of them. Their posture tends to be upright with shoulders straight. Gestures are usually higher than the middle of the chest, perhaps pointing or reaching up. The voice is often quite fast and tends to be high-pitched.

Auditory Processing

Those who process information auditorily literally listen to conversations in their heads over and over again before they make decisions. Thus it takes them a relatively long time to finish the process. They might say, "That sounds right to me" or "That rings a bell." Their eyes will often move from side to side if they are remembering something.

While talking to themselves, they often look down and to the left. Their posture is often a typical "listening" pose, with the head tilted to one side and perhaps with the eyes closed. Gestures tend to be near the middle of the body or rhythmic. They may have musical voices which vary in tone and tempo.

Kinesthetic Processing

People who use this mode process information with their bodies and their feelings. Their eye movement is down and to the right, and they use words like, "I have a feel for that" or "I just want to smooth things over." Their posture is often relaxed with sloping shoulders, or it may reflect the emotions involved with a memory. Gestures are often down and to the right or might be toward the heart or midsection. They may speak slowly and in a deep-toned voice.

With the couple I described earlier, Jennifer was strongly visual and Mark was extremely auditory. It didn't appear to her that he was listening, because he wasn't looking at her. In addition, she was sending information very quickly, and he needed more time to process it. She would get frustrated and talk louder and faster. He would get further behind until he actually did "tune her out." Once they understood the two different modes, it was relatively easy for them to make some significant changes. Jennifer realized he didn't need to look at her in order to listen to her. She also learned to say something, then stop to give him time to process it. Mark learned to literally hold up a hand and say, "Stop, I need more time" if she went too fast.

Learning about these different modes has helped many of my clients improve their communication skills. It can take away a great deal of shaming and blaming to understand that we communicate differently, but that no particular mode is right or wrong.

Many people tend to be primarily visual or auditory, using the kinesthetic process to determine which image or which auditory message feels right. People with excessive anxiety may use all three processes to frighten themselves. They may picture themselves reacting poorly to a situation. They may add in negative auditory messages like, *You can't do that—what if this happens?* Then, before they ever make a reasonable attempt to conquer their fear, they have a kinesthetic response of anxiety and fear—and they get stuck.

Looking Inside and Accepting What's There

Many of us have been raised to believe that certain feelings are right, while others are wrong. The truth is that feelings are just feelings, neither right nor wrong. Therapists usually define five core feelings: anger, joy, love, sadness and sexuality. If we believe some of those feelings are wrong or bad, we try to deny and suppress them. But in reality, feelings work in correlation with each other. We can only experience as much love in life as we can accept our hate. We can only experience as much joy as we can allow sadness. We can only experience true closeness as we learn to accept anger as an important clue when our love has been violated.

When people first begin treatment, they are often fairly self-punitive, telling themselves that there are certain feelings they should have and others they shouldn't, expecting themselves to feel one way instead of another. In the course of my work with clients, I try to teach them, to be curious instead of self-punitive. *Why am I feeling this way now?* This kind of thought leads to much greater self-awareness, while being self-punitive just shuts us down.

Becoming self-aware instead of self-punitive helps us become more responsible for our own feelings and also more able to cope with stressful events in our lives. Years ago there was some important research on Vietnam veterans who suffered with post-traumatic stress disorder.[1] The researchers found that people who came from homes where they were encouraged to express themselves, had a right to their own feelings and where there was open discussion of emotion suffered much less severely than people brought up in families where they were taught there were right or wrong ways to feel or where they were treated critically when they did express themselves. Research has also found that people who are raised in consistent, warm, attentive and responsive environments develop a healthy sense of empowerment. On the other hand, people who grow up in overindulgent, inconsistent, unpredictable or uncongenial atmospheres develop a sense of helplessness and a tendency to blame outside factors for their attitudes or misery.

Love Starts from the Outside In

Ironically, one of the best ways to learn to communicate more effectively with yourself is to communicate with others. Because of our shame, we tend to treat ourselves the same way we were treated—as inadequate, incompetent or insignificant. We've all heard the saying "You can't love anybody else until you love yourself." That's true, but for people who have been shamed, that's only part of the circle. *We cannot love ourselves until we feel loved, and we first need to get that*

[1] *American Journal of Orthopsychiatry*, 62 (1), January 1992.

love from others. But we can't get that love from others until we learn how to communicate with them.

Communication with Others

The world is a very frightening place when we must manage it all by ourselves. As we venture out into the broader world of recovery and possibility, it helps to have others along to support us and share the journey. In fact, it's essential to have a network of people in your life who affirm and support you. There's just one problem with that—you're going to have to communicate with them. One of the most frightening aspects of recovery for many of my clients is learning to communicate effectively and assertively with others.

It helps to realize that relationships are like mobiles. They hang in a particular balance. Personal growth of any sort, and particularly recovery from excessive anxiety, is like someone coming in and moving a piece on that mobile. What the relationship seeks to do is regain its equilibrium and get in balance again. But to restore the old balance would require the person who has changed to go back to being the same as they were before recovery. For some anxious people, that has meant being passive, keeping a low profile and feeling inadequate or in need of protection. Others have kept themselves safe by being so abrasive or rageful that no one will get close to them. Certainly going back to either of those behaviors isn't an option for someone who is just discovering the exciting possibilities in recovery. At the same time, they are fearful of other family members' reactions to the changes they are making. This can produce a great deal of new anxiety.

For that reason, in my program for anxiety, I prefer to have the anxious person bring along a spouse or other support person. I know that the change in family dynamics will be a challenge for everyone involved, even though the purpose of it is to allow all of them to enjoy lives that are happier, healthier and more enriched. Nevertheless, change is always difficult. I find that having spouses go through the program together makes the change easier for both of them. As they both put their shoulders under the yoke, each evaluating their own strengths and weaknesses and learning new alternatives, they are able to grow together rather than changing separately. As spouses begin to see the benefit for both of them in making changes, they tend to be much more tolerant and supportive in spite of the short-term discomfort that comes with recovery.

But even if spouses do come to the program, clients can't bring along every other significant person in their lives. There are still plenty of people out in the world—children, employers, parents, friends—who have come to expect certain behavior from the anxious person and are likely to resist changes in that behavior. As people learn to express themselves more openly and treat themselves with greater respect, all of their significant relationships are going to change. This will obviously cause some discomfort for others. As a result, some of those relationships may not survive. Usually, though, people find out that those who were truly supportive friends before their recovery began will continue to be supportive even if it involves making adjustments. And even others who resist change at first may come around. Respect is contagious. If you treat yourself with respect, most of those around you will learn to treat you with respect as well.

Good communication, whether it is with ourselves or others, is founded on respect.

Taking Responsibility for Your Emotions: Don't Give Your Power Away

Telling people, "You make me angry" gives your power away. People can't make you feel anything. Whether you realize it or not, you are choosing to respond or react in whatever way you do. When somebody does or says something to you, you go through a very rapid process of interpreting that event or statement and arriving at the feeling you respond with.

Let's explore a few other statements that give your power away and then look at some alternative approaches. Here are a few power-diminishing statements:

- You made me sad.
- You hurt my feelings.
- You make me feel so good about myself.

Now consider these alternative responses:

- When you said that, I became angry.
- When you do that, I feel sad.
- When you told me that, I felt hurt.
- When I spend time with people who affirm me, I feel good about myself.

Do you see how the second group of responses places the responsibility for your emotional reaction back in your own lap? This is an important skill in learning to become grounded. Being grounded is learning to think for yourself; learning to stop seeking everyone else's approval for your thoughts, behaviors and feelings; and learning to validate yourself. This is a very important attitude to develop before you're really ready to go out and meet the people who share your world. Without it, meeting people and becoming friends is too threatening. We may feel the need to please others or give them the power to approve or disapprove of us. Such a relationship feels like an all-or-nothing proposition in which we give up all of our power. If we can stay grounded, however, we don't feel that same lack of control and we're more aware of our options. We know we are in control of ourselves and can stop the interaction if we need to.

Start watching your own semantics and changing the way you say things. Instead of saying, "I can't," say, "I choose not to." Instead of "I should," give yourself the option of choosing whether you want to. Instead of saying, "It's not my fault," learn to consider what role you may have played in creating the situation as well as the role someone else may have had. Practice changing your attitude of "life is full of problems." Begin to notice the opportunities life provides for you to grow. Instead of saying, "I hope this will happen," begin to say, "I will make it happen." Instead of remarking, "If only I had known," begin to declare, "Next time I'll know better, and I will do things differently." Our way of saying things gives us a clue about how we see ourselves—as victims or as empowered individuals. As you begin to consciously speak differently, I think you'll be pleasantly surprised to find that you will begin to feel differently about yourself.

Increasing Your Odds for Successful Communication

1. Make "I" statements.

    Most arguments begin with the word "you." Starting off this way immediately gives away your power because you are blaming the other person. Starting with "you" puts others on the defensive, making it likely that they'll come back with a "you" statement of their own. Making a statement that begins with "I want" or "I feel" is just much cleaner and clearer. When you make "I" statements, you take responsibility for your desires or feelings.

2. Speak for yourself.

    Speaking for "we" insults the other person. Often when I begin work with a couple, I will find that one of them routinely speaks for the other: "We're doing fine right now" or "We think such and such." In some cases, such language means the two of them have discussed the issue at hand, and one of them is simply reporting what they both have agreed to. In other cases, the more dominant partner is assuming the spouse shares the same feelings or opinions. When in doubt, simply speak for yourself and assume that others will speak for themselves. It's both their right and their responsibility to do so.

3. Make sure your verbals and nonverbals agree.

    This is particularly important for anxious people who are just learning to be assertive in their relationships with others. A saying from Alcoholics Anonymous is "Fake it till you make it." Even if you aren't comfortable in your first attempts to assert yourself and take your feelings more seriously, act as if you are. Make sure that your chin is up and that you are looking at the other person eye to eye. Speak directly, without apology. If there is silence, just let it be there, resisting the temptation to chatter or backslide.

Remember that we're not talking about your feelings agreeing with your words. You aren't necessarily going to feel confident. Your goal is to sound and look confident and assertive. Feeling that way will come later.

Sometimes people will say things like, "I'm comfortable" while their fingers are drumming on the chair and their legs are jiggling with agitation. That docsn't make what they say very convincing. There's no shame in saying, "I'm nervous, but I want . . ." or "I love you, but I'm upset with. . . ." Comments like these are congruent and seem believable to people.

4. Keep your feelings and your logic in balance with each other.

As our emotions increase about the idea we're expressing, our logic often declines. The optimum time to speak with someone is when your feelings are strong enough to make your point sincere but are also enough in balance with your logic to make your point clear. You may need to vent some of your emotions privately before you talk with the other person. Then your feelings won't crowd out your logic, and you'll be able to communicate more effectively.

5. Ask open-ended questions.

If you want to encourage conversation with someone, don't ask questions that can be answered with a "yes" or "no." For example, you could ask your child, "Did you have a good day at school?" If you want to have a conversation, however, you might say, "Tell me about your day."

6. Contract for time.

If I am upset about something, come into the room where my wife is watching TV, and stand in front of the set or turn it off and say, "I'm upset about this, and I want to talk about it now," the chances that she will be receptive are slim. If you are truly upset about something, remember suggestion 4 on the previous page about finding a balance between emotion and logic. The chances of accomplishing something are better if you cool down and ask the other person, "When would be a good time to talk?" This method shows respect for both yourself and the other person, and you improve your chances of accomplishing what you set out to do.

Pulling It All Together: Getting Ready to Meet the World

Sit down, slow down and clear your mind. Take a deep, cleansing breath and relax the muscles from the top of your head to the bottoms of your toes. Remind yourself, *I do have value. I am important. My feelings count. And if I take it a little at a time, I know I can handle whatever life throws at me.*

As you anticipate engaging in a difficult conversation or situation, imagine the results you want to achieve. Tell yourself that even if something happens that you don't like or didn't plan for, you can calm yourself down, get centered and focus on your goal. Remind yourself that good communication is about mutual respect. The only guarantee you have going into any situation is your own self-respect and the value you place on your thoughts, feelings and wishes. Treating someone else with respect doesn't guarantee that you will be respected in return. As long as you complete the situation having done your best, you're already a winner. Acknowledging that there are times when you may have to compromise, or agree to disagree, is also a winning step forward.

The following statements, taken from the work of Donald Meichenbaum, are designed to help you train yourself to deal with challenging situations.[2] Adapt the statements to fit your specific situations, and practice repeating them to affirm and support yourself.

Preparing for What Is Ahead

- I will be able to cope with the situation, even though I may not be perfectly relaxed.
- It won't be impossible for me to handle.
- It won't be any worse than the discomfort I experience at other times.
- I have coped with much worse situations in the past.
- I can tolerate some temporary stress because I know it will lead me to experience less discomfort the next time.
- I will imagine myself going through the situation and coping with the anxiety.
- My mind and body have learned to feel anxious, and it will take time to unlearn these reactions.

[2]Donald Meichenbaum and Dennis C. Turk, *Facilitating Treatment Adherence: A Practitioner's Guidebook* (New York: Plenum, 1989).

- I will think about the progress I have made so far—just going is a big step!

Confronting and Dealing with Situations

- What is it that I have to do right now—just focus on each moment.
- I can handle this—take it one step at a time.
- I may be anxious, but I can cope with this anxiety.
- This may be uncomfortable, but it is not dangerous.
- This is not pleasant, but it is not the worst feeling I've ever had.
- This may be uncomfortable now, but it is helping me get over my fears.
- It is normal that I feel some anxiety, as I have avoided this experience.
- I will think of facing, accepting and floating.
- This is a good opportunity to breathe slowly and focus on relaxation and my imagined safe place.
- I will stay focused on the present.

Coping with Being Overwhelmed

- I have gone through this before and never gone crazy.
- I may feel overwhelmed, but I am in control.
- I will be able to manage, regardless of what happens.
- I must concentrate on the business at hand.
- I will rate my anxiety 0–10 and watch it change.
- Anxiety is time-limited and will pass—I can ride it out.
- I will focus on giving in to the feeling and not fighting it.
- Face, accept, float.
- Don't be upset by physical feelings; they are superficial.

- This is a good time to practice coping.
- I will not faint, die or lose control.

Evaluating Afterward

- I did pretty good!
- I did not let my anxiety get out of control.
- I am capable of coping with most anxiety-provoking situations.
- I can prepare for, handle and cope with this kind of situation.
- I am proud I am able to do this!
- I felt anxious, but I coped and stayed with it.
- I feel good about confronting my fears.
- I am happy about not letting irrational thoughts get the best of me.

Regardless of whether you are approaching a situation that makes you a little nervous or you are confronting the thing that causes you the greatest anxiety, centering exercises such as these can help you to stay on track and feel as if you accomplished your task. This increases your confidence for the next encounter.

Conclusion

None of the ideas in this chapter can guarantee that you'll get what you want all the time. None of them will let you manipulate those around you so you always get your way. But as you learn to balance respect for yourself and respect for others, it won't be as necessary to get what you want—

because you'll get what you need much more often than you used to. Moreover, you will have learned that you are okay even if you don't get what you want.

Learning to communicate effectively in the world takes practice. It begins by learning to communicate effectively with yourself. Learning to take seriously your feelings, thoughts and perceptions is critical. Learning not to fear your symptoms, but to regard them as messengers—your body's attempts to communicate with you—takes much of the fear out of your anxiety. Learning to relax yourself and get centered or grounded is a skill that improves with time and practice as well. Understanding what your rights are as a human being helps you set appropriate boundaries in relationships.

Sometimes people are surprised when I remind them that communicating effectively takes practice. Some people think it should just come naturally to them, as it seems to come to others. But I suspect those others were born and raised in families that practiced respect for people's feelings and encouraged children to express themselves. Yes, it would have been easier if you had learned as a child to express yourself openly, honestly and assertively. It would have been easier for you to learn a foreign language as a child, too. But just because you didn't learn Russian when you were two doesn't mean you can't learn it now. In the same way, you can learn better ways of communicating. It just takes patience and practice.

Learning to take that deep breath, relax your body, remind yourself of your rights, and express yourself assertively all may seem contrived and mechanical at first. But after a while they will become second nature. Then you can begin to move about in the world with confidence and comfort.

Suggested Exercises

1. Practice becoming grounded. Clear your mind, take a deep breath, relax your body, and remind yourself of your value and your rights. If you struggle with any part of this important skill, consider talking with a professional who can help you begin to feel comfortable in your own skin.

2. Identify the different "voices" within yourself: the Worrier, the Critic, the Victim and the Perfectionist. Practice creating and using an internal supportive observer.

3. If you didn't talk about private things in your family or you weren't encouraged to express yourself, list some resources for meeting people who could support and affirm you as you learn to talk about yourself. Remember, love starts from the outside in.

4. For the next week, listen to the way you speak to people. Do you take responsibility for the way you respond to events? Practice using "I" messages.

5. Practice using open-ended questions when you want to involve someone in a conversation.

6. Practice "contracting for time" when you're upset with someone and want to talk to that person about it.

THE BIG PICTURE:
SPIRITUAL AND EXISTENTIAL
ISSUES IN RECOVERY

This is an adventure that every human being
must go through—to learn to be anxious in order
that he may not perish. . . . Whoever has learned
to be anxious in the right way has learned the
ultimate. . . . The more profoundly he is in anxiety,
the greater is the man. . . . Then anxiety
enters into his soul and searches out everything
and anxiously torments everything finite and
petty out of him, and then it leads him where he
wants to go. . . . [Thus] the individual through
anxiety is educated into faith.

—Søren Kierkegaard

Is This All There Is?

Suppose for a moment that you've made all the changes we have discussed thus far. You've learned how to relax and communicate with yourself, you've explored the shame at the root of your anxiety, you've learned to be assertive and set healthy boundaries, you can work through a conflict, you have a support network, you know how to grieve. And you still don't feel whole. You have a vague sense of tension and unrest. You've worked this hard, you've changed this much, you've come this far—and you're wondering, *Is this all there is? Why is there still something missing?*

Congratulations! You are on the threshold of genuine spiritual growth. You have discovered that long-term recovery from anxiety isn't really the end of the journey. It's merely another step—a major step, to be sure—along the way.

Psychotherapists like Irvin Yalom and Rollo May use the term *existential guilt* to refer to anxiety that arises from not living up to our full potential as human beings. Existential guilt is not about doing anything wrong, per se. It's about the unanswered questions in our lives, the untapped creativity in us, the unused life that leaves us with regrets in our later years. This can lead to a background sense of tension, frustration, unrest, boredom or even quiet desperation, evoked by our sense of incompleteness.

Think about it. A lack of purpose and meaning provides fertile ground for the growth of excessive anxiety and phobias. A periodic glimpse of the overwhelming responsibility we have in authoring our own lives can certainly encourage panic. Feeling trapped, confined or unable to escape provides the underpinnings for various anxiety-related conditions.

Paradoxically, recovery from anxiety can take us back to where we started, face to face with our own need for spiritual meaning. The difference is that now we are stronger, more centered, and able to begin asking and answering the questions "Why am I here? What is my purpose?"

Developing a sense of direction and purpose serves two main functions:

1. It allows us to feel more whole and complete.
2. It leaves us feeling as if we're a contributing member of society.

There are many things that can give us a sense of purpose or direction for a time. Some of them might include:

- Developing a relationship
- Raising a family
- Building a house
- Pursuing our education
- Pursuing our career
- Writing a book
- Supporting a social cause

Nobody can argue with the virtues of these different pursuits, except that they are all short-term goals and the person pursuing the goal need only depend on self for the goal to be accomplished. From pursuing these goals, we may get a glimpse of the bigger picture from time to time. But none of these day-to-day human activities can fully give us a necessary connection with a power greater than ourselves.

John and Linda Friel, in *The Soul of Adulthood*, say "that those who are unable to connect with something beyond themselves often feel pervasively depressed or angry because they discover they can't control their universe." The Friels go on to say, "Those who have a rigid, immature faith end up bitter and angry, because in their concrete, literal understanding of spirituality, they mistakenly believe that life will always be pleasant 'if only they follow the rules' and 'do everything right.'" [1]

I believe that full recovery from excessive anxiety is ultimately a spiritual matter. I'm certainly not advocating spiritually oriented psychotherapy as a substitute for other therapeutic approaches. I'm suggesting it as a necessary

[1] John Friel and Linda Friel, *The Soul of Adulthood* (Deerfield Beach, Fla.: Health Communications, 1995), 218.

addition to them because it adds the dimension of soul. Soul is not so much a thing as a quality or dimension of life in ourselves. Carl Jung said that every psychological problem is ultimately a matter of spirituality. Spirituality is founded on reactions to what is fundamentally unexplainable by family and culture—the meaning of death, the purpose of life and why things happen as they do.

With spirituality we reach for consciousness, awareness and the highest values. Spirituality involves the recognition of a Higher Power and can provide inspiration, security, peace of mind, guidance and serenity. Spirituality is about trust rather than control, about empowerment, surrender, relationship, intimacy, care, hope and subtlety.

Religion and Spirituality Are Not the Same

Let's not confuse spirituality with religion. Religion proposes various belief systems about the nature of a Higher Power and suggests practices that might be important in maintaining a relationship with that Higher Power. Spirituality, on the other hand, is about our own personal relationship and experience with our Higher Power that transcend ourselves, and the human order and understanding of things. This helps us to confront and overcome the most basic sense of fear and insecurity that underlies various sorts of excessive anxiety. A healthy spiritual life helps us to move beyond superficial changes and behavioral techniques in approaching the world around us. It helps us in transforming our whole sense of being—a basic trust and faith, a firm foundation, moral support, courage, and hope for recovery. Spirituality reminds us we are not alone in the universe, and provides us with guidance and support in times of frustration.

In *The Anxiety and Phobia Workbook*, Edmund Bourne suggests five things that spirituality can provide:

1. Security and safety
2. Peace of mind
3. Self-confidence
4. Capacity to give and receive unconditional love
5. Guidance[2]

Security and Safety

Developing a relationship with a Higher Power assures us that we are never alone in the universe and no problem is so great that it can't be managed. Since one of the main concerns for those of us who suffer with anxiety is *I don't have what it takes to deal with whatever challenges life may throw at me,* a spiritual faith can provide additional support and become a source of comfort in times of difficulty. Human beings can sometimes be hard to track down. God is always available.

Peace of Mind

Some of the same skills that are used in treating anxiety behaviorally are practiced in the context of our spirituality, including clearing our mind, visualizing safety, being meditative (or prayerful) and letting go. These skills can lead to an abiding sense of peace of mind or serenity that replaces our anxiety. We can begin to believe "it will be okay."

[2]Edmund Bourne, *The Anxiety and Phobia Workbook* (Oakland, Calif.: New Harbinger, 1990), 319.

Self-Confidence

Anxious people often perceive themselves as inherently flawed or insignificant. To realize that we are "created in the image of God" by a loving God encourages us to see that we are special, loved and worthy of respect. Even if we make errors in judgment, we are inherently a perfect creation.

Capacity to Give and Receive Unconditional Love

While human love is conditional, God's love is unconditional. This is why exploring a person's concept of God (which is often flavored by their relationship to early authority figures) is vital. When we are shamed, we feel flawed and unlovable. When we feel like we're drowning, it's hard not to flail; and as we flail, we may bring down others with us.

When we feel unconditionally loved, we can have greater compassion and care for people, judging them less. We can believe that we ourselves have much to contribute in a relationship. Real love opens our hearts, leaving us feeling less fearful and more trusting. When we're empty, we seek to fill our lives with things to compensate. When we feel loved and lovable, we feel that we are enough and have enough.

Guidance

Our relationship with a Higher Power provides us with guidance in making decisions and solving problems. We can tap into our inner wisdom when we learn to be quiet and listen to our "inner voice."

Aids to Developing a Spiritual Life

Anxious people are often isolated or loners, and are reluctant to consult others for fear of being rejected or appearing foolish. An active spiritual life provides us with greater humility and self-acceptance. These, in turn, allow for greater closeness with others and the ability to tap into the universal wisdom beyond our own intellect. Jung describes this universal wisdom as the "collective unconscious"; for others, it is God or a Higher Power. Many anxious people have found the following practices and actions great aids in developing a rich spiritual life.

Participation in a Spiritually Based Organization, Church or Synagogue

I find it helpful to be involved in a church myself, not necessarily because I enjoy crowding my weekends or my evenings with one more committee. But I find it important to be part of a team of people who are pulling together toward a similar cause. When I participate in meetings, I may be just as frustrated as the next person by the mundane concerns that sometimes take up our time. I'm also impressed by the synergy that can develop when people put their heads together and come up with many more alternatives than I would have come up with by myself. To worship and work together with people also helps me reduce my tendency to be isolated and is a good reminder that "I'm not the only one who struggles with this."

Daily Inspirational Readings

Once we realize that dwelling on negative thoughts can contribute heavily to our anxiety, it only makes sense that a conscious concentration on positive material can encourage us to move in a much better direction. There are many spiritual books available from which to choose, including traditional scriptures, timeless philosophers and modern meditation guides.

Meditation, Yoga or Tai Chi

Meditation, yoga and tai chi are only a few of the many disciplines and exercises that can help you learn to focus. There is a wide range of practices for all interests, ages and physical capabilities, so you can find one that is comfortable for you. Learning a disciplined method of clearing your mind and concentrating on constructive thoughts always pays dividends.

Twelve-Step Programs

The twelve steps of Alcoholics Anonymous have helped hundreds of thousands of people over the years. The original emphasis on alcoholism has broadened to providing support for just about any type of issue that can complicate your life. Groups such as Codependents Anonymous, Emotions Anonymous and Overeaters Anonymous are all examples of the many groups from which people can choose to find others who are serious about bettering their lives. All these groups still use the same basic twelve steps that have been so successful for alcoholics, adapting them for specific purposes and situations. Twelve-Step programs give us a free opportunity to see how living life more honestly can lead to healing.

Life's Existential Givens

There are four unavoidable, existential "givens" in life that we all have to face eventually: death, freedom, isolation and meaning. We may deny these, avoid them or fight them, but we cannot escape them. We can add enormous richness to our lives if we choose to embrace these givens instead of resisting them. The way we do that is through a healthy spiritual life.

Death

Jerry, a member of my anxiety program and later one of my therapy groups, claimed to be agnostic. When he was nineteen, he had found his father dead of a heart attack. Being suggestible, as anxious people are, he suffered his first panic attack with chest pain that night. He had suffered with chest pain and anxiety attacks ever since. At age nineteen, he had gotten a woman pregnant. She chose to have an abortion without consulting him. In the group, Jerry talked tearfully about how he'd felt both angry and ashamed before God ever since. Jerry's agnosticism and anxiety both resulted from his fear and guilt around the issue of death.

In dealing with issues related to death, we're not just talking about dying itself, but the whole continuum of aging and the inherent losses involved. Death is something that we deal with on a daily basis, not just when a person dies. As we age, as we divorce, as we go through job changes, as our kids grow up and don't need us as much any more, we are encountering death experiences.

We learn two basic ways to deal with death. One is *living in a state of forgetfulness*, where we immerse ourselves in the everyday diversions of life and surround ourselves with worries and concerns about the way things are. The second is a *mindfulness of being.* Many people never learn mindfulness of being because it involves developing awareness. Mindfulness of being doesn't celebrate the way things are—but that they are at all. Mindfulness of being allows us to have a childlike sense of awe about some of the simple things in life—a sunset, a rainbow or dinner with the family. It allows us to periodically pull back and gain some objectivity in the midst of all our busyness, giving us a greater appreciation for the things we can otherwise take for granted.

Remaining in a state of forgetfulness is very appealing and seductive. If we can stay in that state, we don't have to think about anything significant. It's similar to using alcohol or other drugs to numb our pain. One of the most frequent ways that Americans maintain a state of forgetfulness is through a chronic state of busyness. If you were to ask most people why they were so busy, they would reply that they were simply trying to climb the ladder of success. But sometimes people are so busy climbing the ladder that they never step back and check to see that the ladder is leaning against the right wall.

We simply cannot always live in a state of mindfulness. It's too overwhelming. But healthy people do learn to develop a balance between immersing themselves in day-to-day busyness and stepping back to appreciate what they've been through. They give themselves choices about what they would like to do with their time in the future.

When we don't take time to realize that our lives are finite and limited, life becomes somewhat less special. As we learn to face our death and recognize that we cannot take life for granted, it can help us make some startling discoveries.

Rearranging One's Priorities

Stephen Covey, in his book *The 7 Habits of Highly Effective People*, illustrates how people's priorities can become confused. He describes life as a container that can be filled with many things, such as rocks, gravel, sand and water. If we begin by putting the big rocks in the container, it can appear full to us when the rocks reach the top. But if we're clever, we can take the gravel and shake it into the spaces around the rocks. Once again, the container can look full. But if we sprinkle in sand, there may be room around the rocks and gravel to absorb much more sand than we would have thought possible. But even when the rocks, gravel and sand seem to fill the container, we can still pour a great deal of water into it.

Covey's point is that many people fill their lives with sand, gravel and water, so there is no room for the big rocks. We can get so involved in the busyness of life, feeling the need to just keep our heads above water, that we never save room for things like vacations, relationships, hobbies or even the development of our spiritual lives.

Experiencing a Sense of Liberation

Often people with anxiety live life as though they are victims. They feel as if they don't have choices. As a result, they end up doing a lot of things out of a sense of obligation and with resentment. When we are reminded that life does not go on forever and that opportunities are slipping away, it can help us to learn to make choices that may be painful but important.

Learning to Live in the Present Instead of Postponing Life

How often do we hear people say, "When I retire, I'm going to start having fun." And then they die in the first year of retirement. The time to begin to develop other facets of ourselves and to learn how to play is now.

Having a Greater Appreciation of the Ordinary and the Awesome

I went on a trip to Mexico recently with my son. Just before we left, I had a mole removed, and the results came back "precancerous." I knew that I would have to have additional surgery when I returned from my trip, and I was also reminded that I could not take for granted that I would ever have the chance to take this trip again. As a result, the feel of the sun on my face, the spray of the ocean, the sights and sounds of the trip, and just sharing time with my son became particularly special.

Experiencing a Deeper Sense of Communion with Loved Ones

We can allow a lot of relatively trivial things to bug us when we think we're going to live forever. But once something shocks us into realizing we can't take anything for granted, we may have a greater tendency to be forgiving or to accept people's idiosyncrasies.

Having Fewer Fears

I had a client who came to me with a fear of needles. The source of her fear became obvious as we explored her history, which included several early traumas with less-than-gentle dentists and doctors. Despite that insight, she still maintained her fear. Then she developed cancer. The pace at which we made progress increased rapidly after that because now she had greater motivation to face her fears head-on so she could take full advantage of the available treatment options.

Most of the ways we learn to cope with death are based on denial, like Jerry's claimed agnosticism. We simply don't want to think about it. Ironically, however, this refusal to think realistically about death means that it haunts us and interferes with life. Many of the people I work with are so obsessed with dying that they really aren't living. They seem to live by the belief *If I'm really careful, nothing bad will happen to me.* I need to remind them that the reality is, if they're really careful, nothing bad *or good* will ever happen to them. Life is a risk, and risking gives life flavor and meaning. *If we risk nothing, we risk everything.*

Healthy anxiety encourages us to enjoy the choices that life provides and to have the spontaneity that stimulates life. Excessive anxiety and a constricted lifestyle can leave us feeling as if we've died long before our time. An active spiritual life can leave us with much less fear of death. Being meditative and quiet allows us to appreciate each moment. I have noticed a high correlation between clients who feel satisfied with their lives and low death anxiety. Recognizing that life doesn't go on forever encourages us to consciously appreciate the moment and establish healthy priorities.

Freedom

Steve was forty-five when he came to see me, but he looked sixty, wheezing with asthma and hampered by innumerable allergies. Growing up, he'd been dominated (or suffocated) by his mother, and he now lived in a relationship with his wife where he felt powerless and continually obsessed with the possibility of her having affairs.

As he recognized his choices and learned to exercise his freedom, Steve reported that he had dramatically reduced his need for medications. In prior years he had quit playing racquetball because of his asthma, but after about a year in therapy, he reported that he had participated in a tournament. Ten years earlier, when he played in a tournament, he had had to stop every few minutes because of lack of energy and the need to use his inhaler. This time he took along the inhaler but never used it. When I asked him the reason for the difference, he said, "The only thing I can attribute this to is my taking back my own power, a growing spiritual belief that's allowed me to live one day at a time, sometimes one hour at a time, and the abiding sense that things will be okay."

I truly believe that God's greatest gift to us is freedom. Most of us want, even demand, freedom, but we aren't excited about the responsibility that comes with it. That responsibility is huge because it means recognizing that we are the authors who create our own lives. We are in charge of our reactions to our world, our choices, our life design and our actions. If we don't like our lives, we can't depend on somebody else to decide what is best for us to do. That responsibility is ultimately in our lap. Accepting it can be empowering, but it can also be frightening. "You mean *I'm* in charge here?"

We can do funny things to avoid that responsibility, such as getting married to people who are more than happy to make decisions for us. We can give our power away, as Steve did in his marriage. We can procrastinate. Or we can simply let life's circumstances make decisions for us. When we don't want to take responsibility for directing our lives, we're living in a state of forgetfulness.

I've received many phone calls from people over the years who indicate part of their problem before they ever walk through the door. They may be suffering terribly with anxiety and are calling in hopes of finding some answers. As I talk to them about what I can do to help them reduce their anxiety and take back the reins of their life, they may say something like, "This all sounds very good. I'll just have to talk to my husband (or wife) to see if they'll let me come." While it may be respectful to talk to a spouse or friend about working out the logistics of getting help for yourself, nobody can determine your needs except you. It might be more reasonable to respectfully inform your spouse about your decision to seek help, rather than to ask your spouse's permission.

The first time Steve had the chance to attend my anxiety program, he gave his power away by asking his wife, "Will you go with me?" and making his participation contingent on her willingness to join him. When she refused, he didn't attend. Once he began to exercise his freedom and personal responsibility, he approached this decision in a very different way. He told his wife, "I'm attending the class. Would you like to come with me?" People who don't own their freedom and who persist in blaming others or outside circumstances for their misery generally do not heal.

The issue of authorship comes up in making other decisions as well. Wouldn't it be nice if there were one inherent right decision? In most cases, there are simply decisions to make, and it becomes our responsibility to recognize how to make the decision right. This redefines the whole concept of making a mistake. I think the biggest mistake we can make is not taking a risk, because that can lead to existential guilt. Some of the most painful regrets later in life are the ones we have because we failed to answer important questions about our capabilities or our potential.

I'll go out a little further on the limb to say that I don't think God often has a specific reason for whatever happens in our lives. It's our responsibility to create meaning out of life's events, including the painful ones. In my own life, the deaths of my mother and my sister were acutely painful events for me. I had the choice to make something good or bad come out of those situations. I could have chosen to become bitter and rigid and blame God for my misery. God was there not to give me a reason for the deaths, but to give me the strength to transform tragedy into good.

Isolation

Eve was a very bright but dependent woman in her mid-forties who came from a conservative Baptist background. She had moved and gone back to school after divorcing her husband, and she came to see me about the time she completed her college degree. She was suffering with panic attacks. These resolved themselves after she expressed her guilt over divorcing her abusive husband and becoming involved with another man before she was legally divorced.

Because of Eve's deep fears of being alone, I thought she needed further work on her dependency. However, she said she felt "just fine" after she went through my program. Besides, because of her job, she didn't have time for more therapy.

Eve came back to me several years later, after quitting a job she was proud to have landed in another state. She had expected to retire in that job. Instead, she became so lonely and anxious that she quit the job and returned to marry the boyfriend she had left behind. She was finally ready to dig deeper and look at the way her dependency cloaked her fears about her existential aloneness and self-sufficiency.

No matter how many people we have in our lives, we are ultimately alone. Nobody else can be born or die for us. Nobody else is responsible for making decisions about the lives we create for ourselves. This existential, fundamental aloneness is not something we can change.

People often confuse aloneness and loneliness. Loneliness is interpersonal isolation—feeling different, disconnected and separate from other people. This is often accompanied by intrapersonal isolation, or a sense of separation from ourselves. Both of these conditions are unnecessary, created for ourselves out of shame and fear. We have the power to change them; that's essentially what this whole book has been about. But existential loneliness is a fundamental part of life, and accepting it is a fundamental part of spiritual growth.

Over the years, I have met with many people who have been overwhelmed by a divorce or the death of a spouse. The loss forces them to pay attention to something that has always been true—the responsibility of their own aloneness. While they were married, they had hidden from that truth by focusing on the illusion of togetherness. I also see people who cling to imprisoning, abusive marriages because they are so afraid of their own aloneness. They pay an outrageous price in integrity for that security and familiarity—and the irony is that the marriage provides no real security at all.

In his book *The Art of Loving*, Erich Fromm reminds us that isolation is the most primary source of anxiety. Of what is man afraid? Of nothingness.

So if we are ultimately alone, is being in a relationship pointless? Of course not. While we are fundamentally alone, healthy love is the key way of compensating for the pain of our isolation. Unfortunately, love often gets confused with many inferior imitations, as I described in chapter 7. Someone like Eve, overcome with fear and anxiety when faced with loneliness, may make a decision about marriage based more on fear than on love. Lonely people are unlikely to be able to reach out with love. Instead, we flail and grab desperately at the people around us so as not to drown. In this situation, we are not relating to people as people, but as objects. It's only as we are able to acknowledge our isolation that we can turn toward others with genuine love.

To truly love, we must understand love's opposite—fusion. In love, we can maintain our separateness and our awareness of our existential isolation. In fusion, we relate to others as tools in our defense against isolation. Mature love preserves our integrity and our individuality. The more two people are separate and whole, the more they can be together. Mature love is an expression of strength and abundance, and comes out of concern, responsiveness, respect, and knowledge vis-à-vis oneself and the other. Fusion, on the other hand, eliminates isolation by eliminating self-awareness. We join with the other, not out of abundance, but out of neediness. In this way, compulsive affection and sex can be used as a distraction, numbing our fear of isolation.

Ironically, those who come from loving, reciprocally

respectful families can separate from their families. They have been given the self-confidence and strength to tolerate separation and loneliness. The more disturbed the family, the harder it is to leave. Those who are ill-equipped to separate cling to family and friends for shelter against their isolation.

When I began treatment, I tried desperately to avoid my aloneness by my dependency on other people. I tried to plan constant activities with others so I wouldn't have to be by myself. I was not a very good friend to myself, and I used my creativity to scare myself. As a result, I lived in a state of forgetfulness as much as possible.

My therapist pointed out to me that I really had no friends. I had to laugh. Throughout school I had been the captain or the head of whatever organizations I was a part of. I was extremely popular and the life of the party. And yet she persisted in saying that I had no friends. Eventually I realized that she was right. Nobody knew me. I lived behind an image, distracting myself by taking care of everybody else so I would not have to be by myself. I found my existential aloneness too terrifying to face.

Now I have a healthy balance in my life of togetherness with people and spending time in solitude. I have learned to value aloneness to process, listen and consult with myself and with God about my next step. A first step in construc-tively grappling with this issue of isolation is to learn the process of deep breathing and relaxation, which is in itself a desensitization and exposure to being alone. Once we learn to soothe and be comfortable by ourselves, our spirituality can allow us to become empowered and healed in the pres-ence of our God in quietude. We must learn to turn loneli-ness into solitude.

Meaning

Meaning and purpose give our lives direction, color and depth. Without meaning, we can feel rudderless. This leads to a real sense of anxiety and a feeling of being out of control.

Almost anything can give us short-term meaning or direction, such as excelling in our careers, building a house or raising a family. Deeper meaning comes through our spirituality, which can enlarge our sense of purpose in the world and beyond.

It's difficult for people to develop that deeper meaning when they have an inherent sense of being flawed and inadequate as a result of being shamed. Those who have been shriveled by shame don't believe they have the right to live fully instead of merely to survive. They have not been able to fully develop their will.

Otto Rank, a well-known psychologist, described three types of will that people need to learn in growing up: counter will, positive will and creative will.[3]

Counter Will

We begin to learn counter will when we are entering the toddler stage and the "terrible twos." This is a very important step for children, because they are learning to see themselves as separate from their caregivers and are learning to set their own boundaries for the first time in their lives. Parents who understand the importance of this stage encourage their children to think for and express themselves.

[3]Otto Rank, *Will Therapy and Truth Reality* (New York: Alfred A. Knopf, 1945).

Positive Will

When we first develop positive will, we learn to get those things that we need simply to survive. Later, we learn to ask for what we want and need. With positive will, we learn our preferences for different foods and clothing styles, and how to express ourselves as individuals.

Creative Will

Some people never learn creative will. It involves willing what we want. If parents teach their children that expressing their emotions is undesirable and that asking for what they want is bad, two basic consequences will result. First, children grow up suppressing their emotional life. They literally learn how not to feel. Second, children develop a stunted, guilt-laden will.

Often people know what they should do, what they ought to do and what they must do, but they have no idea what they really *want* to do. In fact, when they begin to ask for what they want, they feel guilty. But this creative will is not selfishness. Quite the contrary: It is the part of us that urges us to reach for more in life—to use our abilities, fulfill our dreams and grow spiritually. Developing creative will helps us become "more than," able to make a contribution to our world.

Part of the role of therapy in general is to help people learn to will and to will without guilt. This is an important part of people's spiritual journey and enables them to build a sense of purpose. People begin to develop creative will when they start to replace their sense of worthlessness with an awareness of being a child of God, created by a loving God.

Viktor Frankl, the Jewish psychiatrist who was put into a concentration camp during World War II, learned much during his imprisonment that helped him in his work with people after the war. He found that people who survived the ugliness of the camps were those who had something to look forward to, some meaning that they had yet to fulfill, some purpose in their suffering.

The people I work with in my practice have not suffered the torments of the Holocaust. But they have suffered. For every man and woman who walks through the door of my office, I hope to have the chance in some way or other to help them explore the meaning of their lives.

The goal of recovery from anxiety is not simply to become more comfortable in the world. My job is to help people rethink the overall focus and direction of their lives, to explore their belief systems, their connections with others, their long-range hopes and goals, their creative interests and pursuits. There is nothing more rewarding than to work with people who at first feel frightened, impotent, inadequate or directionless. A few months or years later, these same people leave therapy with a clear sense of excitement and a knowledge of their own potency, spontaneity and purpose. The opportunity to help people make those changes adds a great deal of meaning and depth to my own life.

Conclusion

We are not human beings having a spiritual experience. We are spiritual beings having a human experience.

—Teilhard de Chardin

Spirituality is not a technique to be learned, but a very personal journey. This chapter has attempted only to touch on the matter of spirituality in hopes of encouraging you to explore it deeply for yourself. Developing your spirituality can prepare you to deal more effectively with life events—not only with the immediate and superficial concerns of life, but with the ultimate issues of confronting death, exploring your freedom, facing your isolation and creating purpose in your life.

If you decide to explore these issues, I suggest you find a therapist who is comfortable discussing these matters with you. On the other hand, I would suggest you run from any therapist or spiritual counselor who claims to have "The Answer." Spirituality is a mystery for which sometimes there are no answers. Our prayerfulness, meditation and serenity don't so much give us answers as allow us to accept the mystery.

Suggested Exercises

1. Who or what do you rely on to provide you security and safety? Peace of mind? Self-confidence and self-worth? Guidance?
2. What were your experiences with religion when you were younger? Do you think you can develop a relationship with a Higher Power that could enrich your life?
3. Do issues around death and aging, accepting the existential responsibility for authoring your life, facing your fundamental aloneness or learning about the meaning and purpose in life bother you? How do you go about confronting those issues?

12

SAILING OUT OF THE HARBOR: EMBARKING ON YOUR OWN JOURNEY

Would you rather be a ship anchored safely in a harbor, or are you ready to sail? My suspicion is that you wouldn't have read this far if you weren't interested in pulling up anchor, filling your sails and heading out to sea. I hope the ideas in this book will help you chart your journey.

I still remember the giddy feeling I had when I ended treatment for my anxiety. I kept saying to my wife, "I can't believe life can be this easy. I can't believe I can feel this good." I had come to believe that misery and discomfort were just my fate. Previous to treatment, I was uncomfortable before I opened my eyes in the morning, wondering, *What's going to happen to me today?* No matter what it was, I didn't feel prepared to tackle it—not comfortably, anyway. I estimated that my stomach was in knots due to worry 98 percent of the time I was awake, and I had a lot of nightmares while asleep that left my poor wife literally bruised.

Now my life is not without its stress. The many irons I have in the fire and the goals I set for myself see to that. But it's the normal anxiety that everybody feels when they're trying new things.

People who suffer with anxiety are generally highly motivated and capable people who have high standards for themselves. Even in recovery, such people are "doomed" to anxiety forever. But it's a very different kind of anxiety than what brought me into treatment. Robert Gerzon, in his book *Finding Serenity in the Age of Anxiety*, refers to this as "sacred anxiety," the anxiety that comes with finding out what we're capable of, confronting the unknown, and living with a sense of awe, full sensual aliveness, authentic self-expression and passionate commitment to our dreams.

While previously I spent 98 percent of my time miserable and worrying, now if I spend 5 percent of my time excessively anxious, I'm surprised.

It sounds exciting, doesn't it? Well, it is. When we start to realize that when we risk nothing, we risk everything, our excitement is piqued. We begin to wonder, *Just what am I capable of?* instead of *What do I have yet to endure?* The mentality of *When in doubt, don't* is replaced with *When something causes me this much anxiety, I know it's important for me to face it.*

Possibilities for Change

Over and over again my clients demonstrate the exciting possibilities and dramatic changes which can result from a commitment to their own recovery.

> *Recovery is about long-term effectiveness, not short-term comfort.*

Cynthia had lived most of her life in misery. She could remember feeling like dying back in elementary school. She was shy and insecure. By the time I met her, she was in her thirties and had never been involved in a long-term relationship.

I was about to say she was never involved in a serious relationship, but that's not true. Every relationship for Cynthia was serious. The thing she feared the most was her inability to manage if and when a relationship came to an end.

During the time we worked together, she did meet a man, they dated, it ended, and she did feel as if she were coming apart at the seams. For a time she questioned her sanity, her will to live and whether she was capable of a better life. But this time, because of her commitment to recovery, she used her pain to motivate herself to keep exploring. She expanded her social network and learned to ask for what she wanted. She became able to accept affirmation, something that had seemed "beyond her" before we met.

One afternoon, a few months before she left the group, she announced that she had been invited to go camping with a new female acquaintance. "The thought of it was mighty uncomfortable," she said. "But this time I decided that must mean it was important for me to try."

She went camping and ended up having a good time. A short time later she attended a college reunion, despite some discomfort due to knowing she would see people there who had been less than kind to her. Cynthia was beginning to face the situations in her life that she had previously avoided. She had learned to be opportunity-minded instead of problem-minded.

When we risk nothing, we risk everything.

Ray came in with his girlfriend the first time they came to my office. She had been referred to me for panic attacks and anxiety, but it didn't take long for me to suspect that her panic was related to her cocaine use. I really didn't expect her to be back for her next appointment.

I was right. Instead, when I opened the door, Ray was there. He asked if he could meet with me. I can't say I was bubbling with enthusiasm about the idea. Ray had long, greasy hair, his clothes were unkempt, and he hadn't impressed me on the first visit as having any motivation to change. But I had the hour available, so we met.

This time, I'm glad to say, I was wrong. Ray's eyes looked

like those of a panic-stricken deer caught in the headlights. At thirty, he was rudderless in his life, working in a series of dead end jobs. He drank too much, had a history of putting whatever he could into his system to numb out and smoked like a chimney. I had no idea how he could even afford our sessions. Yet he continued to meet with me weekly.

When I described my sixteen-week program to Ray, his eyes opened even wider. "There's no way I could do that with all those people there."

But Ray was committed to getting better. Shortly thereafter, he stopped drinking, using drugs and smoking. By now we had the beginnings of a good therapeutic relationship established. In fact, I'd begun to look forward to our sessions. Ray's humor started to show through, as well as his intelligence.

By the time my next treatment program was to start, Ray was ready to join it. He went a step further and joined a therapy group I usually reserved for the most highly motivated clients who had finished the program. Ray had a lot to work through, but he faced his issues with courage in the group and became an inspirational leader. He enrolled in college at night. By the time he left the group, he had been accepted into a graduate program.

If I'm really careful, nothing bad or good will happen to me.

Gwen was another of my clients, in her mid-fifties when her doctor referred her to me. She'd been holed up inside of her home without answering the door or the phone for the past few years. As she described her life and her history to me, I really wondered just what we could accomplish together. She had no education past eighth grade and very little sophistication. Her children, mostly grown by that time, felt free to literally abuse her physically and emotionally. She had moved to Rapid City with her first baby thirty years earlier, hitching a ride on a truck from across the state. With no money or means of support, she had fled from a husband whose beatings had knocked out most of her teeth. Later she met her current husband, who was an alcoholic, and several of her children had been the result of what she described as marital rape. What were the chances that this woman, who had no support, no job and little apparent hope, could get better?

She proved that you can't predict human behavior based on the external cover. By the time Gwen completed my anxiety program, she requested to be involved in the therapy group. She fairly quickly began to set healthy boundaries with her children and her husband, to ask for what she wanted, and to begin to dream. By the time she left therapy, she had begun her own business and was happier than she'd ever been in her life. She had previously lived by the motto "If I'm really careful, nothing bad will happen to me," which anyone could understand given her history of abuse. But now she began to live by a very different motto: "Ready or not, here I come!" Her courage and determination helped her to replace the vacant, hopeless look in her eyes with laughter and a great deal of compassion for others. She was engaging in life passionately and loving it.

Ships in a harbor are safe,
but that's not what ships are built for.

–John Shedd

Phyllis was a very tightly controlled woman in her mid-forties when I met her. She had a checking compulsion. She couldn't leave the house without going back many times to make sure she had turned off her stove and unplugged other appliances. She was an only child whose parents had controlled and belittled her. She was still working in her parents' business even though they had cancelled her health insurance without warning. (She only found out about it because she opened the mail at the office.) I could tell she liked me after we'd met a few times, although she chronically apologized: "I'm sorry, did I take your chair?" "I'm sorry I'm late." "I should have written this check before I came in."

Not surprisingly, Phyllis was married to a man who was critical of her as well. Even though she had a job, he controlled their finances and gave her just enough money for groceries every week. He refused my requests to meet with him: "I don't have any problems; she's the crazy one."

Phyllis epitomized a woman who had no "self," no feeling of worth, no idea of herself except as a bother. But she flourished as she felt listened to in our relationship. Her constant question at the end of each session, "Now when do you think I should come back?" followed by my smile and question, "I don't know. When would you like to come back?" began to change as she began to realize she had feelings and rights and that it was safe to dream here.

Phyllis went through the anxiety program and flourished

with the help of new information. It was also helpful for her to meet other people who were suffering needlessly. "They don't look crazy; maybe I'm not either." Her humor touched the other members of the program, and she thrived on some of the first affirming comments she ever remembered receiving.

She began to trust herself—her adequacy, her feelings and her ability to make good decisions about her life. Her checking behavior disappeared. Her husband didn't like the new Phyllis, but his disapproval of her meant less and less. She quit her job despite her parents' warning, "You'll never find another job as good as this one." She decided to go back to school to pursue her dream. About the time she finished school, she ended her marriage. Her children were proud of her, although her parents still felt she had made another dreadful error.

I lost touch with Phyllis for a while, but just recently got a card from her. She said she had been single for a year while she got acquainted with her new career. Then, when she wasn't looking, she'd met a man who treated her well. They had been dating for a year and were considering marriage.

All of these people went through a great deal of effort to make the changes they made. But they learned that recovery was not about short-term comfort anymore, but about long-term effectiveness. They were willing to face the unknown and see where it would take them. It's extremely rewarding and terribly exciting to see people who question their worth when they begin treatment and who have started to reach for the sky by the time they end.

Another exciting phenomenon is watching people who have previously been paralyzed by indecision, "not wanting to make a mistake," begin instead to simply make a decision and to learn how to *make it right.* They have learned to make a decision based on what they know at the time instead of taking on the impossible task of trying to anticipate all the factors in the future. They also allow themselves, if new information becomes available, to change their minds, then to make their new decision right.

Human beings just aren't predictable, and that's what makes this work exciting. Whenever people begin therapy, I tell them I can't guarantee a thing. This is simply because it's up to them to apply what they learn. But I've seen such frequent examples of success that I know the only limits people have are the limits they put on themselves.

The examples in this chapter are all illustrations of the fact that our symptoms don't have a life of their own. We give them life. All these are people who have made a concerted effort and commitment to their own quality of life. They have learned that anxiety and depression are not illnesses, but a part of being human. As a result, they have also learned that the answer was not to be found in a "cure" for what ailed them. Instead, they needed to learn to provide ongoing care for themselves, the kind of care every one of us as human beings has a right to and deserves.

I hope that the stories throughout this book have provided the same kind of inspiration for you as they do for me. I feel honored to have the opportunity to walk the path with these courageous people each day in my practice.

Treatment Options

It is my hope that you use this book as a springboard to launch your own recovery. But as you begin to reach for the sky, you might find it useful to have a little down-to-earth information about various treatment options.

There is no one right way to get help. Every anxiety sufferer has particular needs, issues, styles, interests and beliefs to consider. But from my own personal experience in being in treatment and from having provided treatment over the past twenty years, I will say that some methods are more effective and efficient than others.

Determine What You Need

In seeking help, you first need to consider exactly what you're interested in. There are two levels of recovery: symptom management (or short-term problem solving) and broad-based change and growth.

Symptom Management

A person's first panic attack can be terrifying. Other forms of anxiety are just miserable. In both cases, it is normal to think, *I just want to get back to the way I was before*. That's not necessarily a good idea since where you were before this started is what led you to suffering with the symptoms.

Still, at the beginning, regardless of the type of treatment you decide on, symptom management is an important thing to learn. Recognizing that our anxiety symptoms follow our thoughts removes a lot of the fear that something serious is happening. Learning to take a deep breath and relax our bodies fully, while giving ourselves comforting and affirming messages, is extremely helpful. Taking medications can also make the symptoms more manageable.

However, I'm not satisfied with that level of recovery. I've seen too many people who have stopped their treatment at that point and have seen their conditions deteriorate and the anxiety return.

Research has indicated that people who get medications exclusively for treatment of anxiety relapse 80 percent of the time within a year after they stop taking the medications. On the other hand, for those who take a medication and also learn behavioral and attitudinal alternatives and life skills, the relapse rate is closer to 20 percent. I suspect we would find similar results for those without medications who are only seeking short-term symptom management.

I tell people that I'm really not terribly interested in just getting them to a point where they feel much better but are frantically looking back over their shoulders wondering when their symptoms might return. Instead, I'd like to help people to look forward with confidence and excitement, understanding what they have done to encourage and create this positive feeling so they can remain confident of maintaining it in the future.

Broad-Based Change and Growth

In the very first session I spend with clients, I go over all the issues that I talk about in my sixteen-week program—the same issues summarized in this book. (See Appendix A for a brief description of the treatment program.) I find that after people have heard about all their choices, almost all of them are interested in "going for the gold." Many of them are surprised that, as I describe the personality types of people who suffer with anxiety and the typical issues they need to attend to, I am describing them perfectly before I've even really gotten acquainted with them. I do this intentionally so they know the treatment I provide is a well-trodden path and that they are not "different."

A plan for broad-based change and growth is what I've tried to offer you through this book. It requires exploring the more subtle aspects of your personality and the approach you take to your life, your belief systems and assumptions, your worst habits, compulsions, or addictions, and what gives your life direction and meaning. This is hard work, but it is effective. It can help you stop reacting to life and learn how to respond to life.

Once you're clear about what you're seeking and the goals that you have for yourself in recovery, there are several different options you might want to consider in seeking professional help and support.

Medical Management and Medication

People who are suffering with anxiety symptoms usually see their primary care physicians first. This is an important step. You want and need their assurance that there is nothing physically wrong with you before they determine that your symptoms are related to stress and anxiety. Most of my referrals come from physicians. I find it a particular honor that they trust me enough to refer patients to me once they have determined there is no physical cause for a person's symptoms.

One option physicians can offer is medication. I think it's unfortunate that many doctors provide immediate medication to their patients without describing any other choices for them. Physicians are taught in medical school that anxiety and depression are illnesses. Since the symptoms often respond to medication, I can understand this line of thinking. Physicians often refer these patients to psychiatrists, who also tend to see anxiety and depression as diseases and to prescribe medications. The problem comes when medication is seen as the primary or only treatment approach.

I, too, sometimes refer people to a psychiatrist or their physician for medications once I've had a chance to talk with them about all their alternatives. Some of my clients do benefit from medications. However, many of the people I work with don't want to be on medications at all, and they certainly don't want to use them as a long-term solution. Once they hear about the possibilities for broad-based change and growth, they can put the idea of medications into a healthier perspective as only one part of recovery.

Hypnotherapy

People often perceive hypnotherapy as magical. Perhaps that's because of some of the entertaining shows that can be performed with hypnosis. Like many therapists, I have had some basic training in hypnotherapy and do use it from time to time with my clients.

While hypnotherapy can be useful in helping people deal with specific issues and traumas in their lives, I believe that a broader form of treatment is necessary for complete recovery. I suspect there are many professionals using hypnotherapy who recognize this need and do provide a broader base of training to clients. On the other hand, I've seen a number of people over the years who want the magic that they hope hypnotherapy can provide and don't see the bigger picture. If you're interested in this as a treatment option, I encourage you to see a reputable hypnotherapist whose training is not limited to just this one approach and who does not promise magical results.

Eye Movement Desensitization Reprocessing (EMDR)

This is a rather formidable name for a treatment for psychological trauma that has emerged in the last decade. Francine Shapiro discovered and developed a method of treatment that has been nothing less than remarkable. She has tested her methods with severe trauma victims and persons who had suffered severe post-traumatic stress in the Vietnam War and who hadn't responded to other traditional forms of therapy. She had such exciting results with her work that I went for training in providing EMDR myself.

This treatment uses clients' eye movements as a guide to helping them "reprocess" traumatic experiences and begin to recover. It is especially useful for people who are suffering with post-traumatic stress disorder, phobias, obsessive-compulsive disorders, panic and addictions. I have used EMDR to help my clients effectively recover from the kinds of shame-based traumas that leave them with beliefs about themselves such as *I am inadequate, I don't have what it takes to deal with this,* or *I'm not lovable.*

People do not need to have gone through severe emotional trauma to benefit from this type of treatment. I would strongly urge you to look into this kind of treatment for help with your own anxieties. I especially like the fact that the EMDR Institute emphasizes that EMDR is best provided in the context of a broader base of treatment and training, helping people to transcend issues that have left them stuck in the past.

Cognitive Behavioral Treatment

Over thirty years ago, therapists found that there were more effective treatments than the psychoanalytical approach of lying on the couch and free-associating two or three times a week. They found it was much more effective to help people recognize the thoughts that contributed to their anxiety and then to teach them behavioral methods of calming themselves, such as deep breathing to allow themselves to relax. Cognitive behavioral approaches to treating anxiety and depression continue to be an important contribution to the field. If you are looking for a therapist to help you with anxiety or depression, it would be important to ask during an interview whether they are comfortable with cognitive and behavioral techniques.

Group Psychotherapy

I find group psychotherapy to be an incredibly powerful form of treatment for many different reasons. I think individual psychotherapy certainly provides a piece of what is necessary because the person seeking help needs to develop trust with one human being first. I see people in a group setting for my sixteen-week program for many of the same reasons. Many people think they are the only ones suffering and find it therapeutic simply to meet other people who also suffer needlessly. People are not required to talk in the anxiety program; otherwise many of them would be too fearful to even attend. But after the first few classes, and after I have shared bits and pieces of my story mixed with humor, it creates an atmosphere where people do begin to share their lives. Not only does this help them to realize they are not alone, but as others begin to obviously get better, the message is "If they can do it, I can do it."

While people can learn important information in the anxiety program, many people, once they learn about alternatives, want and need a chance to experience and practice them. Group psychotherapy provides a safe environment for people to experience the "family they never had." The confidential group setting gives people courage to share things that would have been too risky to share with their families at home. It also helps them realize that healthy disagreement, and even conflict, can lead to greater closeness instead of abandonment and being shamed.

I have said that the only way to fully recover from shame is to develop healthy, intimate human relationships. A therapy group gives people a chance to develop that type of intimate relationship. Even those who never develop close friendships with other members of the group do learn the skills to form intimate relationships with people outside the group. When people have learned to manage their lives actively and have developed a network outside of the group, they no longer need group psychotherapy. They "graduate" and set out to use their new skills in the real world.

Twelve-Step Programs

These programs began exclusively for alcoholics, but they were so successful that they have proliferated in providing support and guidance to people who struggle with all types of issues. Al-Anon is a support group for those who have lived with alcoholics. Emotions Anonymous is for persons who want to learn how to express their emotions more openly in general. Co-dependency Anonymous is a program for those who have learned to take care of everybody else to the exclusion of themselves. These are just a few examples of the different support groups available. I suggest you check your local area to find out more about the free support that can be provided through these wonderful organizations.

So Where Are You Going from Here?

From this point on, your recovery is up to you. I've tried to give you some information that can help you make the changes you want to make. I've suggested some resources and treatment options if you choose to find professional help in your recovery. But the commitment and the desire to make those changes has to come from you.

The following chapter includes letters from some of my clients who have made exciting and dramatic changes in their lives. I hope reading them will help give you the encouragement and inspiration to take control of your own life. They have done it; you can, too. I hope you will.

THE SKY'S THE LIMIT

Throughout this book, I have described the techniques, attitudes and skills that are helpful for people as they seek to reduce the unnecessary anxiety in their lives. However, I want to emphasize again that the most crucial element in recovery is your own commitment. If you decide to make changes, if you are willing to persist and plod along even when the results are not as quick as you might hope–then the sky is the limit in terms of the possibilities. The only limits you have in recovery are the limits you impose upon yourself.

I wish I could allow you to speak face to face with the many people I've had the honor to help over the years. Many of these people are so appreciative of the changes in their lives that they do end up volunteering to speak to others who are considering treatment for their anxiety. When I was told that I would have the opportunity to publish this book, I notified some of my current and former clients. The following letters came from some of those people. They wanted to share their stories to encourage others who might be reading this book and asking themselves, *Is it worth it?* I hope the following success stories will inspire you to create one of your own.

Growing up in a family where I was sexually molested, and emotionally and verbally abused, I became withdrawn and depressed. I couldn't figure out what was wrong with me. I felt so alone and worthless and ashamed of myself. I got married and had two children, but nothing made me happy. I kept trying to be happy by being as perfect as I possibly could. Nothing worked. Sleep was the best part of my day. I was tired all the time and slept or laid in bed as much as possible.

At thirty-nine I began seeing a psychologist and attended group therapy. Later that year, I attended a weeklong experiential therapy workshop. During both of these programs, I worked through the sexual abuse from my childhood. Several months later, when I was still feeling depressed, I joined a therapy group for survivors of sexual abuse. Meeting and working with others like myself helped me feel less lonely. I was still anxious and depressed. The following year my husband and I joined Rex's class on anxiety. My husband and I began communicating better. (He also attended the experiential therapy workshop and a Twelve-Step program.)

Presently I attend a weekly therapy group with Rex. We work on real-life problems. The group is the support I've never had before. Gradually I'm starting to shed the shame I've carried around most of my life and feel like a valued human being. I'm sleeping less and less, and feeling better. I feel like I'm a participant in life instead of watching life go by. I'm closer to my kids, who are now twelve and sixteen. I've quit trying to portray this perfect image of myself and can now accept others and allow them into my life. I've learned that I can't live life alone and that I enjoy others' company. I'm not so hypervigilant around people, watching their every move. I'm beginning to think about things I like to do and pay attention to myself. Sometimes I allow myself to relax and do nothing. I sit and talk with my kids. I am not always in a hurry anymore. I've gotten to know my sister and value her friendship.

I feel like now I can soak up life instead of flying through it. Life now seems worth living.

Childhood: *My life as a child living under my parents' roof was like living in an emotional desert or wasteland. My mother and father never said, "I love you" to me. My mother and father never hugged me. Criticism was the norm. To give them credit, I never saw them hug, kiss or show mutual affection toward each other at home or in public. Passive-aggressive behavior, rage, shame, verbal abuse and belittlement,*

and emotional and physical neglect and abuse were the norm. Emotional and physical boundaries were violated. Controlling and manipulating others' behavior was in the whole mess, too. I think you get the picture.

Teen/Young Adult: I started drinking and partying at age fourteen. The drinking continued until I "discovered" drugs. Then I did them both. I used to hang out at the bar six nights a week. I mixed "speed" with beer. Then I found a high-paying job. I discovered fast cars and motorcycles. Yep, I got real good at finding things to make me feel good. I found the sun very soothing. I hung out at the beach, lying in the sun every day I could, as long as I could. Yep, I had a "savage tan."

In the middle of all this, I was getting into relationships that did not last. I vaguely remember that I would give up the "addiction of the moment" when I met that "someone." When the relationship would end, I would find a new "addiction of the moment." Then came the "darkest night." Another relationship had ended. Another full circle in the repeating cycles I was setting up for myself. Frustration, hurt, hopelessness, rage and a suicide attempt. The cry for help—unanswered.

Midlife: Still being haunted by the never-ending thoughts that I had when I was younger, only now they got really strong. Is this all there is? Is this what life is? It was so overwhelming. It was like a black cloud that is always there to ruin your day. I called it a midlife crisis at that point because the time thing entered into the picture. I felt (and still do) that my life was half over (I'm thirty-seven), and I was still stuck, still spinning my wheels. I had tried everything I could think of, but I felt like life was repeating itself. Here I go again, I would say to myself.

Rex enters my life: I first met Rex because my marriage was in bad shape. My wife and I took his anxiety classes after quite a few sessions of individual and couple counseling. At that point I thought my wife was the one with all the problems. It was a heavy denial on my part that I did not have problems. (I say this somewhat embarrassed *now.) As soon as the class was done, I remember thinking,* All right then! Smooth sailing from here on out! *We also stopped seeing Rex for counseling at that time.*

Things stayed the same. The "power struggle" was in effect between my wife and me. So we lived in the same house basically as roommates, not as husband and wife. Finally it got so bad two or three years later that we went back to Rex. My wife admitted she had thought of leaving the marriage. More couple sessions, and then Rex suggested we take the class again. In the meantime I had reached my "critical mass." I was scared that my marriage was ending. I had to save my marriage. I had to take myself off the pedestal. I had to admit fault. And all the years of running, and why I was running, and what I was searching for were revealed to me. I cussed, I spit, I obsessed. Sleepless nights, rage, sadness—the whole spectrum of emotions came up. When the class started and we went to it the second time, I was ready. *I basked in the words that Rex spoke and the knowledge that he gave.* Then I realized that I had to save myself.

The class made a huge difference in my life. It is not a magic cure— if you are not ready to do the work or face certain things, the benefits may not be as noticeable to you. If you go to this class or to therapy with an open mind, ready to change your life, it can help you get to where you want to be. But not overnight. It takes time and a lot *of hard work. I consider Rex to be my push-off platform for the second half of my life. I know him and trust him. Now I can start my life.*

I come from a long line of anxious women. However, everyone called my grandmother and mother "high-strung" or "go-getters." I learned early on that the "appearance of perfection" was very important. For a while my childhood did seem "perfect"—my father a lawyer; my mother

a pretty wife and mother of three darling children; nice home, nice vacations. . . . Until my mother started drinking, and I started noticing she was always worried about my grandparents' drinking. By the time I was twelve, I could sense there was "something to be tense about, something to worry about." But by then I was an expert at denying there were any problems because our family did not have any problems! We were so very perfect! I was a good student and a very good girl, and I certainly liked the attention I got for that. What a setup!

In college I started getting real crazy with my weight and appearance. I began going to Al-Anon meetings when I got out of college and started to get a glimpse of some family dysfunction. It evolved slowly, but I truly did get some handle on my life. By this time, I was living and working on my own, making some decisions for myself and enjoying my independence. I developed a spiritual direction for myself and surrounded myself with healthy friends. Coincidentally, my mother was in recovery at this time, and there was a lot of clarity and closeness in our relationship. My father got involved in Al-Anon and was making his own progress.

I moved back to my hometown (happily), met "the man" and got married. My husband was a recovering alcoholic—we were so enlightened—life seemed grand! Within the first year of our marriage, we had a child, and my husband lost his job. Financially things were not going well. But I was a "good" girl, and my experience was to deny any problem—so I worried in my own little mind. Why bother someone with my problems? I began to isolate myself. My husband moved to a new job, and I just carried on as if nothing was a problem. I am the master of "everything is fine."

As time went on, I began to experience panic attacks. They were beginning to come so fast and furious that I was beginning to believe I had cancer. Something was terribly wrong with me. I went to my doctor a few times, complaining of dizziness and weakness, but she never found anything physically wrong with me. Finally, I could take it no longer. I sat in my doctor's office and suggested that I take an antibiotic for the flu that was going around. I was sure that would cure me! My doctor left the room and came back with a pamphlet on depression. I said, "Oh, no, I'm not depressed—sometimes I'm anxious, but. . . ." She told me depression and anxiety go hand in hand. I knew immediately this was it. I was happy I didn't have a brain tumor but embarrassed that I was depressed. It made sense though—I was becoming afraid of driving and people; little by little my world had become tiny.

I heard about Rex's anxiety course in the paper. Tentative and scared, I called him on the phone, and he invited me to join the class. "Well, I'd like to come to your class," I said, "but I get dizzy and I might faint." Rex responded, "What better place to faint than in my class!" The course was a gradual understanding of the condition of anxiety and all the things that relate to it: family dynamics, stress, etc. I found it to be a safe and nurturing environment to explore myself. There was no magical potion; rather, an open exchange of knowledge and experience of anxiety. A former sufferer of anxiety, Rex was an authentic example and teacher. I began to try out my new knowledge and skills and found I had fewer panic attacks. I started very small and moved slowly out of my little world. I opened up and discussed with my family and a few close friends the place where I had found myself. I talked with other course members and found such solace in knowing I was not alone—other people had anxiety issues, too. I felt like a five-year-old child getting a new way of life. Just being freed from a little of the anxiety I had lived with for so long was pure joy.

Today, I am still actively playing the game of life! I have problems and issues, but without the debilitating anxiety. I think this has been maintained since the course by taking care of myself (physically, emotionally and spiritually). I stay connected with friends, with a therapy group and with readings and writing.

For many years I suffered from stress and anxiety; not only the day-to-day type of anxiety, but also performance anxiety, which hindered my professional development. My doctor referred me to Rex in an attempt to help me deal with stress, anxiety and panic attacks. The only other option was medication.

I first met with Rex in the fall of 1997. At our first meeting, he discussed the concept that anxiety was shame-related. This explained why, coming from a family where positive performance was an absolute requirement, I had learned to worry about every little detail that could possibly go wrong in an attempt to avoid the shame associated with a less-than-perfect performance. I started developing ulcers in college. I was incredibly anxious in my first postcollege job. I hated every day of professional school and finally developed debilitating panic attacks.

With Rex's help, I looked back at my life through the lens of shame. I could see that the avoidance of shame was the prime motivator in my life. Once Rex opened my mind to the concept of shame as a motivational factor, he helped me analyze my life, finding positive motivational factors to replace shame.

During one of our sessions, I explained to Rex that I was angry all the time and that I hated my job. In my chosen profession, being prepared is not only a good idea, it is an absolute necessity. Failure to be prepared could, and most likely would, lead to unsatisfactory results. In an attempt to be prepared, I would try to anticipate all the possible arguments that the advocate for the opposing party could make during meetings, conferences, negotiations or trials. The only problem was that, instead of rationally analyzing the pros and cons of each position, I would get into arguments in my head with the opposing advocate. As such, I was arguing internally all of the time, both at work and at home. I was never able to resolve the arguments successfully. The by-product of this thought process was that I was angry. When one of my children would ask me a question after work, I would yell at them. Why? Because I had been arguing in my head for some time, and I was angry with the opposing party.

After I explained this, Rex told me what I was doing. I was appalled that what had started out as such a good idea (anticipating the position of the opposing party) had developed into such a negative way of thinking that it was making my life miserable.

I can truly say that Rex made a positive difference in my life and that my life is better because of him.

It is of course hard to sum up in a few words what a life-altering experience your program has been for me, but I feel you should know what a significant difference your program has made in my life. You, of course, are aware that I spent years going from doctor to doctor in search of an explanation for my stomach problems, as well as some sort of magic pill that would make the hours I spent in the bathroom dissipate. All I ever heard from the medical field was "irritable bowel syndrome" or "spastic colon." These diagnoses were not treatable, and I just wasn't willing to live the rest of my life in the bathroom. Luckily one nurse suggested that my symptoms might be stress-related and referred me to your office.

Almost immediately you began to show me, through one-on-one therapy and the classes, that I was making myself ill. My body was trying very hard to communicate with me, but for years I had not understood what it was saying. Now I was starting to understand. I had a lot to learn about how I dealt with stress and how to listen to my body, but I know without a doubt that my life has not been the same since our first visit. Not only have I gained hours formerly spent in restrooms, but I also have used your lessons in immeasurable ways to communicate with myself and with others.

I am very grateful to you and your classes for setting me on the right path to a better life with myself. I have no doubt that many people will benefit from a book outlining your methods. I only wish I had been lucky enough to have learned all of this much earlier in my life, thus saving many wasted years.

I first met Rex Briggs through my husband. I was my husband's support person in one of Rex's anxiety classes. Through this experience, I learned that I had plenty of personal work to do—my life was not good. Rex suggested that I join one of his therapy groups; I quickly declined.

Several months passed, and I phoned Rex to tell him that I was ready to join his group. I felt I needed to join because I had contemplated suicide. I was a very unhappy (as a matter of fact, I didn't even know what "happy" was), selfless woman who was angry and lacked self-confidence.

Through the group process, which was hard work—sometimes I felt worse rather than better—I learned that I mattered, that what I thought counted, that I was smart and, most importantly, that I had rights. I could say "no," and that would be okay. I learned to trust, and believe it or not, I am happy. With Rex's guidance, I have learned that life can be better.

My relationship with myself is better. I know I'm okay just the way I am. My relationship with my husband is better. I used to tell him that I trusted him more than anyone. My husband knew what that really meant—I trusted him about 50 percent of the time, and that wasn't good enough. Now I trust him 100 percent.

I learned that it took a huge amount of energy to hide things. I had a tough-kid exterior to cover my very sensitive interior. After I let everything out, it was very freeing. It's okay to be sensitive, and now my insides match my outsides.

The quality of my life is better. I'm more positive and not angry about how my life was. I'm much more self-confident, and I know that it's okay that everyone doesn't like me. And I don't have to change me to make anyone else happy.

I became more active. If I didn't like a situation that was unchangeable, like work, I tried to change my attitude toward it. I'm not always right or wrong. Things aren't black or white. And everyone isn't out to get me.

I tried to look for the good in things. I can now appreciate the beauty of a sunrise or sunset that I never even noticed before.

I remember the first time I came to your office desperately seeking help for the panic attacks and depression I had been suffering. After months of trying to find a physical cause for my problems, I didn't know where else to turn. When you named the problem "anxiety" and told me my life didn't have to be miserable, it became a turning point for me. Through self-examination and uncovering layers of emotion I had never dealt with, or allowed myself to face before, I have gradually seen a self-confidence emerge that had been lacking my whole life. Though the process has taken courage and patience, it has revealed a new "me" that I always felt existed within me; now it's becoming a reality. I feel like I have been given a new lease on life. Although I know I will never be completely free of anxiety, I have been given the resources to control it so that it will never control me again.

Before I began counseling with Rex Briggs, I always set myself up to be a victim. I would subconsciously place myself in situations where I would not be able to succeed. For example, I remarried my ex-husband, following his stroke, knowing in advance that it was not a healthy environment for me to return to. Prior to counseling, I was unable to make the connection between the direction my life was headed and where my childhood and adolescence had affected the decisions I made in my adult life. I did not feel comfortable in making a decision without first checking with family members or friends. I felt I needed my opinions and decisions validated and that I was not capable of making the correct choice.

During the course of counseling, my friends told me that I began to blossom. I became more outgoing and began finding interests and hobbies outside of the home. For the first time in my life, I envisioned myself as an adult, rather than as a child. I began to make small decisions that eventually grew to life-changing decisions. I began to see the need to leave the business that I was part owner of, due to the negative impact that it was having on my health, my emotions and my future. I found that if I did not solicit the opinions of those around me, prior to making a decision, that the world did not come to an end when the decision was wrong. I began taking steps to improve my health, and I was eventually able to walk away from the business that I had helped to create.

Now that I have completed counseling, the quality of my life has greatly improved. I began a new job, which I enjoy, and which has assisted in improving my self-esteem. My social circle has grown to include a boyfriend—a positive relationship in my life. I have learned to understand that my children are very important to me, but I do not dwell as often on the opinions they have of my life or my future. My new job affords me the opportunity to continue to travel, something I enjoy but did not pursue as often prior to counseling. I have realized that I am a person of worth and self-respect, and I enjoy spending time in my own company now.

I find this a very difficult letter to write. Not because of all the pain it may bring me to recall my past experiences, but for the enormity of everything I have been through and have survived. To go to the beginning of what brought about my fears and my anxieties and put that on paper would be a whole book in itself. I came to Rex when the weight of all my life finally came crashing down on me. I had a fear of social situations and going anywhere that might bring me in contact with other people. I also feared being in rooms I could not escape from. I believed everyone could see my pain, and I was afraid of that. I truly was ashamed of myself.

My love for my husband and my children is what brought me to seek help from Rex. I had seen many other healthcare professionals, and they could not give me the answers or understanding I was looking for. Rex was the first person who gave me answers to why I was feeling so terrible. I began to see him on a one-to-one basis, and at the same time I took classes that he offered. These gave me the opportunity to learn about my anxieties and fears in a setting with other people who had the same struggles and issues. Even this was difficult. Every time I walked up those steps to those classes, I felt like I couldn't breathe and I would die. I always placed myself for a quick getaway, but I never ran.

Through sheer determination I stayed and proudly never missed a class. Even though I was extremely uncomfortable, what I was learning kept me coming back. Rex suggested I join his group therapy a few months after I began seeing him. I was terrified. I had been to a treatment center before coming to Rex, and the experience was one of shaming and control. So I joined the group with much trepidation.

I made myself sick each time I went to group by trying to hold in all my pain and fears. I still didn't believe anyone would understand. But as I allowed myself to trust the people in my group to give me what I needed, I began to trust the world around me, and gradually my life changed. It wasn't overnight, and it wasn't a magic pill. It took time and a lot of patience from Rex and the people around me. Rex always said that he knew his job was done when I didn't need him anymore and found my own support system in my life.

Five years later I found that I was strong enough to leave the group. There are times I miss it because it was so safe, but I found many good friends in group. And when life hands me some tough things, I know they are only a phone call away. I enjoy being in the middle of life and even challenge myself to take on new things just to see what I can do. My life is pretty good, and I'm enjoying it!

This letter is to acknowledge the lengthy path I have traveled for the past several years and the progress I have made. Any success has come out of desperation, determination, courage, acceptance and most of all through your help and guidance.

In 1991 I was diagnosed by my family physician with an anxiety disorder and depression. I had suffered through several "panic attacks," not knowing what was happening to me, and I had an extreme fear of dying. I did not know that many other people were suffering from the same disorder and symptoms. For two years I took medication to control the attacks and help with the depression, and I had short-term psychiatric care. It was not until 1993 that I was desperate enough to determine the reasons for the depression and physical symptoms that accompanied my panic attacks. I thought finding an explanation would be a matter of instruction in behavioral management and personal examination. I was resolute in finding a mental health professional who specialized in anxiety disorders or at least had experience in handling individual cases. It was important for me to know about the positive results of other individuals who had had or were currently in treatment for this disorder.

Upon receiving a recommendation to seek treatment with you, I signed up for your instruction program on anxiety disorders. Immediately I realized I was not alone in experiencing either unhealthy anxiety or panic attacks. Through the instructional program, I acquired "tools" to address and change my behavioral and thought patterns. It took all my energy to just control the panic attacks and continue my life's ambition and career as an archaeologist and supermom. However, I did not tackle my depression, fears and the reasons for them at this time. I had put a dressing on my wound, but I just couldn't heal.

In 1998, at a time when I was again feeling desperate, I knew it was time to penetrate my humanness and deal with my depression and fears. I no longer suffered from panic attacks, but I was not happy or content. I had very few relationships with others, and those were cursory. I began individual therapy and started to acquaint myself with who I was. Up until this time, I had not allowed time just for myself in my busy life of being a wife, mother, student and finally a professional in my scientific field. In time I joined group therapy. I have been a part of that group for one year and have certainly embraced the opportunity to explore myself and to become aware of issues in my life that need work. There are times when I become very uncomfortable, confused, frustrated and sometimes afraid. It is then that I develop an awareness, face myself and begin to work on improving my quality of life.

I'm going through the anxiety program for the second time with my husband. We are seeking understanding and awareness of our relationship and how to better share our lives with each other and others. We can only do this by understanding ourselves as individuals.

The program is not a quick fix or a shortcut to easy relationships or happiness. I have found through the program and individual and group therapy that improving one's quality of life is a continuum. It takes courage, determination and hard work.

I'm writing this letter to thank you for the continued guidance and sincere care in helping me to realize my humanness, to begin to know myself and like myself, and to seek fullness and contentment in life's sometimes ambiguous journey. The self-worth that I have gained helps me with existential issues. I have set goals, deepened my relationship with my husband and others, and I have a dream. I have given myself hope and a future through your earnest tutelage and devotion to your field of mental health.

I originally thought that writing down my thoughts on why I went to see Rex would be easy. This was not the case.

It is hard to put into words how low and miserable I was when I first walked into Rex's office. Everyday life was almost too much to handle. I was really having a hard time dealing with the death of my father from cancer and also the death of a dear friend from ALS (Lou Gehrig's disease).

My first session with Rex paid immediate dividends. He asked me to close my eyes and tell him how I felt and what my "self-talk" was about. I started to cry when I realized I was saying, You're going to die, *over and over in my head. Was it any wonder that I was miserable and had reached such a low point that I could barely function at work or anywhere else? I had become a shell of my previous self. I no longer enjoyed activities that previously brought me happiness and joy. Through much intense work with Rex, I learned that a combination of shame-based issues that I had never recognized, along with an obsessive-compulsive disorder, were causing me most of my stress and heavy-duty anxiety. It got to the point where I was convinced I had ALS and was dying. I even developed twitches and other ALS symptoms that further convinced me I was going to die. Rex helped me understand that this was merely a "paper tiger" I had created in my mind. Once I recognized this, it lost all its power over me. I was now free to work through shame issues from childhood which also held quite a bit of power over me.*

I think just being able to understand what was going on started my healing and growing. The individual sessions as well as the group therapy I was involved in changed my life!

I should add that not every day is easy and fun, but now I have quite a bit of knowledge and skills to be able to keep everyday problems just that. This was not possible for me before my therapy. Therapy was tough, scary, fun, interesting, sad, exciting and much, much more.

I guess in closing I would like to thank Rex for his help and support. He used his vast knowledge and personal experience to help me understand what I am all about. With this knowledge and confidence I now have my life back and am continuing to grow and prosper.

When I first came to see Rex, I was actually skeptical of my need to be there. My wife needed to be there, and I just wanted to show her how easy it was to go and maybe "inspire" her to do the same.

What I found was that after years of dealing with her depression, I had put my needs and feelings aside for the noble cause of helping her. The reality was that I wasn't helping her, but enabling her and at the same time killing myself.

I developed asthma and allergies that became increasingly debilitating to a point where just breathing was difficult.

Then I met Rex. I can honestly say that he helped me back from the brink. He helped me to understand and deal with my anxiety, overcome my self-doubt and regain my self-respect.

I owe Rex my life, and I thank him. And I thank God for his gift.

January 2, 1998, was a day I will long remember. I had just survived two of the longest days of my life. A point in my life, I hope, that I can always look back on as rock bottom. I just can't imagine feeling any worse. That day I reached out in despair and found a voice that offered a glimmer of hope.

For the previous two years, I had watched my life fall apart. My job as a special education teacher was becoming a nightmare. At that time I blamed the students and their parents. I dreaded going to work and dealing with the students, much less their parents. The actual teaching was still something I enjoyed. Every relationship in my life—professional, family and friends—was disintegrating. Even my relationship with myself stopped. I couldn't stand to be with myself, and consequently no one wanted to be around me. It was a vicious circle. The more people avoided me, the worse I felt about myself, and the more I wanted to be with other people.

Physically I was also a mess. The stress had taken its toll and was fighting to get noticed. I was at an all-time high with my weight, something I had fought with all my life. I got maybe two hours sleep a night. I felt hot all the time, especially at night. I had constant headaches, as well as muscle and joint pain. I had always stuttered under extreme stress, but now I was finding it difficult to control under any circumstances. It had even begun to interfere with my teaching, and any kind of conversation was nearly impossible. Then I began scratching. It seemed that everything itched—head, arms, face, chest, legs, everything.

And I could not ever scratch hard enough. The itching would return as soon as I stopped scratching. I would often scratch hard enough to leave bruises or a rashlike spot. I was quite a sight.

My whole life I had been taught to turn my attention to others and do what was needed to please them, to make them happy. Focusing on others' needs was my number one priority. My needs could be addressed if there was any time and energy left over. What I wanted or needed didn't matter. All of my relationships and contacts with people were about them.

When I was young, I swore never to have any close friends. I don't remember making the statement, but I do know it is one I have always lived by. If I didn't care about anyone, open up to them or let them care about me, then I couldn't get hurt. I had to learn to take care of myself. I avoided people so that I wouldn't accidentally let them in. The only people I ever confided in were my family. So growing up, I never had another reference for relationships. My family was safe.

I lived like this for the next twenty years. I knew a lot of people and was pretty good at keeping our relationships as acquaintances. I learned about everything I could so I would not have to rely on anyone. I let everyone else make every decision and speak first; that way I wouldn't have to take the risk of being wrong. Everyone thought I was a very nice, quiet person.

At the age of thirty I developed a close friendship with M. Through that friendship I began to see that my perceptions about relationships were not healthy. Unfortunately, I focused all my attention and life on this friend, just as I had been taught. Our friendship continued for a few years with all the focus on M. I think back on it now, and the pressure I put on her, and I am surprised M remained my friend. However, in the process of those two years, I pretty much succeeded in driving her away. Finally M couldn't take me anymore. She wrote a letter telling me how messed up my life was and that she was willing to help me if I got professional help.

With my friend pushing me away, I felt lost. There was no one else for me to focus my attention on. With no one to please, how was I to know how to act, behave. . . . I had no idea how to live my life for me. What I perceived myself to be had been stripped away. I truly believed I did not have the power to do anything. I had no options. My thoughts kept going to suicide. However, because of my being raised to think of myself last, suicide was not an option. I have always believed that suicide is an extremely selfish act in which the person puts themselves first. So I felt that I could not even end the pain I was in. The most I could do was to hope that God would put an end to my misery. Out of desperation to keep my friend, I told her that I would seek help like she had asked, if only she would help me. That first call wasn't for me; I was trying to save that friendship. Again to please someone else.

I met Rex on January 5. I was scared and nervous. Never in my life had I spoken with any type of counselor, not even while attending school. I had never felt I was very good at meeting new people or talking very much. I had no idea what to expect. I don't remember everything that was said at that first meeting, but I remember coming away with a feeling of hope. With the next few meetings, I began to feel better; maybe there was some hope after all. Even the slightest chance would be better than the hell I had been living in. At Rex's suggestion I joined a class he was teaching on how to cope with anxiety and relationships.

Over the next four months my life began to change dramatically. At least the way I perceived my life did. What I learned in the class and the individual counseling I was receiving opened my eyes. For the first time in my life I could see what I had done to myself. I began to learn about what beliefs I had based my life on, how false they were and how they had affected my life. I started to learn how to change things in my life. Because my life had been so empty, the changes in those first few months were dramatic. I had set my goal on becoming a "real" person.

I have now been seeing Rex for over a year, and my knowledge about myself has grown tremendously. I have learned that I don't have to know everything or always have the right answer. I have learned that I do need and want people around me and that it will require risking myself. But through risking myself I can become a stronger person, like myself better and not give in to everyone. I am still learning how to take back—not lose—my power and my person. I don't have to give myself up to keep a relationship. Just the opposite. I have to keep my own identity so that I can keep any relationship going. I can now recognize when I am giving my power away, and more importantly, I can sometimes stop myself.

My friendships and professional relationships are better. I am at a stage right now where I am anxious to meet new people. I am more comfortable with myself. I can spend the day alone and not worry excessively. I understand that if someone isn't around me, that doesn't mean they no longer like me. I can express some of my feelings. Sometimes those old insecurities still come back, but I recognize and work through them. M and I are still friends, but my focus is no longer completely on her.

The slowest progress of all has come with my family. This is pretty much what I had expected. My habits with them will be hard to break. After all, they have been over thirty-five years in the making. It is hard to make myself stop and think, to respond to them instead of react the way I always have. I am slowly working through each member of my family, deciding what I want our relationship to be like. I love my family and want to be able to like them as well.

The biggest change has been with how I feel. The best way to describe that feeling is "freedom." I can make decisions for myself— what to do, where to go, who to do things with or if I want to be alone. I can try new things. I can talk to people and not be terrified of seeming stupid. I still get nervous about that, but I realize that it's okay and I am not stupid. I am enjoying my life. I am laughing more, and even singing, something I hadn't done for years. For the first time in my life, I can look forward to the future and know that I will have a great chance at happiness.

Working with Rex has changed me dramatically. And I know that he will continue to listen and ask the questions that will lead me to the choices that are the best for me. To Rex I can only say, "Thank you! I now see a real person emerging."

I have been attending group counseling for about two years. Before this I had seen counselors on two other occasions. I first came to Rex Briggs to attend anxiety classes with my husband. And realizing the sadness I had inside, I decided to join a group. I grew up in an alcoholic home, until my father died when I was ten, in a car accident while driving drunk. Being raised by an alcoholic father, I had many feelings of abandonment and shame. I was a people-pleaser, trying endlessly to keep the people around me happy. It was easy for me to see what they needed and try and give that to them. But at a cost—the cost of being me. I had lost myself—who I was, what I liked and didn't like, what I needed to be happy. I was not able to make friends, always thinking, Who would want to be friends with me? To know me is to hate me. *So I spent all my energy hiding the person inside, the person who was so sad and inadequate, insecure and alone. Let's say my insides never matched my outsides.*

Over the last two years I have worked hard at finding that lost person inside. Tried to deal with some of the shame, sadness and even anger I have found. I am now forty-five years old, and for the first time in my life I am feeling good about who I am. I am learning what I need to be happy. One of the most exciting things is that I am trusting myself, which makes it easier for me to trust others. Instead of living each day feeling guilty about the past or worried about the future, I try hard to live in the present, which isn't an easy task. I allow myself to feel happy, let my guard down, without thinking that something terrible will happen because I do. My insides are starting to match my outsides, which is another first for me.

I am looking forward to continued work with my group and Rex; the progress I have made and will continue to make is with their help.

It was 1993, and my wife had just asked me for a separation. She couldn't stand to live with me anymore. Insulated in my own little world, this came as a complete surprise to me. I knew things had not been going well in our marriage, but I thought it was the pressures of work, kids, home and finances. The end of a meaningful relationship seemed the least of our problems. I had had blinders on for years. I had been depressed for so long I couldn't tell the difference.

Depression, for me, started in college. I don't know the clinical reason, but depression seems to run in my family. My father and grandfather both suffered all their lives and both died in their mid-sixties.

In a desperate attempt to save my marriage, I decided to seek professional help. I had been to various marriage counselors with my wife on many occasions, but this time I was serious. This therapy would be for me, or so I thought. In reality, it was just one more thinly disguised attempt to understand why this wasn't my fault.

I contacted Rex Briggs because I heard good things about his program and I knew him from church. I was sure I could attend his sixteen-week course and all would be well. My wife would see all my work and would love me again. All would be right with my world. No muss, no fuss.

It was at Rex's first class that I realized the problems I was having were all related. I was also amazed I was not the only person in the world who felt like this. The course really opened my eyes. I finally thought I understood. I was so excited. I ran home to tell my estranged wife of the wonderful progress I was making. She said, "Ho hum."

But things really were changing for me. I was starting to feel like a human being again. I completed the course and felt better than I had in years. I now had the tools to work with to make some basic changes in my life. This time I was doing it for me.

My wife wasn't back, but now it wasn't the end of my world. I was becoming stronger, a more complete person in my own right. I was relating better to people all around me whom I had ignored for years. I was feeling something again.

Rex then asked me if I would be interested in joining a group. I had no idea what a group did, but I was ready. I was actually feeling good about myself again. I thought I might have something to contribute. I started group and was amazed at the bond I could feel with other people. It was an experience I hadn't had in a long time. I was starting to grow as a person. Amazingly enough, my ex-wife noticed this and became interested again. Imagine that. We moved back in together soon after.

Not long after this, our son was killed in an accident. I was devastated. My world turned upside down overnight. In my old life that would have been the end for me. I don't think I could have survived. Now I had the tools and the support group to help me live with this tragedy and believe I could survive. I had something left over to comfort and support my wife—and the capacity to be comforted and supported by her. We got through this somehow and continue to survive it every day, one day at a time.

We were remarried a year later in a small ceremony with only family and close friends. It was one of the best times in my life. It was also one of the first times in my life I could enjoy such an intimate experience.

I'm gone from the group now, but the group isn't gone from me. The lessons I learned from Rex and other group members will be with me for the rest of my life. Thank you, Rex! You saved my sanity, my health and my marriage. You saved my life.

I hope reading these letters has helped you decide that recovery from anxiety is possible and worth the struggle. Most of all, I hope you will decide that you are worth it. I feel honored to have had the chance to share my ideas with you and would welcome your reactions to them. God bless you as you learn to live the kind of exciting life that you deserve.

Rex Briggs, M.S.W.
811 Columbus Street
Rapid City, SD 57701
E-mail: *calm@rapidnet.com*

Appendix A

My Sixteen-Week
Anxiety Treatment Program

Most people I work with are referred by their physicians or by friends who have been through my program. As soon as people are referred, I try to get them in for an initial session. I find that, since anxiety waxes and wanes, if I wait too long, their anxiety may ease and they may not see as urgent a need for help. If they come in somewhat scared or miserable, they are more motivated to make a commitment to their recovery.

After an initial evaluation and possibly some individual sessions, many clients decide to join my sixteen-week program. I strongly encourage people to bring a support person with them, whether that be a spouse, a lover, a family member or a friend. I find that people respond much better in treatment if they have a support person with them. They will then have someone in daily life who speaks the new language they are learning.

This program is a class rather than group therapy. Each two-hour session begins with a lecture and includes discussion for any class members who choose to share. Sometimes there are "homework" assignments, and we often do exercises during the session. People are encouraged, but not required, to participate. The first six sessions are designed to help people learn how to manage their anxiety better. They learn to recognize their negative thinking patterns and how they contribute to their anxiety. The remainder of the program is designed to promote wellness and to help people be healthier than they've ever been before. Following are brief descriptions of each session.

Session One–Introduction. I give a brief overview of the program and describe the personality dynamics of those who suffer with anxiety. I also describe healthy family development. Participants begin to evaluate their own strengths and weaknesses and their families of origin. This first session is intended to provoke thought and make people feel welcome and curious.

Session Two–Losing Our Fear of the Symptoms. I emphasize that whatever physical symptoms have brought people to treatment, those symptoms are not in and of themselves dangerous. They are messages that each person needs to heed. I teach them the four functions of healthy anxiety and remind them that our goal is to eliminate unnecessary anxiety, not all anxiety.

Session Three–Deep Breathing and Deep Relaxation.
I first help people learn to do deep breathing, and then I
teach the deep relaxation process described in chapter 4. By
now, people are beginning to feel more comfortable with
each other, and the process of getting down on the floor
together to learn deep relaxation is an equalizer.

**Session Four–Learning Cognitive Distortions That
Lead to Fear.** I illustrate Albert Ellis's process–from event
to thought to feeling to behavior–during this class. We talk
about typical false beliefs, and I encourage people to start
recognizing their own fallacious beliefs. I teach the three
ways (visual, auditory and kinesthetic) that people process
information.

**Session Five–Shame, the Driving Force Behind
Anxiety.** I give a detailed description of the difference
between guilt and shame, helping people to recognize ways
they may have been disempowered in growing up or in their
current lives. This session generally stirs up a lot of discussion and thought for group members and makes their individual psychotherapy more focused and effective.

Session Six–Goal Setting. Most people I work with set
very high goals for themselves because they are perfection-
ists. In this session I help people define their mission in life
to give them a better sense of direction. Then we discuss
ways for them to set realistic goals, break those goals down
into manageable steps and give themselves credit for their
achievements.

**Session Seven–Learning to Be Curious and Going
with the Flow.** People who suffer with anxiety tend to either
shut down or to punish and shame themselves with "I

should" and "I shouldn't." Instead, I teach people to become
curious and ask, "Why might I be feeling this way now?"
We explore feelings in general and help people learn how to
enjoy and appreciate their feelings.

**Session Eight–Learning to Be Reasonable with
Yourself and Setting Boundaries.** This session explores
our rights as human beings and explains the different components of passive, aggressive and assertive behavior. I teach
people how to value what they think and feel. We discuss
finding a balance between respecting their own rights and
those of others, and asserting rights in a way that is respectful of themselves and others.

Session Nine–Healthy Sexuality. This session explores
a little bit about showing affection as it relates to our sexuality. But its focus is primarily on how we feel about ourselves as men and women and how our sexuality is shaped
by our role models. I also talk about sexual abuse since so
many anxious people have been sexually violated in one
way or another.

Session Ten–Learning Healthy Conflict Resolution.
People who suffer with anxiety often avoid conflict and
maintain low profiles in relationships because they never
saw healthy conflict modeled when they were growing up. I
describe the difference between healthy anger and rage. I
illustrate three steps that are necessary if two people are to
grow closer as a result of conflict instead of feeling separated
from each other. We discuss anger as a prerequisite to a loving relationship and an important way to "become known"
to each other.

Session Eleven–Developing and Maintaining Loving Relationships. I describe the things that are confused with loving relationships and some of the building blocks in establishing and maintaining loving and intimate relationships. This is a session from which people leave quietly because it presents very challenging information.

Session Twelve–Dealing with Our Losses. I explain that we deal with loss on a daily basis, not just when there is a death. Loss is another one of those feelings in life that can either isolate us or help us develop greater closeness.

Session Thirteen–How Do We Relate to Others? This session explores the different kinds of relationships that we may share with others, including relationships where we feel inferior to others, where we are caretaking or (rarely) where we actually feel like an equal. We discuss here what we can do to realize how these types of relationships were created and what our options for change are.

Session Fourteen–Learning to Communicate with Self and Others. My goal in this session is to teach people how to listen to their own bodies and to recognize what their choices are. Once we have learned to communicate more openly with ourselves, we naturally become much better communicators with others.

Session Fifteen–Learning to Deal with the Existential Givens in Life. Everyone must learn to deal with some of the givens in life, such as death, freedom, isolation and meaning. I describe some of the typical ways people have learned to avoid thinking about these ideas. We then explore how a healthy spiritual life can provide people with support and guidance as they deal with the existential as well as everyday issues of life.

Session Sixteen—Reviewing What We've Learned. We summarize, review and discuss some of the alternatives people have for maintaining their progress. Some people find that the program provides enough to make them feel comfortable trying their new skills on their own. Others use the program as a first step and go on to group therapy or individual sessions.

I have written a manual to accompany this sixteen-week program, and I have most of the lectures on audiotapes. If there is sufficient need and interest, I will consider making the program available to the public.

If you're interested in more information about the program, manual or tapes, please contact me.

Rex Briggs, M.S.W.
811 Columbus Street
Rapid City, SD 57701
E-mail: *calm@rapidnet.com*

Appendix B

Other Resources

Anxiety Disorders Association of America
11900 Parklawn Drive, Suite 100
Rockville, MD 20852-4004

The OCD Foundation
P.O. Box 9573
New Haven, CT 06535

The EMDR Institute
P.O. Box 51010
Pacific Grove, CA 93950-6010

All of these organizations have national clearinghouses for information pertinent to their fields. They can provide you with names of people in their respective specialties who practice near you. They are also willing to provide information to help you decide if you're interested in pursuing help in their area of specialization.

Appendix C

Anxiety Disorders— Behaviors and Symptoms

Agoraphobia. A condition causing a person to avoid everyday situations, like driving or going to the mall, because they're afraid they might feel out of control, helpless or panicky.

Generalized Anxiety Disorder. Characterized by a constant state of anxiety, agitation, worry and difficulty relaxing.

Obsessive Compulsive Disorder. Usually entails an obsessive thought (*did I turn off the coffee pot?, maybe I'll hurt someone*) combined with a ritual (excessive checking or washing). It could also be a thought without a ritual or a ritual without a thought.

Panic Disorder. Adrenaline rushes that create feelings of being out of control, which can lead to various symptoms such as racing heart, difficulty breathing or many other frightening symptoms. Periodic panic may be uncomfortable but does not lead to avoidance.

Post-Traumatic Stress Disorder. A traumatic event that can lead to flashbacks: memories that can interfere with a person's ability to function spontaneously.

Simple Phobia. Specific phobias such as fear of heights, fear of public speaking, etc. People generally do not seek professional help for these problems, but merely avoid the anxiety-provoking activity.

Social Phobia. Avoidance of situations where a person fears being humiliated or feeling foolish in social situations.

Bibliography

Alberti, Robert E., and Michael L. Emmons. *Your Perfect Right: A Guide to Assertive Living.* New York: Impact Publishing, 1970, 1995.

Barbach, Lonnie Garfield. *For Yourself: The Fulfillment of Female Sexuality.* New York: Signet Books, 1975.

Beck, Aaron T., Gary Emery, and Ruth L. Greenberg. *Anxiety Disorders and Phobias: A Cognitive Perspective.* New York: Basic Books, 1985.

Benson, Herbert, M.D., and Mariam Z. Klipper. *The Relaxation Response.* New York: Avon, 1990.

Bourne, Edmund. *The Anxiety and Phobia Workbook.* Oakland, Calif.: New Harbinger, 1990.

Bradshaw, John. *Healing the Shame That Binds You.* Deerfield Beach, Fla.: Health Communications, 1988.

Burns, David D., M.D. *Feeling Good: The New Mood Therapy.* New York: Signet Books, 1992.

Chambless, Dianne L., and Alan J. Goldstein. *Agoraphobia: Multiple Perspectives on Theory and Treatment.* New York: John Wiley & Sons, 1982.

Colgrove, Melba, Harold Bloomfield, and Peter McWilliams. *How to Survive the Loss of a Love.* New York: Bantam Books, 1976.

Cornett, Carlton. *Soul of Psychotherapy.* New York: Free Press, 1988.

Covey, Stephen. *The 7 Habits of Highly Effective People.* New York: Simon & Schuster, 1990.

Diagnostic and Statistical Manual of Mental Disorders. 4th ed. Washington, D.C.: American Psychiatric Association, 1994.

Eliot, Robert S., M.D. *Is It Worth Dying For: A Self-Assessment Program to Make Stress Work for You, Not Against You.* New York: Bantam Doubleday Dell, 1991.

Ellis, Albert, and Robert A. Harper. *A Guide to Rational Living.* 3rd ed. North Hollywood, Calif.: Wilshire Book Co., 1975.

Emery, Stewart. *Actualizations.* Garden City, N.Y.: Dolphin Books, Doubleday & Co., 1977, 1978.

Erickson, Erik. *Childhood and Society.* New York: W. W. Norton, 1950.

Fossum, Merle A., and Marilyn J. Mason. *Facing Shame: Families in Recovery.* New York: W. W. Norton & Co., 1989.

Friel, John, and Linda Friel. *Rescuing Your Spirit.* Deerfield Beach, Fla.: Health Communications, 1993.

———. *The Soul of Adulthood.* Deerfield Beach, Fla.: Health Communications, 1995.

Fromm, Erich. *The Art of Loving.* New York: Bantam, 1956.

Gawain, Shakti, and Laurel King. *Living in the Light.* Mill Valley, Calif.: Whatever Publishing, 1986.

Gerzon, Robert. *Finding Serenity in the Age of Anxiety.* New York: Bantam Doubleday Dell, 1998.

Goleman, Daniel P. *Emotional Intelligence.* New York: Bantam Books, 1997.

Hardy, Arthur. *Terrap Foundation Manual.* Menlo Park, Calif.: Terrap Foundation, 1981.

Hay, Louise. *You Can Heal Your Life.* Santa Monica, Calif.: Hay House, 1984.

Jeffers, Susan, Ph.D. *Feel the Fear and Do It Anyway.* New York: Fawcett Books, 1992.

Kabat-Zinn, Jon. *Full Catastrophe Living: Using the Wisdom of Your Body and Mind to Face Stress, Pain, and Illness.* New York: Bantam Doubleday Dell, 1990.

Kaufman, Gershen. *Shame: The Power of Caring.* Cambridge, Mass.: Schenkman Books, 1980.

Lerner, Harriet. *The Dance of Anger.* New York: HarperCollins, 1989.

Love, Patricia. *Emotional Incest Syndrome: What to Do When a Parent's Love Rules Your Life.* New York: Bantam Doubleday Dell, 1991.

Marks, Isaac, M.D. *Living with Fear.* New York: McGraw Hill, 1978.

McCullough, Christopher J., and Robert W. Mann. *Managing Your Anxiety.* New York: St. Martin's Press, 1985.

Meichenbaum, Donald and Dennis C. Turk. *Facilitating Treatment Adherence: A Practitioner's Guidebook.* New York: Plenum Press, 1987.

Moore, Thomas. *Care of the Soul: How to Add Depth and Meaning to Your Everyday Life.* New York: HarperCollins, 1992.

Peck, M. Scott, M.D. *The Road Less Traveled.* New York: Simon & Schuster, 1978.

Peurifoy, Reneau Z. *Anxiety, Phobias & Panic: A Step-by-Step Program for Regaining Control of Your Life.* Sacramento, Calif.: Life Skills, 1988.

Pittman, Frank. *Private Lies: Infidelity and Betrayal of Intimacy.* New York: W. W. Norton & Co., 1990.

Rank, Otto. *Will Therapy, Truth and Reality.* New York: Alfred A. Knopf, 1945.

Schnarch, David, Ph.D. "Inside the Sexual Crucible." *Family Therapy Networker*, March/April 1993: 40-48.

———. *Passionate Marriage: Love, Sex, and Intimacy in Emotionally Committed Relationships*. New York: W. W. Norton & Co., 1997.

Shaw, George Bernard. *Man and Superman*. New York: Viking Penguin, 1903, 1987.

Sheehan, David, M.D. *The Anxiety Disease*. New York: Charles Scribner's Sons, 1983.

Wilson, R. Reid, Ph.D. *Don't Panic: Taking Control of Anxiety Attacks*. New York: HarperCollins, 1996.

Yalom, Irvin. *Existential Psychotherapy*. New York: Basic Books, 1980.

Index

A

abandonment, 59–61
abuse, 65
  emotional, 65–66
  mental, 66
  physical, 65
  sexual, 66–67
  spiritual, 67–68
activity addiction, 74–75
Actualizations (Stewart), 21
addiction, 49–50, 74, 288, 296
aggressive behavior, 116, 117, 322
aging, 258
agoraphobia, 27, 327
Al-Anon, 55, 291, 298
Alberti, Robert E., 114, 121
alcoholic family, 298, 314
Alcoholics Anonymous, 55, 240
  See also Twelve-Step programs
aloneness, 266–67, 268
anger
  distinguished from rage, 69,
    138–39

essential in healthy
  relationships, 5
healthy aspects of, 138,
  139–40, 153–54
learning to express in healthy
  ways, 143–49
levels of, 142
necessary for protection, 207
prerequisite to loving
  relationship, 69, 139
as protector of boundaries, 141
unhealthy, 136–37
anxiety
  definition of, 28, 43
  denied grief leading to, 221
  distinguished from excitement,
    230–31
  effect on beliefs and actions,
    35–37
  emotional component in
    excessive anxiety, 43
  forms of, 6
  goal of recovery from, 271

anxiety *(continued)*
  healthy, 262
  normal response to, 33–38
  as outcome of not feeling, 137
  perception of in others, 21–22
  physical aspects of, 2–3, 40
  physical reflex against, 29–30
  as promoter of change, 41
  as reaction to stress, 28, 33
  relapse, 285
  result of conflict of insides and
    outsides, 143
  result of shame, 56
  result of societal change, 39
  as safety mechanism, 32–38
  shame as factor in, 11–12
  as spur to maturation, 30–31
  sufferers' high priority on
    comfort, 14–15
  symptom of family's
    "responsible child," 3
  symptoms of sufferers, 6–7
  thought process behind, 44–46
  after treatment for, 276
  in victims of sexual violation,
    199–201
anxiety attacks, presence of
  rationale behind, 40
anxiety disorders, 27–28, 306–8
Anxiety Disorders Association of
  America, 325
*Anxiety Disorders and Phobias: A
  Cognitive Perspective* (Beck,
  Emery and Greenberg), 28,
  33
  definitions in, 42–44
  thinking process of excessive-
    anxiety sufferers, 44–46
anxiety management, alternative
  methods of, 106–10

The Anxiety and Phobia Workbook
  (Bourne), 254
anxiety resources, 325
anxiety sufferers
  creativity of, 32–33, 228
  thinking process of, 44–46
anxiety treatment program,
  319–24
appreciation, 261
arrogance, 70
The Art of Loving (Fromm), 267
assertive behavior, 322
assertive rights, 121–28
assertiveness, 114–19, 240–41
attentiveness, 167–68
auditory processing, 232–33, 234
authorship, 264–65
autonomy, 51–52
avoidance, 82

B
balance, 236, 241, 242
balancing people's rights, 129–31
Barbach, Lonnie, 192
Beck, Aaron T., 28. *See also Anxiety
  Disorders and Phobias: A
  Cognitive Perspective*
blame, in shame-based families, 68
blaming, 72–73
Bloomfield, Harold, 209
boundaries, confusion over,
  113–14
boundary setting, 322
Bourne, Edmund, 254
Bradshaw, John
  becoming a human doing, 58
  on healthy shame, 53–54
breathing
  deep, 202, 227, 321
  proper, 90–91

broad-based change and growth, 285–86
Burns, David, 46

C
Care of the Soul (Moore), 33
caretaking, 73–74
catastrophization, 45
challenging situations, 242–45
change, examples of, 277–83. *See also* recovery stories
children, relationship with caregivers, 51–52
choice, 34, 112–13
church, 256
clearing the air, 149–50
closeness, loss leading to, 219–21
codependency, 311–12
Co-dependents Anonymous, 257, 291
cognitive behavioral treatment, 289
cognitive distortions, 321
comfort, 14–15, 18–20
commitment, 169–70, 293–94
communication, 323
    increasing chances for success in, 240–42
    with oneself, 224–36, 246
    with others, 236–42
    people pleasing through, 223–24
    preparing for difficult situations, 242–45
communion, sense of, 261
compulsive-addictive behaviors, 49–50, 74–76
    activity addiction, 74–75
    eating disorders, 74
    feeling addictions, 75

life re-enactments, 75–76
    recovery from, 55
    thought addictions, 75
confidence-building, 5–6, 13
conflict, 290
    avoiding, 65
    two people required for resolution of, 154–57
conflict resolution, 156, 322
confrontation, risking, 172–73
contempt, 70
contraception, 193–94
control, 68, 81
cooling off, 151–52
counter will, 269
counterdependence, 171
Covey, Stephen, 260
creative will, 270
creativity, use of, 228–29

D
The Dance of Anger (Lerner), 140
danger, 82–83
"dark side," recognition of, 142–43
death, 258–62
decisions, right vs. wrong, 20–22
deep breathing, 202, 227, 321
deep relaxation, 91–92, 202, 227, 321
    creating a safe place, 99–100
    techniques, 93–98
    value of including emotional experiences, 98–99
demobilization, 30
denial, 68, 309–10
dependency, 164, 268
dependent personality, 160–61, 164

depression, 66, 299, 303, 306–8,
        315
    result of shame, 56
    result of suppressing feelings,
        138
desensitizing, 23, 100–6
developmental stages, 51–53
diet, 106–7
direction, sense of, 251–52
discipline, 173–75
discomfort, 18–20
disqualification, in shame-based
        families, 68
divorce, process of grieving,
        209–10
DSM-IV, 27, 28
dying, 262

E
eating disorders, 74
Ellis, Albert, 45, 82, 85, 321
EMDR. See eye movement
        desensitization reprocessing
EMDR Institute, 289, 326
Emery, Gary, 28. *See also Anxiety
        Disorders and Phobias: A
        Cognitive Perspective*
Emery, Stewart, 21
Emmons, Michael L., 114, 121
emotion, sharing of, 219
emotional abandonment, 59–60
emotional incest, 165–66
Emotional Incest Syndrome (Love), 166
Emotional Intelligence (Goleman), 157
emotions
    options for dealing with, 145
    taking responsibility for,
        238–39
Emotions Anonymous, 257, 291
enabling, 74

Erickson, Erik, 51
event-behavior continuum, 45, 82
excessive anxiety
    anxiety as emotional
        component in, 43
    causes of, 38, 41
    characteristics of, 26–27
    fear as cognitive component in,
        42–43
    feelings of insignificance at
        core of, 54
    loss resulting from, 208–9
    panic as physical component
        in, 43
    phobia as belief component in
        excessive anxiety, 43–44
    related to thinking, 41–46
    symptoms as indication of
        poor self-communication,
        224–25
excitement, distinguished from
        anxiety, 230–31
exercise, 107
exercises
    about acquiring shame, 78
    about anger and conflict
        resolution, 158
    about assertiveness, 133
    about beliefs that govern
        behavior, 48
    about communication, 247
    dealing with challenging
        situations, 242–45
    desensitization, 104–6, 110
    about developing closer
        relationships, 78
    about existential issues, 273
    about facing situations, 24
    about grieving, 222
    about Higher Power, 273

journaling about avoidance
behavior, 24
journaling about methods of
thinking, 48
journaling about self-image, 78
about life goals and purposes,
16, 24
about loss, 222
about love, 178
about physical symptoms, 48
about relationships, 178
relaxation, 93–98, 110
about religion, 273
about role models, 204
about sexuality, 204
about shame and anxiety
symptoms, 78
existential givens, 323–24
death, 258–62
freedom, 262–65
isolation, 265–68
meaning, 269–71
existential guilt, 251, 265
expectations, 5
eye movement desensitization
reprocessing, (EMDR),
288–89

F
facing extremes, 18
Facing Shame: Families in Recovery
(Fossum and Mason), 68
failure-to-thrive syndrome, 61
fallacious beliefs, 84–86, 321
family dynamics, 237
Family Therapy Networker, 184
family tragedy, 316
fear
of airports, desensitizing
process for, 105–6

of being alone, desensitizing
process for, 104
cognitive component in
anxiety, 42–43
common denominators leading
to, 87
dcfined, 42–43
of dentists, desensitizing
process for, 104–5
of flying, desensitizing process
for, 105–6
having less, 261–262
learning to go on in spite of,
11–13
limiting choice, 1
physical reflex against, 29–30
related to shame, 11
of symptoms, 81–83
Feel the Fear and Do It Anyway
(Jeffers), 11, 12
feeling addictions, 75
Feeling Good (Burns), 46
feelings, acceptance of, 234–35
Finding Serenity in the Age of Anxiety
(Gerzon), 276
For Yourself (Barbach), 192
forgetfulness, living in state of,
258–59
Fossum, Merle, 68
Frankl, Viktor, 271
freedom, 262–65, 313–14
Friel, John, 252
Friel, Linda, 252
Fromm, Erich, 267
fusion, 267

G
gender identity, 63–64
generalized anxiety disorder, 5,
27, 327

Gerzon, Robert, 276
goal setting, 321
goals, 20, 23
Goleman, Daniel, 157
Greenberg, Ruth L., 28. *See also*
    Anxiety Disorders and Phobias:
    A Cognitive Perspective
grieving, 206–7
    avoidance of compounding
        loss, 212–14
    healing aspect of sharing,
        217–19
    loss brought on by anxiety
        symptoms, 208–9
    no time limits on, 211–12
    as a process, 209–11
    small losses, 214–16
group psychotherapy, 289–90
guidance, 255
guilt, 50, 53, 146

H
Hardy, Arthur, 84
hate, 139
healthy anxiety, 320
healthy conflict, stages in, 149–53
healthy love, 166, 167–75
healthy relationships, as aid in
    recovery from shame, 290
healthy shame, 53–54, 55
Higher Power, 54, 55, 253–55
hinting, 120–21
Holocaust survivors, 271
homosexuality, 197–98
hypervigilance, 30
hypnotherapy, 287–88

I
image, living behind, 161–62
imagination, 228

impotence, 195–96
incompleteness, in shame-based
    families, 68
independence, risking, 170–71
individual psychotherapy, 289
information, methods of
    processing, 231–34
inhibition, 30
inspirational readings, 257
intensity, 165
intentions
    awareness of, 131–32
    paying attention to, 147–48
internalizing right and wrong,
    52–53
intimacy, 166, 184–86
intimate communication, 167
isolation, 265–68

J
Jeffers, Susan, 11, 12, 22
journaling, 24, 48, 78, 201, 227
Jung, Carl, 253, 256

K
kinesthetic processing, 233–34

L
lack of talking, in shame-based
    families, 68
learning and resolution, as stages
    in resolving conflict, 152–53
Lerner, Harriet, 140
liberation, experiencing sense of,
    260
life mission, 15–16
life re-enactments, 75–76
Living with Fear (Marks), 12–13
living in the present, 217, 261
loneliness, 266, 268

loss, 206–7, 221
  compounded by failure to
    mourn, 212–14
  dealing with, 323
  excessive anxiety as, 208–9
  feelings and actions resulting
    from, 213
  healing from, 209–11
  hierarchy of, 215–16
  leading to closeness, 219–21
  leading to unfinished business,
    216–17
  opening up after, 221
  risking, 168–69
  of self, 207–8
love
  as compensation for pain of
    isolation, 267
  flawed belief systems about,
    160
  healthy, 166
  healthy anger as prerequisite
    to, 139–40
  unhealthy, 163–66
Love, Patricia, 166
lust, 165

M
magnification, 44–45
Man and Superman (Shaw), 23–24
Managing Your Anxiety
  (McCullough and Mann),
  33
manipulation, 119–20
Mann, Robert, 33
Marks, Isaac, 12–13
martyrdom, 164
Mason, Marilyn, 68
masturbation, 191–92
maturation, 30–31

May, Rollo, 251
McCullough, Christopher, 33
meaning, 269–71
medical management, 286–87
medication, 108–10, 286–87
meditation, 227, 257
Meichenbaum, Donald, 243
Melody, Pia, 74
midlife crisis, 296
milestones, 205–6
mindfulness of being, 259
minimization, 44
modeling, 57–58
Moore, Thomas, 33
motivation to change, 14–17

N
neglect, 60–61
  vs. abuse, 60–61, 65
  emotional, 62
  gender, 63–64
  mental, 62–63
  physical, 61
  sexual, 63–64
  spiritual, 64–65
nonverbal messages, 59

O
obsessive compulsive disorder, 27,
  288, 308–9, 327
OCD (Obsessive Compulsive
  Disorder) Foundation, 326
Overeaters Anonymous, 257
overwhelming feelings, dealing
  with, 244–45

P
pain, 217–19, 221–22
panic, 288
  defined, 43

panic *(continued)*
    as physical component in
        excessive anxiety, 43
panic attacks, 5, 27, 298–99, 303,
    306, 328
participation in spiritually based
    organization, church or
    synagogue, 256
Passionate Marriage (Schnarch), 186
passive behavior, 115–16, 117, 322
peace of mind, 254
Peck, M. Scott, 166
people-pleasing, 73–74, 137,
    223–24, 311–12, 314
perfection
    appearance of, 297–98
    in shame-based families, 68
perfectionism, 70–71
performance anxiety, 300
phobias, 27, 43–44, 288, 305–6
physical abandonment, 59
physical anxiety symptoms,
    29–30, 32
    as attention-getting devices,
        226–27
    management of, 147
    as messengers, 246
    scale of, 102
    of sexual violation, 200
    of suppressing feelings, 137–38
Pittman, Frank, 140, 166
positive will, 270
post-traumatic stress disorder, 27,
    235, 288, 328
power, 71–72
    sexual abuse and, 67
    sexual violation as facet of,
        199
    and taking responsibility for
        emotions, 238–39

power struggle, 297
powerlessness, feelings of, 113–19
premature ejaculation, 196–97
priorities, rearranging, 260
Private Lies (Pittman), 140, 166
purpose, sense of, 251–52

R
rage, 69–70, 75, 138–39
Rank, Otto, 269
recovery
    beginning of, 54–55
    bottom line of, 11
    challenge of anger, 137
    change in family dynamics, 237
    coming to terms with sexual
        behavior, 203
    commitment as key to, 293–94
    discovering roots of belief
        systems, 83
    fallacious beliefs in, 85
    goals of, 8, 46–48, 271
    hard work of, 19
    impeded by shame, 7
    importance of communication
        in, 236
    importance of recognizing roles
        assumed, 202
    importance of relationships in,
        175–78
    importance of self-
        communication to, 226–27
    managing and reducing effect
        of symptoms, 88–89
    requirements for, 13
    role of medications in, 108–10
    as spiritual matter, 252–53
recovery stories, 294–317
    addiction, 296
    alcoholic family, 298, 314

anxiety disorder, 306–8
codependency, 311–12
denial, 309–10
depression, 299, 303, 306–8,
   315
family tragedy, 316
freedom, 313–14
midlife crisis, 296
obsessive compulsive disorder,
   308–9
panic attacks, 298–99, 303, 306
people-pleasing, 311–12, 314
perfection, appearance of,
   297–98
performance anxiety, 300
phobias, 305–6
power struggle, 297
relationships, loss of, 310
risking self, 313
self acceptance, 302 3, 314 15
self-esteem, 304–5
sexual abuse, 294–95
stomach ailments, 301–2
unemotional parents, 295–96
victimization, 304
See also change, examples of
Reikian body therapy, 202
rejection, risking, 168–69
relationships
   approach of anxiety sufferers
      toward, 162–63
   change in as a result of
      recovery, 237–38
   components of healthy love in,
      167–75
   developing and maintaining,
      323
   healing shame through, 76–77
   loss of, 310
   recovery through, 175–77

relaxing
   goals for, 89–90
   learning about, 88–93
   practicing, 92–98
   value of including emotional
      experiences, 98–99
religion, distinguished from
   spirituality, 253–55
resentment, 260
resources, 325
respect, 237–38
responsibility, in communication,
   240
retreating, 103
rights, communication of, 227
risk, 81–82, 262
risking self, 313
The Road Less Traveled (Peck),
   166
role models, lack of, 162 63

S
sacred anxiety, 276
safety, 17–18, 254
Schnarch, David, 184–86
security, 254
selective abstraction, 44
ꭗ self-acceptance, 302–3, 314–15
self-alienation, 207
self-awareness, 228, 234–35
self-confidence, 255
self-defeating beliefs, result of
   shame-based experiences, 83
self-esteem, 3–4, 195–97, 304–5.
   See also shame
semantics, importance of, 239
separateness, risking, 170–71
separation, 268
Seven Habits of Highly Effective People
   (Covey), 260

sex without intimacy, 184–86
sexual abuse, 294–95
sexual activity, 194–95
sexual attraction, 165
sexual dysfunction, 195–97
sexual fantasy, 192–93
sexual interest, 184–86
sexual role models
  changing, 182–84
  traditional, 181–82, 184
sexual thoughts, 192–93
sexual violation
  anxiety in victims of, 199
  symptoms of, 200–1
sexuality, 322
  as aspect of health, 201–2
  messages that lead to shame
    about, 191–95
  shaming of, 180
  talking openly about, 189–90
shame
  abandonment, 59–60
  abuse, 65–68
  arrogance, 70
  vs. autonomy, 51–52
  beginning recovery from,
    54–55
  blaming, 72–73
  caretaking, 73–74
  compared to guilt, 50
  compulsive-addictive
    behaviors, 74–76
  contempt, 70
  development of, 57–68
  factor in anxiety development,
    7–8, 15
  factor in thinking of anxiety
    sufferers, 47–48
  as force behind anxiety, 321
  healing of, 76–77

healthy, 53–54
healthy relationships as aid in
  recovery from, 290
interference with healthy
  relationships, 77
as limiter of self-confidence,
  227
modeling, 57–58
as motivational factor, 300
neglect, 60–65
of sexuality, 180, 190–95
passed along generations, 58
people-pleasing, 73–74
perfectionism, 70–71
power, 71–72
rage, 69–70
recognition of, 5
related to compulsive and
  addictive disorders, 49–50
related to fear, 11
roots of, 50–53
rules of shame-based families,
  68
severing relationships with, 56
strategies of defense against
  pain of, 69–76
verbal messages, 59
withdrawal, 73
shame-based families, rules of, 68
Shapiro, Francine, 288
Shaw, George Bernard, 23–24
shutting out life, 18–20
simple phobia, 328
sleep, 108
social phobia, 328
social/emotional symptoms, of
  sexual violation, 200
soul, 253
The Soul of Adulthood (Friel and
  Friel), 252

spiritual life, aids to developing,
    256–57
spiritual symptoms, of sexual
    violation, 200
spirituality, 253
    distinguished from religion,
    253–55
    as journey, 272
spiritually oriented
    psychotherapy, 252–53
stimulus and response
    putting distance between, 47
    relationship between, 41–42
stomach ailments, 301–2
stress, anxiety as reaction to, 28
stress management, alternative
    methods of, 106–10
support network, need for,
    175–77
Surviving the Loss of a Love
    (Bloomfield), 209
symptom management, 284–85
symptoms
    eliminating causes of, 80
    losing fear of, 81–83, 320
    as messengers, 5, 79–88
synagogue, 256

T
tai chi, 257
therapy
    effects of, 3, 5
    realistic goals of, 46–48
thought addictions, 75
thought-sorting, 87–88
touching
    communication of, 187–89
    necessity of, 186–87

toxic thoughts, 157
treatment options, 284–91
    symptom management,
    284–85
    broad-based change and
    growth, 285–86
trust vs. mistrust, 51
Twelve-Step programs, 55, 76,
    177, 257, 291

U
unconditional love, 255
underlying conflicts, 31–32
unemotional parents, 295–96
unhealthy love, 163–66
unreliability, in shame-based
    families, 68

V
vaginismus, 197
verbal messages, 59
victimization, 304
visual cliff reflex, 29
visual processing, 232, 234

W
will, 269–70
The Wisdom of Anxiety
    (McCullough), 33
withdrawal, 73
withdrawn personality, 160–61

Y
Yalom, Irvin, 251
yoga, 227, 257
Your Perfect Right: A Guide to
    Assertive Living (Alberti and
    Emmons), 114–15, 121–28

A New Season of
Chicken Soup for the Soul

Chicken Soup for
the Single's Soul
Code #7060—$12.95

Chicken Soup for the
College Soul
Code #7028—$12.95

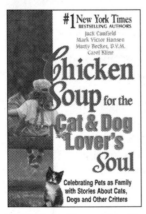

Chicken Soup for the
Cat & Dog Lover's Soul
Code #7109—$12.95

Chicken Soup for the
Unsinkable Soul
Code #6986—$12.95

Each one of these heartwarming titles will bring inspiration both to you and the loved ones in your life.

Also available in hardcover, audiocassette and audio CD.
Available in bookstores everywhere or call **1.800.441.5569** for Visa or MasterCard orders. Your response code is **BKS**. Prices do not include shipping and handling.
Order online at *www.hci-online.com*